Stuart Spouses

Stuart Spouses

A Compendium of Consorts from James I of Scotland to Queen Anne of Great Britain

Heather R. Darsie

First published in Great Britain in 2024 by
Pen & Sword History
An imprint of Pen & Sword Books Limited
Yorkshire – Philadelphia

Copyright © Heather R. Darsie 2024

ISBN 978 1 39909 591 4

The right of Heather R. Darsie to be identified as
Author of this Work has been asserted by her in accordance
with the Copyright, Designs and Patents Act 1988.

A CIP catalogue record for this book is
available from the British Library

All rights reserved. No part of this book may be reproduced or
transmitted in any form or by any means, electronic or mechanical
including photocopying, recording or by any information storage and
retrieval system, without permission from the Publisher in writing.

Typeset by Mac Style
Printed in the UK by CPI Group (UK) Ltd, Croydon, CR0 4YY.

Pen & Sword Books Limited incorporates the imprints of After
the Battle, Atlas, Archaeology, Aviation, Discovery, Family History,
Fiction, History, Maritime, Military, Military Classics, Politics,
Select, Transport, True Crime, Air World, Frontline Publishing, Leo
Cooper, Remember When, Seaforth Publishing, The Praetorian Press,
Wharncliffe Local History, Wharncliffe Transport, Wharncliffe True
Crime and White Owl.

For a complete list of Pen & Sword titles please contact

PEN & SWORD BOOKS LIMITED
47 Church Street, Barnsley, South Yorkshire, S70 2AS, England
E-mail: enquiries@pen-and-sword.co.uk
Website: www.pen-and-sword.co.uk
or
PEN AND SWORD BOOKS
1950 Lawrence Rd, Havertown, PA 19083, USA
E-mail: uspen-and-sword@casematepublishers.com
Website: www.penandswordbooks.com

For my wonderful husband Kris Piereth, without whose love and encouragement I would not be the person I am today. He has supported my historian/writing career since the day we met and shares the joys and lackluster bits equally with me.

Contents

Acknowledgments viii
Timeline of the Stewart/Stuart Monarchs ix
Family Trees xiii
Introduction xvii
A Note on the Auld Alliance xix
Prologue: Who Were the Stuarts? xxii

Chapter 1   Joan Beaufort   1
Chapter 2   Mary of Guelders   16
Chapter 3   Margaret of Denmark   28
Chapter 4   Margaret Tudor   38
Chapter 5   Madeleine de Valois   54
Chapter 6   Marie de Guise   63
A Note on the Scottish Reformation and Mary, Queen of Scots   80
Chapter 7   Francis II of France   83
Chapter 8   Henry Stewart, Lord Darnley   92
Chapter 9   James Hepburn, 4th Earl of Bothwell   104
Chapter 10 Anna of Denmark   119
Chapter 11 Henriette Marie of France   132
A Cromwellian Interlude: Elizabeth Bourchier and Dorothy Maijor 142
Chapter 12 Catherine of Braganza   148
Chapter 13 Anne Hyde and Maria of Modena   156
Chapter 14 Mary II & William III   175
Chapter 15 George of Denmark   184

Epilogue: The Introduction of the Hanoverians 192
Appendix: A Selection of Poems 193
Bibliography 230
Index 235

Acknowledgments

As always, my heartiest thanks to my friends for their patience and support. Thank you to Sarah-Beth Watkins for her attention to this work and patience. Thank you to Amy McElroy for teaching me how to create family trees the new-fangled way, instead of hand-drawing them. Finally, thank you to Nathen Amin for his feedback and general banter about book-writing.

Timeline of the Stewart/Stuart Monarchs

2 March 1316	Birth of Robert II
2 March 1320	Birth of Elizabeth Mure
1329	Birth of Euphemia de Ross
1336	Wedding of Elizabeth Mure and Robert II
1337	Birth of Robert III, born John Stewart
1350	Birth of Anabella Drummond
May 1355	Death of Elizabeth Mure by 1 May or earlier
2 May 1355	Wedding of Euphemia de Ross and Robert II
1367	Wedding of Anabella Drummond and Robert III
22 February 1371	Robert II becomes king of Scotland
1386	Death of Euphemia de Ross
19 April 1390	Death of Robert II; Robert III becomes king of Scotland
July 1394	Birth of James I
1401	Death of Anabella Drummond
1404	Birth of Joan Beaufort
4 April 1406	Death of Robert III; James I becomes king of Scotland
12 February 1424	Wedding of Joan Beaufort and James I
16 October 1430	Birth of James II
1434/1435	Birth of Mary of Guelders
21 February 1437	Death of James I; James II becomes king of Scotland
15 July 1445	Death of Joan Beaufort
3 July 1449	Wedding of Mary of Guelders and James II
July 1451/May 1542	Birth of James III
23 June 1456	Birth of Margaret of Denmark
3 August 1460	Death of James II; James III becomes king of Scotland
1 December 1463	Death of Mary of Guelders
July 1469	Wedding of Margaret of Denmark and James III

17 March 1473	Birth of James IV
14 July 1486	Death of Margaret of Denmark
11 June 1488	Death of James III; James IV becomes king of Scotland
28 November 1489	Birth of Margaret Tudor
8 August 1503	Wedding of Margaret Tudor and James IV
10 April 1512	Birth of James V
9 September 1513	Death of James IV; James V becomes king of Scotland
22 November 1515	Birth of Marie de Guise
10 August 1520	Birth of Madeleine de Valois
1534	Birth of James Hepburn, 1st Duke of Orkney and 4th Earl of Bothwell
1 January 1537	Wedding of Madeleine de Valois and James V
7 July 1537	Death of Madeleine de Valois
18 June 1538	Wedding of Marie de Guise and James V
18 October 1541	Death of Margaret Tudor
8 December 1542	Birth of Mary, Queen of Scots, who spelled the family name as Stuart
14 December 1542	Death of James V; Mary becomes queen of Scotland
19 January 1544	Birth of Francis II of France
1546	Birth of Henry Stewart, Lord Darnley
24 April 1558	Wedding of Francis II of France and Mary, Queen of Scots
10 July 1559	Francis II becomes king of France
11 June 1560	Death of Marie de Guise
5 December 1560	Death of Francis II of France
29 July 1565	Wedding of Henry Stewart and Mary, Queen of Scots
19 June 1566	Birth of James VI
10 February 1567	Death of Henry Stewart, Lord Darnley
15 May 1567	Wedding of James Hepburn and Mary, Queen of Scots
24 July 1567	Mary forcibly abdicates the throne in favor of her son, James VI
12 December 1574	Birth of Anne of Denmark
14 April 1578	Death of James Hepburn
8 February 1587	Death of Mary, Queen of Scots, by beheading, under her cousin Elizabeth I of England's watch
20 August 1589	Wedding of Anne of Denmark and James VI of Scotland

Timeline of the Stewart/Stuart Monarchs

19 November 1600	Birth of Charles I
24 March 1603	James VI of Scotland becomes James I of England after the death of his cousin, Elizabeth I of England; Anne of Denmark becomes queen of England
25 November 1609	Birth of Henrietta Maria of France
2 March 1619	Death of Anne of Denmark
27 March 1625	Death of James VI and I; Charles I becomes king of Scotland and England, etc.
1 May 1625	Wedding of Henrietta Maria and Charles I
29 May 1630	Birth of Charles II
14 October 1633	Birth of James VII and II of Scotland and England
12 March 1637	Birth of Anne Hyde
25 November 1638	Birth of Catherine of Braganza
30 January 1649	Execution of Charles I; Protector's Privy Council takes over England, Charles II becomes king of Scotland
4 November 1650	Birth of William III
2 April 1653	Birth of Prince George of Denmark
5 October 1658	Birth of Maria of Modena
3 September 1660	Wedding of Anne Hyde and James VII and II
29 May 1660	Charles II become king England, etc.
30 April 1662	Birth of Mary II
21 May 1662	Wedding of Catherine of Braganza and Charles II
6 February 1665	Birth of Queen Anne
10 September 1669	Death of Henrietta Maria
31 March 1671	Death of Anne Hyde
23 November 1673	Wedding of Maria of Modena and James VII and II
4 November 1677	Wedding of Mary II and William III
28 July 1683	Marriage of Queen Anne and Prince George of Denmark
6 February 1685	Death of Charles II; James VII and II becomes king of England and Scotland
23 December 1688	James VII and II is deposed during the Glorious Revolution
13 February 1689	Mary II and William III are offered the crown
28 December 1694	Death of Mary II
16 September 1701	Death of James VII and II
8 March 1702	Queen Anne becomes queen of England and Scotland
31 December 1705	Death of Catherine of Braganza

1 May 1707	Acts of Union, uniting England and Scotland as the sovereign state of Great Britain
28 October 1708	Death of Prince George of Denmark
1 August 1714	Death of Queen Anne and the end of the Stuart Dynasty
7 May 1718	Death of Maria of Modena

The Early Stewarts and Their Spouses

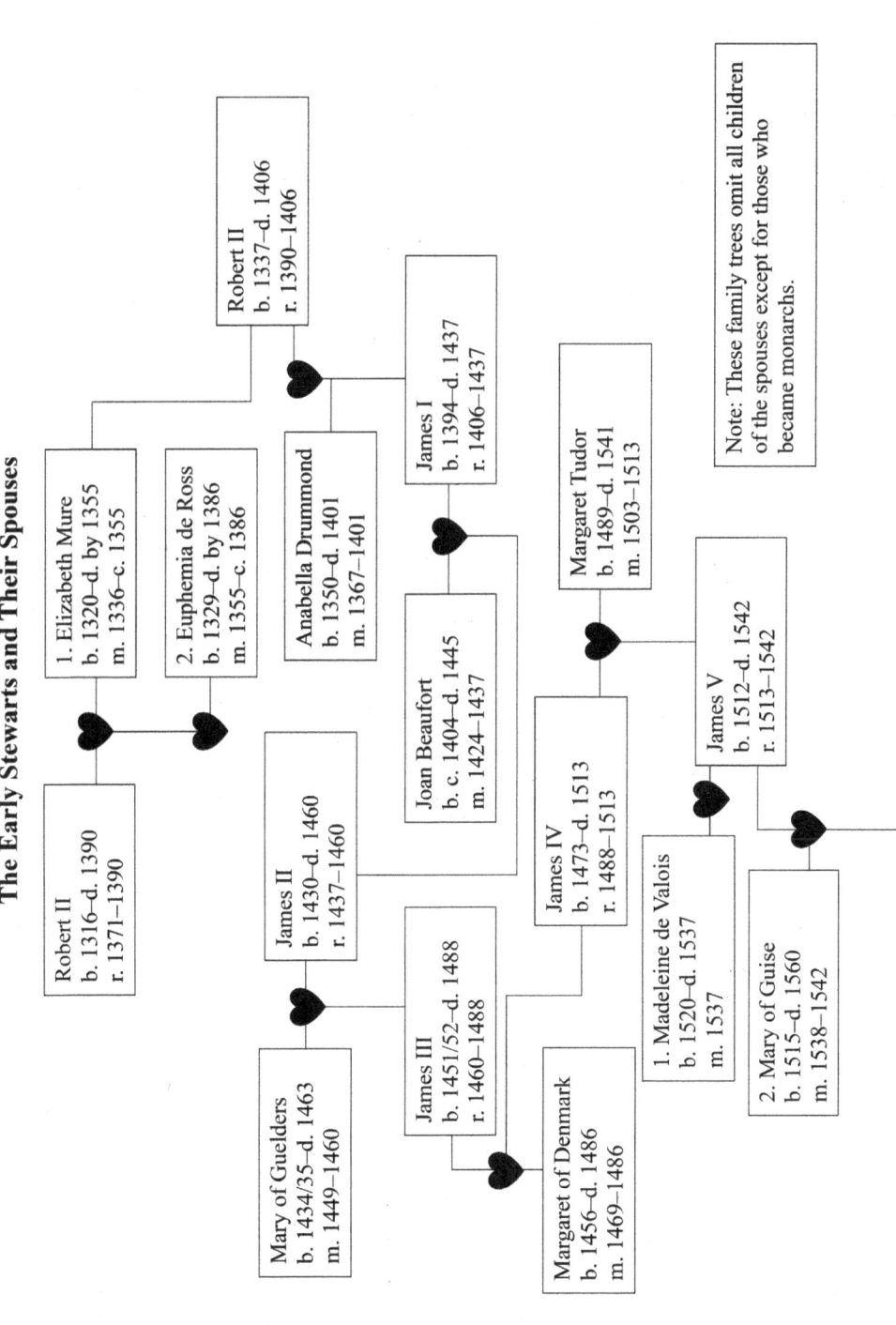

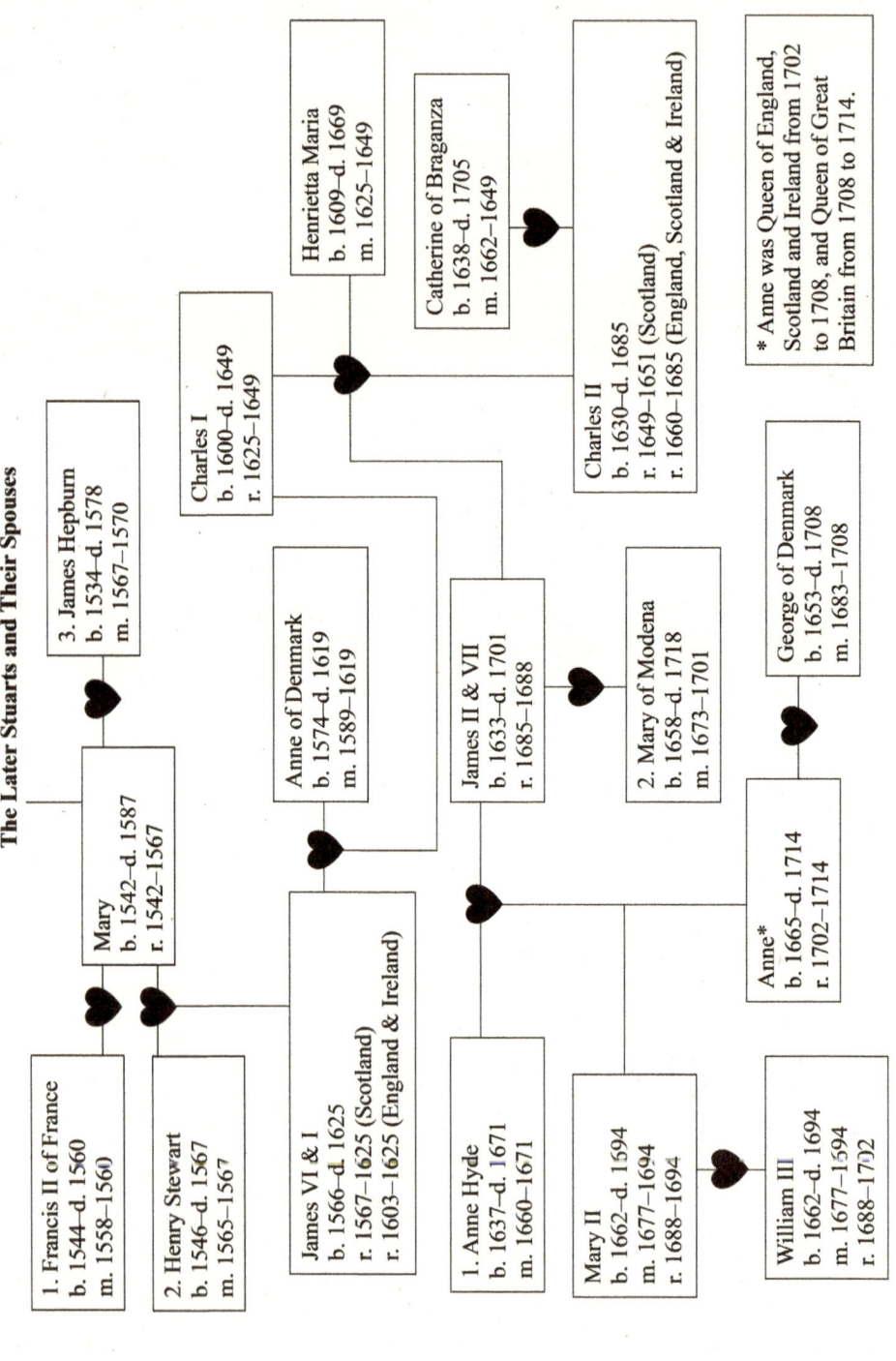

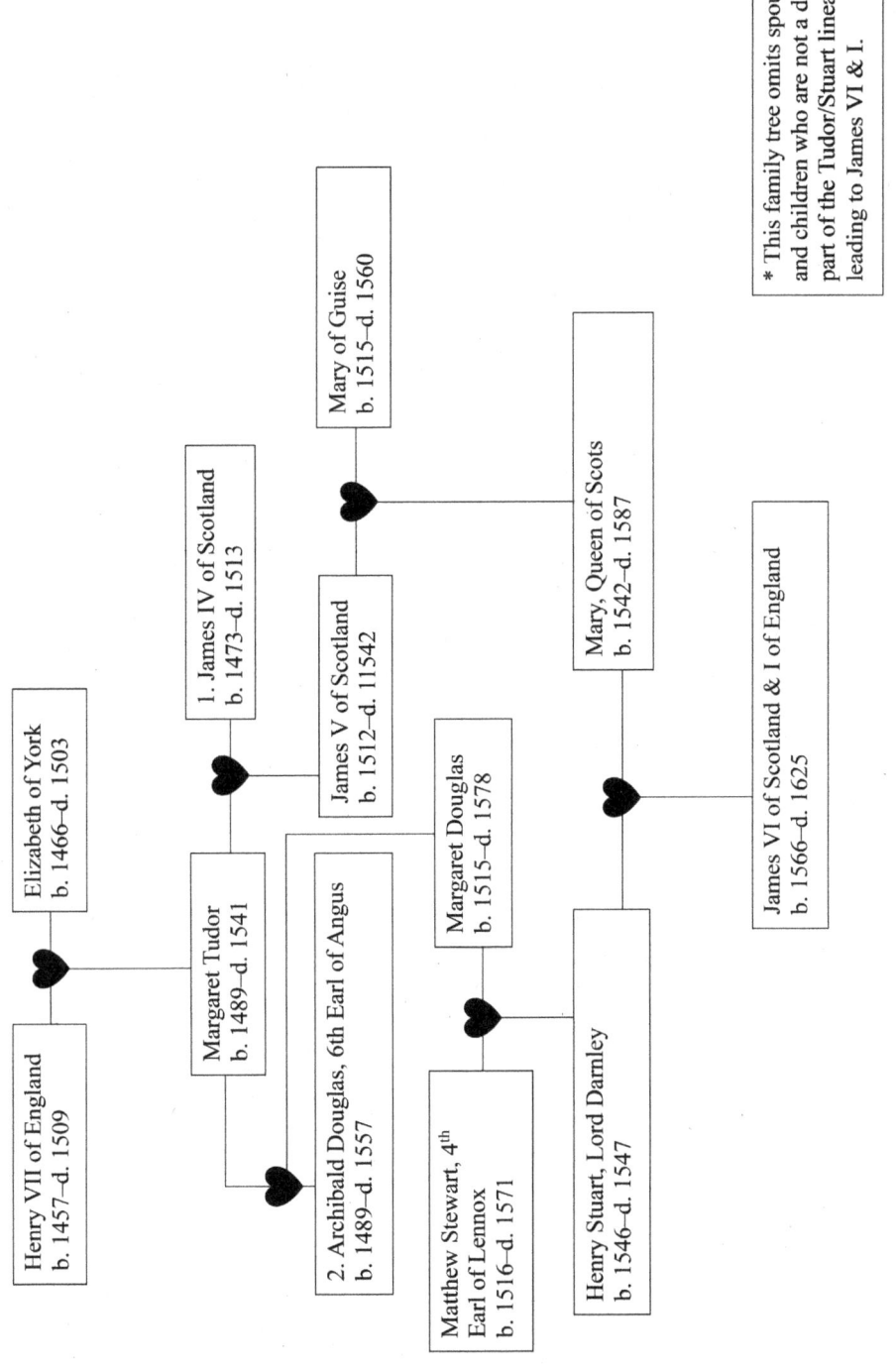

The Hanover – Stuart Lineage

- Henry Stuart, Lord Darnley
  b. 1547–d. 1567
- Mary, Queen of Scots
  b. 1542–d. 1587
- James VI & I
  b. 1566–d. 1625
- Anne of Denmark
  b. 1574–d. 1619
- Elizabeth Stuart
  b. 1596–d. 1662
- Frederick V, Elector Palatine
  b. 1596–d. 1632
- Sophia of the Palatinate
  b. 1630–d. 1714
- Ernest Augustus, Elector of Hanover
  b. 1629–d. 1698
- George, Duke of Brunswick-Lüneburg
  b. 1582–d. 1641
- Anne Eleonore of Hesse-Darmstadt
  b. 1601–d. 1659
- George I of Great Britain
  b. 1660–d. 1727

* This family tree omits children who are not a direct part of the Hanover/Stuart lineage leading to George I of Great Britain.

Introduction

The Stuart monarchs came from an ancient Scottish family who eventually came to rule the thrones of Scotland, England, and Ireland after the Tudor line failed in England. James VI of Scotland became James I of England and Ireland after his cousin Elizabeth I of England died in 1603 without an heir. The sequence of Stuart monarchs continued, not without rebellious interruption, for the next century until the death of Queen Anne in 1714.

During the reign of the Stuarts in Scotland, Ireland, and England, they did, of course, marry and produce children. This book familiarizes the reader with the spouses of the various Stuart monarchs. There is source material for some more than others. The farther away from the present in which the spouses lived, the less source material exists. In addition, consorts were frequently in the shadow of their beloved monarchs, so there can be a frustrating paucity of information at times. Overall, due to the general nature of this work, the curious reader is encouraged to seek out more in-depth biographical works for the monarch and the monarch's spouse who draws the most interest.

The work begins with describing the Auld Alliance, which most believe they understand but might only genuinely know a little about. Gaining insight into the Auld Alliance helps explain some of the Scottish and Stuart monarchs' political and marital decisions.

The prologue visits the very first Stuart consorts. This introduces the reader to a few of the queens consort from relatively far back in time. The substantive portion of the book, beginning in Chapter 1 with Joan Beaufort, is the point at which more detail is given about each person married into the Stuart family.

I spell the family name "Stewart" until Mary, Queen of Scots, is sent to France. In France, she began spelling the family name "Stuart" and continued upon returning to Scotland. However, Mary, Queen of Scots' second husband, was Henry Stewart, Lord Darnley. Presumably, their son adopted "Stuart," and thus, the spelling was solidified.

Although certainly not a Stuart spouse, Oliver Cromwell's wife, Elizabeth Bourchier, is included in the middle of this work. She still left her mark on what would become Great Britain. It is hoped that the reader will forgive the author for including the non-Stuart Elizabeth Bourchier in her appropriate place in the timeline. There is a brief appearance by Elizabeth's daughter-in-law Dorothy Maijor, who married Richard Cromwell. The book then returns to its regularly scheduled programming.

Chapter 14, concerning William III and Mary II, discusses them both because they are dual Stuart spouses. The final chapter, about Queen Anne's husband, George of Denmark, necessarily has a portion that concerns the many, many sorrowful deaths of the couple's children.

The appendix is a collection of poems relevant to the spouses discussed. I have left the poems in their original language with a modern English transcription, where appropriate. The Scots are phenomenal poets, and it seemed undesirable to leave out these essential poems in a discussion about Stuart consorts.

I hope this book will serve as an introduction to the Stuart spouses and monarchs. The book is not meant to be a conclusive authority about the complex and lengthy Stuart dynasty, the history of Scotland, or England, or Great Britain. It does give a general overview of the intrigues and machinations of the dynasty as it spread across multiple kingdoms.

A Note on the Auld Alliance

Background

The Auld Alliance, an ancient alliance between the French and the Scots, extended back to at least the 13th century. Appeasing the needs of tradition, both sides claimed the alliance began with Charlemagne in the 8th or 9th century. This was highly unlikely, especially given that Scotland was known as Albion at the time. No country of France existed, either.

In truth, the Auld Alliance was put in place by Philip IV of France and the Scottish Council of Twelve in October 1295. Scotland was represented by John Balliol, who signed the treaty on 23 October 1295 in Paris. The basis of this alliance was to defend against Edward I of England and his attempts at exerting control over Scotland. The death of Alexander III left a concerning gap in the governance of Scotland, providing Edward I an opportunity. The Auld Alliance was fully ratified at Dunfermline in Scotland on 2 February 1296.

The Maid of Norway

Alexander III of Scotland died on 18 or 19 March 1286. He was determined to visit his wife, Queen Yolande. Yolande turned twenty-three on 20 March 1286. In his pursuit of seeing her at Kinghorn in Fife, Alexander decided to ride at night through a wicked storm. He never made it to Yolande, being found the next day along the shore with a broken neck. Yolande, upon hearing the news, announced that she was pregnant. If so, she was only a month or two along, and Alexander might not have known of it. Yolande delivered a baby later that year, and it was either stillborn or died shortly after birth. The exact details are lost to time. By the end of November 1286, the Scottish nobles were meeting to determine the next steps for the succession. England's ambitious Edward I had set his eye on Scotland, so it was best to secure the situation.

Alexander's toddler granddaughter, Margaret of Norway, was chosen as Queen of Scotland. Given her tender age, Margaret stayed in Norway for four years. Edward I of England negotiated a marriage for Margaret with one of Edward's sons, causing more worry to the Scots.

Margaret left for Scotland in August 1290. She fell ill along the way, landing at Orkney in late September 1290. Margaret succumbed to her illness quickly after landing in Orkney and was never crowned queen. John I Baliol was made King of Scots after Margaret's death.

Subsequent Overtures and Ratifications

Robert the Bruce and Charles IV of France renewed the Auld Alliance in April 1326 at Corbeil, and it was subsequently ratified on 12 July 1326 in Stirling.

David II, King of Scots, fled to France in 1334 after the Scottish loss at the Battle of Halidon Hill in 1332. David II and Philip VI of France were on friendly terms, and Philip sent back-up from France to assist the Scots by the beginning of the Hundred Years' War in about 1338. In 1346, David was captured by the English at Neville's Cross. Ten or so years later, John II of France, the successor of Philip VI, was captured and joined David. David was released in October 1357 and sought to renew the Auld Alliance with John II's son, the future Charles V of France. They renewed the Auld Alliance in Paris on 29 June 1359.

The Hundred Years' War continued. Robert II, King of Scots, renewed the Auld Alliance once again with Charles V of France on 30 June 1371. Robert II agreed to continue providing aid to the French king, Charles V. The tradition of renewing the Auld Alliance whenever a new King of Scots or King of France was crowned was now in place. Thus, it was restored once more when Charles VI became King of France, with the alliance being re-ratified on 3 March 1391.

The Auld Alliance was renewed on behalf of the captured James I of Scotland on 6 January 1408. A few years later, Charles VI of France was taken into custody by a combined Anglo-Burgundian force, and many Scots were sent to aid the French over the following twenty years or so. With the Scots' help, the French could cast out the English under the weak rule of Henry VI, taking back much of the territory that England previously held.

James III, King of Scots, and Louis XI of France toward the last half of the 15th century failed to renew the Auld Alliance. They were the only monarchs from 1295 to 1558 who did not reaffirm the alliance. This is not to say that the old bonds of friendship and military support were cast aside, but only that no formal action was taken toward ratifying the Auld Alliance between the two kings. James IV subsequently confirmed the Auld Alliance with Charles VIII of France in 1492.

James IV died at the Battle of Flodden in September 1509, leaving his wife Margaret Tudor as the regent of their infant son, now James V. Margaret wed Archibald Douglas in August 1514, removing her as James V's regent. Conveniently, though, Margaret's sister Mary was wedded to the French king, Louis XII. The Auld Alliance was ratified on James V's behalf on 2 January

1515 in Edinburgh, with the Scots being oblivious that Louis XII had died the day before. After some political wrangling between Francis I of France and representatives on James V's behalf, the Auld Alliance was renewed between the monarchs in May 1518.

Between 1518 and 1521, Henry VIII of England, brother of Margaret and Mary as mentioned, was busy agitating against Francis I of France. Attempts at restoring peace came to naught, leading to another renewal of the Auld Alliance on 28 December 1521 in Edinburgh. Henry VIII tried to convince Francis I that he, Francis, should not deal with the Duke of Albany, who was part of James V's regency council, because Albany was a danger to the Scots and Margaret. Margaret had different thoughts, writing on 4 February 1522 to Francis I that the "state of the kingdom [is in order] and that he would be pleased to know that her son [James V], your good brother, cousin, considered son, and ally, and herself" were plenty pleased with the Duke of Albany, further writing to Francis I that, "my cousin the duke of Albany, our commander who, since his return, has put all his efforts, and at great expense and trouble, to the reduction of Scotland to the obedience of my son, the king; [including] the rebels and other great personages malignantly inclined towards this kingdom." The French continued supporting James V throughout his reign.

Finally, James V's daughter Mary, Queen of Scots, renewed the Auld Alliance in 1558. She married the future Francis II of France, joining the Scottish and French crowns. The military aspect of the Auld Alliance ended in 1560 with the Treaty of Edinburgh between the English and Scots.

With this background in mind, it is time to meet the Stuarts.

Prologue
Who Were the Stuarts?

Family Origin

The Stuart family line began in the 12th century with Walter Fitzalan. He was born around 1106 to 1110 and died in 1177. An English baron, Fitzalan came to serve David I of Scotland in roughly 1136. By about 1150, Fitzalan had risen in rank to become Steward of Scotland. It is from Fitzalan that the Stuart family gets their name. By the 13th century, Fitzalan's descendants adopted "Stewart," an alternative spelling of Steward, as a last name.

When he was a young man, Walter Fitzalan was a knight in England, possessing land in Shropshire, which borders modern-day Wales. Fitzalan found his way to Scotland by 1136, with his presence as a witness during the founding of Melrose Abbey being recorded. It is possible that Fitzalan went to Scotland because he, like David I of Scotland, supported the claims of the deceased Henry I of England's daughter Matilda to the English throne.[1]

Fitzalan served King David, and it is thought that the position of steward at this time put Fitzalan in charge of the king's hall, rather than the king's private chambers. The position of High Steward became hereditary likely under King David. When David I died, Fitzalan was reconfirmed as steward by Malcolm IV, and subsequently by William I. Upon Fitzalan's death in 1177, his son Alan Fitzwalter became High Steward of Scotland. Walter Fitzalan's grandson and Alan Fitzwalter's son, Walter Stewart, became the third High Steward of Scotland in 1204.

The Stewart family rose to royalty through Robert II of Scotland, son of Marjorie Bruce and Walter Stewart. Marjorie Bruce's father was Robert the Bruce. Robert the Bruce's son became David II of Scotland when Robert died, but David II died without any children. None of Robert the Bruce's other sons were legitimate, and those that were had predeceased David II. The illegitimate

---

1. The Empress Matilda, Holy Roman Empress by marriage, was elected Henry I of England's heir. His son and heir, not to mention a couple of other children, died when the *White Ship* sank. David I of Scotland was Matilda's uncle and supported her claim to the throne over that of her cousin Stephen of Blois. Matilda invaded England to assert her rights in a civil war known as the Anarchy. In the end, Stephen held the throne between 1135 and 1154, but it was Matilda's son who succeeded him as Henry II of England.

sons of Robert the Bruce could not become King of Scotland when David II died in 1371. The line then fell to Marjorie and her children.

Robert II's mother Marjorie died in 1316 or 1317 when she was roughly twenty years old. Robert, born 2 March 1316, was an infant at the time of his mother's death. The tale surrounding Marjorie and Robert is that Marjorie was pregnant with Robert when she fell from her horse, causing her to go into premature labor. She died shortly after Robert's birth. Another version of the tale is that Marjorie was pregnant with a second child when she fell from her horse in autumn 1317 and subsequently died. Either way, the young woman seems to have died from a riding accident when she was young and pregnant.

Shortly after Marjorie's death, Robert was declared by Parliament in 1317 his grandfather Robert the Bruce's successor should Robert the Bruce fail to have any legitimate sons. When Robert's uncle David II was born in 1324, Robert was no longer the heir of his grandfather. When Robert's father, Walter Stewart, died in 1327, Robert became High Steward of Scotland. He served his grandfather, Robert the Bruce, until the latter died in 1329. Afterward, Robert served his uncle David II until David died in 1371. With David died the House of Bruce.

At the spritely age of almost sixty-five, Robert Stewart became King Robert II of Scotland in February 1371. He was the first Stewart king, and his family would rule for almost 400 years until the death of Anne, Queen of Great Britain and Ireland. Between Robert II and Queen Anne, the Stuart family produced fifteen monarchs and a name change.

Elizabeth Mure, Mother of a Stewart King

Robert enjoyed the favors of Elizabeth Mure when he was a young man. He married her in 1336. This initial marriage ceremony was not done according to Catholic rite, making it uncanonical. The argument that their first marriage was invalid would be a thorn in their children's side in later life.

Not much is known about Elizabeth Mure other than that she was of the minor nobility and possibly born in the area by Rowallan Castle. The castle was built around the 13th century and held by the Mure, or Muir, family. Rowallan Castle is in Ayrshire, in the southwest of Scotland.

Elizabeth's first child, named John, was born in 1337. His exact date of birth is unknown. It is possible that Elizabeth suspected or knew she was pregnant in 1336, and Robert decided to marry her. If true, that might explain why the couple had an uncanonical marriage—it was rushed.

Elizabeth bore ten children who survived to adulthood but may have had as many as thirteen. Perhaps realizing he stood a strong chance of becoming King of Scotland, Robert sought a papal dispensation in 1347 to remarry Elizabeth.

The French Pope Clement VI granted the dispensation in November 1347, and the couple remarried in 1349, following all proper Catholic rites for the ceremony. Elizabeth died in early 1355, sixteen years before her husband became Robert II of Scotland. She never had the chance to be recognized as Queen of Scotland or the mother of Scottish princes and princesses.

Euphemia de Ross, First Stewart Queen Consort of Scots

Euphemia de Ross was the daughter of Hugh, Earl of Ross, and his second wife, Margaret de Graham. Hugh's first wife was Matilda or Maude Bruce, who was the sister of Robert the Bruce. Robert the Bruce ruled as King of Scots between 1306 and 1329, as mentioned previously. It is unknown exactly when Euphemia was born, but she appears to be named after her paternal grandmother, Euphemia de Berkeley.

Euphemia was married twice. Her first husband was John Randolph, 3d Earl of Moray. John's father had a close relationship with Robert the Bruce. John enjoyed a military career which began in at least 1332 but led to his death in 1346. John served as joint-regent of Scotland alongside Robert Stewart, the future Robert II. Euphemia and John did not have any children.

Euphemia's second husband was Robert Stewart. The couple needed a papal dispensation to wed due to consanguinity, although the fourth degree by which they are related is unknown. In addition, Euphemia's first and second husbands were cousins, which also required a dispensation.

Euphemia de Ross married Robert Stewart on 2 May 1355. Their first child, David Stewart, was born around 1357. Scottish records show that,

> In the year 1371, after the incarnation of the Lord, on 26 March at Scone, Robert the Steward of Scotland, earl of Strathearn, nephew of the lord David [II] de Bruce of glorious memory, the illustrious king of Scots who recently died, was crowned and anointed as king by the reverend father in Christ the lord William de Landels, bishop of St. Andrews. At which coronation and anointing, the lords prelates, earls and barons and all the nobles written below were present, with a great assembled multitude of people from all parts of the kingdom of Scotland.

The day after, fealty was paid to Robert II,

> And so, after the aforesaid coronation and anointing had been celebrated duly, amicably and solemnly in all ways, as was proper, the next day, with the king sitting on the royal throne upon the hill of Scone, as is the custom,

the prelates, earls and barons and nobles written below assembled and compeared in his presence.

When Robert II enjoyed his coronation on 26 March 1371, David was created the Earl of Strathearn. David died between 1386 and 1389, leaving behind a daughter. She was named Euphemia Stewart, after her paternal grandmother Euphemia de Ross, and became Countess of Strathearn when David passed away.

Euphemia de Ross's second child and second son with Robert II was named Walter. He was born around 1360. Walter had a dubious demise after being part of a plot to murder James I of Scotland in 1437. Walter was caught, tortured, and died on 26 March 1437—more on that escapade in Chapter 1. Walter was the Earl of Atholl, Strathearn, and Caithness during his lifetime and likely received at least one of those appointments on his parents' coronation day.

Euphemia de Ross had two daughters, as well. The first, Elizabeth Stewart, was born before her father was elevated to King of Scots. Her exact date of birth is unknown, with a range of birth years between 1356 and 1370. She might have been her mother, Euphemia's oldest child. Elizabeth, aged anywhere between five and nineteen years old, had established a relationship with David Lindsay in 1375. He was the father of at least one of her children. Elizabeth Stewart's second son was considered illegitimate, so it is possible that Elizabeth married David years after the birth of some of their children.

In early 1371, non-parliamentary records show that there was some concern over the living conditions of Euphemia and her recently crowned husband,

> On 3 May next following afterwards at Edinburgh, the king then residing there, it was ordained in his secret council concerning the standing and means of living of the king himself and also the queen [Euphemia de Ross], and concerning the regulation and governance of their households, and concerning the keepership and sustenance of the castles by the means which is contained in another register made concerning such non-permanent ordinances and deeds. Present in the said council were the lord [William de Landels], bishop of St. Andrews, the lord [William Douglas, 1st] earl of Douglas, Sir John de Carrick, chancellor, Sir Walter de Biggar, chamberlain, Sir Robert de Erskine, Sir James de Douglas, Sir Hugh of Eglinton and John Lyon, keeper of the privy seal of our lord the king.

Euphemia enjoyed life as a queen until her death in 1386.

Anabella Drummond

After the death of Robert II of Scotland in April 1390, his eldest son with Elizabeth Mure became Robert III, King of Scots. Robert III, back when he was still known as John Stewart, married Anabella Drummond in 1367. Her father was, amongst other things, Chief of Clan Drummond. Anabella was born around 1350.

Anabella had six children with her husband before he sustained a severe and crippling injury. Their first two children were girls, causing drama over whether a woman should be allowed to become Queen of Scots in her own right. Anabella's vexatious brother-in-law, Robert, Duke of Albany,[2] was believed to be behind the effort to remove Anabella's daughters from Scottish succession. Thankfully for Anabella's 16th-century descendant, Mary Stuart, nothing came of the attempt to bar women from the throne. Anabella and her husband, John, still worried about their daughters' future. John handed over his earldom of Carrick to his father, Robert II. Robert then bestowed the earldom on both Anabella and John and allowed for the inheritance of the earldom to pass down the female line. That way, their daughters Margaret and Mary, plus any others, would have some financial security.

Anabella's first son was named David and born on 24 October 1378. After David came Elizabeth and Egidia. David and Elizabeth survived to adulthood and married. Egidia may have survived to adulthood but died unmarried. Another boy, Robert, was born to Anabella and Robert III. Baby Robert did not survive infancy.

In 1384, Anabella's husband had a serious accident involving a horse. The exact nature of the accident is unknown, with it being described as a riding accident due to him being kicked by a horse. Either way, Robert III's physical health was never the same.

The couple's coronation at Scone Palace was held in summer 1390. Scone, in Perth, was its own kingdom and began in the 9th century serving as the official place for a King of Scots to be crowned. John Stewart gained permission to use "Robert" as his regnal name, and became known as Robert III, King of Scots after his coronation.

Robert III was concerned about maintaining Anabella's dignity, and so had her financial needs duly tended to. In 1391, a charter was passed for Annabella's benefit,

---

2. The various dukes of Albany had a special talent for being a thorn in the Scottish monarchy's side over the centuries.

Robert, by the grace of God king of Scots, to all good men of his whole land, clerics and laymen, greeting. Because in [our] parliament [held] at Scone in the month of March in the first year of our reign it was considered by the three estates of the kingdom, decreed and determined we should honourably and reasonably [... ...] cause to be assigned to our most beloved consort Anabella [Drummond], queen of Scotland, for trappings and other things required for her standing and life [... ... ...], 2,500 merks sterling from our great customs of our burghs written below, to be levied and received for her by the hands of our custumars who shall be in that place for the time, for all the time of her life, at the feasts of Whitsun [May/June] and St Martin in winter [11 November] by equal portions.

Robert seems to have intended more benefits for Anabella. The remainder of the charter is lost. Given how much money was granted to Anabella by parliament, it can be safely assumed that the Scots approved of their Queen.

Anabella and Robert III welcomed their last child, a little boy whom they named James, in July 1394. During the last weeks of her pregnancy, Anabella received a letter from Richard II of England. Richard's letter does not survive. It was likely written in Norman French, especially given that Richard was born in Bordeaux and that his successor, Henry IV, was the first English monarch since the Conquest in 1066 to speak English as a primary language. Anabella's response, written on 1 August 1394 from Dunfermline castle, was in Norman French and likely dictated by her to a scribe. It is not known if Anabella herself spoke Norman French. The same scribe who physically wrote the letter may have translated it from Scots to Norman French for Anabella. Anabella mentions the recent birth of her son James and her safe delivery of the baby. The overall letter seemed to be in response to Richard's thoughts on marriages between members of the English royal family or nobility and those of Scotland. Anabella mentioned that she was pleased with Richard's propositions.

Anabella was the force behind the throne. Her injured husband grew increasingly emotionally and mentally incapacitated as the years came and went. Anabella did her best to promote the interests of her son David. One of the more overt activities was organizing a jousting tournament in early 1398 when David was roughly twenty years old. As part of the tournament, David was knighted. In April of that year, David was created Duke of Rothesay.

Anabella's brother-in-law Robert, Duke of Albany, recognized that his brother the King of Scots was increasingly decrepit. He tried his best to exert control over his nephews, particularly David. Anabella pushed back. She is thought to have had a hand in having David declared Lieutenant of the Realm in January 1399. This was a counterbalance to Robert, Duke of Albany having himself appointed King Robert III's chief advisor. David would be in charge for the next three years, to the exclusion of the Duke of Albany.

In the late summer of 1400, Henry IV of England tried to take advantage of Robert III's declining state. English troops invaded Scotland, eventually finding themselves attacking David at Edinburgh Castle. The English retreated fairly quickly, allegedly because of Anabella and their respect for her.

The Mysterious Death of Anabella's Eldest

David Stewart was an interesting character, who ultimately fell under the control of his paternal uncle after Anabella's death. David made curious marital decisions in the 1390s, including rushing into a marriage with Elizabeth de Dunbar in 1395. A papal dispensation was needed for the couple to lawfully wed in the eyes of the Church. The couple decided not to wait. Some of the delays were occasioned by Antipope Clement VII in September 1394, followed by the installation of Antipope Benedict XIII later that month. Of course, Boniface IX was safely installed in Rome back in 1389. Part of David's foolish behavior could be due to the seventeen-year-old being fed up with his parents writing to the "wrong" pope, thus delaying things. This is pure conjecture, but teenagers have always been teenagers, armed with the knowledge that their parents are idiots who do not understand.

Much to David's chagrin, the Pope was unimpressed and declared his marriage to Elizabeth void in 1397. The couple would be allowed to remarry with the Church's blessing after spending some time apart. It was a fine enough solution, except that the Douglas family, rivals of the Dunbars, wished to see a Douglas married to David. David's sickly father Robert III was easily manipulated into approving a marriage between Marjory Douglas, born after 1371, and David. Elizabeth, who had lived openly with David for two years, was a ruined woman who never remarried. Robert III and David alienated the Dunbar family, who gave up Scotland and went to the court of Henry IV of England.

As mentioned before, Anabella saw to it that David was created Lieutenant of Scotland in 1398, a post which he was supposed to occupy until at least 1401. Anabella, a strong supporter and benevolent influence on David, died in the autumn of 1401 at the palace in Scone. She was buried in Dunfermline. David's sickly father was still alive, but completely impotent as a ruler.

In February 1402, months after Queen Anabella's death, David was arrested whilst on his way to St. Andrews. He was arrested in part because his appointment as Lieutenant of Scotland had expired. This was a flimsy excuse, but enough of one to seize David. According to Walter Bower, who lived a religious life and wrote the *Scotichronichon*, a 15th-century chronicle,

A little earlier the lord king in council appointed certain councillors [powerful barons and knights] under oath to control and advise Sir David Stewart...Prince of Scotland, because it appeared to the king...that he engaged too often in unruly games...so that he too was bound by wiser council and swore to conform to the control and advice of these men.

David had gone on a bender of bad behavior after Anabella's death. Reportedly,

But on the death of the queen [Anabella] his noble mother, who used to curb him in many things, it was as if a noose had become worn: he hoped to free himself and, spurning his council of honourable men, gave himself up wholly once more to his previous frivolity.

David's uncle Robert, Duke of Albany, and David's brother-in-law Archibald, 4th Earl of Douglas, were part of the group who received King Robert III's plea.

David was casually on his way to St. Andrews to take the bishop's castle until a new bishop was put in place. The former bishop had died recently. David was captured by the Duke of Albany "between the township of Nydie and Strathtyrum as...he rode towards the castle of Saint Andrews in simple fashion... and led [David] by force to the castle." David was kept at the castle while a plan for what to do with him was sorted. The Duke of Albany and Earl of Douglas were in control of young David.

The Duke of Albany had David transported to Albany's residence of Falkland Palace,

the duke of Albany with second Sir Archibald earl of Douglas forcibly moved him to the tower of Falkland mounted on a mule and dressed in a russet tunic, and there they condemned him to be kept in a certain decent small room, in which he was long guarded...until after languishing with dysentery (as some will have it) with hunger he died on [the evening of] the day before Easter ((which fell on 26 March) or on the morning of Easter Day [1402], and was buried at Lindores.

A sad end for Anabella's eldest son.

Anabella's Son James

Anabella's young son James was the heir apparent once news of twenty-three-year-old David's death reached court. The Duke of Albany secured the position of Lieutenant of Scotland for himself, shoving Anabella's husband into the background. In 1404, Robert III managed to oust Albany. He spent the rest of 1404 and most of 1405 securing the Stewart lands for James. In late 1405, Robert III decided to send James to France for safekeeping. James was eleven years old.

Unfortunately for James, no one thought to plan how to conduct the little prince to France carefully. In February 1406, the prince and his protectors moved through Douglas territory to reach the sea. They had forgotten that James's brother had died of suspicious circumstances not four years earlier, and that the circumstances involved a member of the Douglas family. James and his escort encountered trouble from the Douglas family. James managed to reach the Firth of Forth, which is to say they barely made it. James's father thereafter either ordered that Sir Robert Lauder take James to his family's island of Bass Rock, where the Lauder family had a castle, or that is where James landed when he fled.

A ship heading to France finally passed by the Bass in March 1406. The ship picked up James. He was finally on his way to France. The ship was intercepted by English pirates off the coast of Yorkshire, at Flamborough Head. Likely extremely delighted at having captured the Scottish prince, the English pirates made certain that James was presented to Henry IV of England. James then began a very long period in English custody. His father, Robert III, died days later on 4 April 1406 at Rothesay Castle. Robert III was the last King of Scots to die a natural death until 1625. James was now King of Scots.

Parting Thoughts on Anabella

One final glimpse of Anabella's character is given through an imagined conversation between her and Robert III. The chronicler Walter Bower, who likely saw the king in his lifetime, reflected upon Robert's character shortly after Robert's death. In particular, Bower saw Robert as a humble king who was "tall in stature though lame; he had a very handsome face with a luxuriant beard; he had the attractiveness of snowy-white old age, with lively eyes which always spread good humour, and rather long and ruddy cheeks blooming with every mark of amiability." Sounds like Anabella had a suitably attractive husband and kindly companion.

Presumably five or six years before his death, when Anabella was still alive, she discussed with Robert what he wanted for his tomb. Of this imagined interaction, Bower wrote,

> One day when the noble Queen Annabel (the wife of this most gentle king in her lifetime) asked him why he was not making arrangements for

an honourable monument like other kings who had been his predecessors, and what words of appreciation he had in mind to be written as his epitaph.

Robert replied that he was not worthy of a grand monument, and he wished for his epitaph to say, "Here lies the worst of kings and the most wretched of men in the whole kingdom." For whatever reason, Robert III did not believe in himself. This exchange written by Bower shows Anabella's care and concern for her husband, and his thoughts about himself.

Not much else is known about Anabella directly.

Chapter 1

Joan Beaufort

Joan, like too many women in history, is known through her male relatives. Born a granddaughter of John of Gaunt, Joan was the second or third of six children born to John Beaufort and Margaret Holland. She was likely born around 1404.

One of the first meaningful mentions of Joan comes from her future husband, James I of Scotland. As discussed in the prologue, James came into the custody of Henry IV of England in March 1406, when James was eleven years old. Henry IV had been on the throne for about seven years at this point. He saw to it that James received an excellent education, and he cultivated an appreciation for English culture in James.

When Henry IV died in 1413, nineteen-year-old James stayed on at the English court in the custody of Henry V. James was first moved to the Tower of London, then eventually housed in Windsor Castle. Henry V, born in 1386, was about eight years older than James. It is from Henry V that James is said to have learned the skill of governing a kingdom. Henry V was also a grandson of John of Gaunt, making him a cousin of Joan Beaufort's. Henry V took James on campaign with him in France in 1420 and 1421, too. The relationship between James and Henry slowly changed from that of prisoner and jailer to that of guest and host.

Whilst in the midst of his ongoing captivity and feeling a particular sense of despair, on a fine day in May 1423, James looked out a window at Windsor Castle. He beheld the lovely Joan walking in the garden. The garden in which Joan walked might have been the King's Garden, where herbs were grown. The garden was to the north of the Upper Ward. A second herb garden may have been by the Great Hall, which is in the Lower Ward of Windsor Castle. It is unclear through which garden Joan walked, but she was in the fullness of her beauty and wearing her finery. James's heart was immediately shot through by a dart of love.

Joan is Seen by Her Future Husband

James wrote of his espying Joan for the first time in *Kingis Quair*, or King's Quire, a poem of 197 stanzas written around 1423. It is a good example of early

Scots in its original form. In the following extract, the language is transcribed into modern English for ease of reading. James I wrote,

> Bewailing in my chamber thus alone,
> Despairing of all joy and remedy,
> A-weary of my thoughts, and woe-begone,
> Unto the window did I walk in hye,
> To see the world and people walking by,
> As at the time, though I of cheering food
> Might have nought else, to look it did me good.
>
> Now there was made fast by the tower wall
> A garden fair, and in the corners set
> A herbery green, with wands so long and small
> Railed all about; and so with trees close-set
> Was all the place, and hawthorn hedges knit,
> That no one though he were near walking by,
> Might there within scarce anyone espy.
> ....
> And therewith cast I down my eyes again,
> And walking, as I saw, beneath the tower,
> Full secretly new coming her to pleyne [play],
> The fairest and the freshest youthful flower
> That e'er I saw, methought, before that hour,
> For which surprise so sudden, did astert [started]
> The blood of all my body to my heart.
> ...
> Then in my head I drew right hastily,
> And presently I leaned it out again,
> And saw her walk, so very womanly,
> With no one more, but only women twain.
> Then did I study in myself and seyne [say]
> 'Ha! sweetest are you sure a worldly creature,
> Or truly heav'nly thing in form of nature?'
> ...
> Of her array the form if I should write,
> To wit her golden hair and rich attire
> In fretwise trimmed and set with pearls so white
> And balas rubies sparkling as the fire,
> With many an emerald and fair sapphire;

And on her head a chaplet fresh of hue,
Of plumes par coloured red, and white, and blue;

And full of quiv'ring spangles [sequins] bright as gold,
Fashioned in shape like to the amorétts [love knots],
So new, so fresh, so pleasant to behold,
The plumes eke like unto the flow'r-jonétts [St John's wort],
Others were shaped like to the round krokétts [curled tufts],
Besides all this, there was, as well I wot [knew],
Beauty enough to make a world to dote.

About her neck, white as the fire amaille [enamel],
A goodly chain of small orfevery [goldsmith's work],
Whereat there hung a ruby, without fail,
Like to a heart it shaped was verily,
That, as a spark of flame, so wantonly
Seemed burning bright upon her snowy throat;
A partner good she'd make, full well I wot!
…
In her was beauty, youth, and humble port,
And bounty, riches, womanly facture [mien],
God better wot than pen of mine report:
Wisdom, largess, estate, discretion sure
In ev'ry point so guided her mesúre,
In word, in deed, in shape, in contenance [demeanour],
That nature could no more her child advance.

Through which anon I knew and understood,
That she a mortal was this bright creature;
On whom to rest my eyes, so much of good
It did my woeful heart, I you assure,
That it was to me joy without measure.

James spotted Joan walking in the herb garden, despite the secluded nature of it. As a point of interest, this portion of *Kingis Quair* gives an idea of what the herb garden was like for someone strolling through it. James, who might have been lodged in the large round tower of Windsor Castle which still stands today, saw Joan walking beneath. James describes Joan as young, beautiful, and blonde, wearing expensive clothing. If she did have spangles on her clothes, those certainly would have stunningly caught the sunlight. Safe to say, James was in love, and he left to posterity a simple description of Joan Beaufort.

Joan's Family Background

Joan's family was considerably well connected. Her father John Beaufort, 1st Marquess of Somerset and 1st Marquess Dorset, was born around 1373. He was later elevated to 1st Earl of Somerset. His father, Joan's paternal grandfather, was John of Gaunt. John of Gaunt, Duke of Lancaster was born in Ghent. "Gaunt" was the English word for Ghent, Netherlands.

John of Gaunt was the third or fourth son of Edward III of England. He had an impressive fourteen children, between three wives and a mistress. In addition, John of Gaunt's son became Henry IV of England after Henry overthrew his cousin and John of Gaunt's nephew Richard II.

John's third wife, Katherine Swynford, started as John of Gaunt's lover. Her first child was John Beaufort, who was born before Katherine married John of Gaunt. The two later wed and their children were legitimized by their half-brother Henry IV. Upon their legitimization, John of Gaunt's children with Katherine Swynford adopted the surname of Beaufort. This is, of course, a simplification of John of Gaunt's life, but it brings us around to the birth of Joan Beaufort.

John Beaufort was married to Margaret Holland by at least 1401. Margaret was a great-great-granddaughter of Edward I of England. The couple had four sons and two daughters. Joan Beaufort was their second or third child. She was also the half-niece of Henry IV. She would have had a typical education for a girl of her station, which likely included reading, but perhaps not much in the way of writing.

James I Pursues Joan

Whether or not James did behold Joan outside his window, or met her at court, it is clear that he was smitten by her. There needed to be a proper plan for returning James to Scotland. At the same time, there was a distinct advantage to having James married to a high-ranking English woman.

An embassy from Scotland went to England in August 1423 to negotiate the release and return of their king. Part of that release included marrying Joan. The marriage gave a sense of security in England since it prevented James from marrying a French woman. After the finances of James's ransom and Joan's dowry were negotiated, the wedding was set.

Joan married James on 12 February 1424. She was roughly twenty years old, and he was twenty-nine. After their wedding at St. Mary Overy, which is now Southwark Cathedral in London, they went to Winchester Palace. Now ruins just off Clink Street in London, Winchester Palace was the London residence for the Bishops of Winchester. Joan's uncle, Cardinal Henry Beaufort, hosted the couple.

After celebrating their wedding, Joan and James headed to Scotland. After James signed a pact in Durham on 28 March 1424, pledging a truce with England for seven years, the couple finally entered Scotland. James had been absent from his country for eighteen years.

Life in Scotland

The couple celebrated their coronation on 21 May 1424 at Scone Abbey. The Bishop of St. Andrews performed the ceremony. Having conceived quickly, Joan gave birth to her first child on Christmas Day 1424. It was a little girl, and she was named Margaret. On 19 March 1425, parliament agreed that it was "ordained that each bishop give bidding by his letters patent to his clergy that they make processions and special prayers for the welfare and healthy estate of our lord the king and our lady, the queen [Joan Beaufort] and their children." The health and safety of Joan and her hoped-for brood of children were certainly important to the Scots.

Perhaps still wishing for Joan to have more successful pregnancies, Parliament issued another piece of legislation in March 1426, penalizing those who would not make proper orations for Joan, her husband, or her children in church,

> since previously the estate of the clergy wilfully granted to cause certain orations to be made through all their subjects for our lord, the king, our lady the queen [Joan Beaufort], and their children born of them, therefore, having considered now the great favours and gracious zeal and maintenance that our said sovereign lord, the king, bears and shows to the holy church and its ministers, the said whole estate of the clergy has wilfully granted that each bishop of the realm shall cause it to be ordained and statute in the next "seigne" that each priest, whether religious or secular, of his diocese, shall say certain collects each time he says mass for the prosperity of our said lord, the king, our lady, the queen, and their children, under a certain pecuniary pain and censure of the holy church. And that they shall make a general statute thereupon at their next general council of the clergy.

The prayers and orations seemed to work because Joan was delivered of her daughter Isabella in late 1426.

Another daughter, Joan,[1] arrived in about 1428. That same year, in July, all the leading Scottish prelates were ordered to swear fealty to Joan as they had to James I,

> On which day our lord, the king, from the deliberation and consent of the whole council, decreed that all and singular successors of the prelates of the kingdom whomsoever, and also all and singular future heirs of earls, barons and all freeholders of the lord king should be held to make a similar oath to our lady queen [Joan Beaufort], and no prelate henceforth should be admitted to his temporality, or the heirs of any tenant of the lord king to his tenancy unless he has previously performed that oath to the queen.

Despite this, Joan still had not given birth to the ever-important son.

A few days later, on 19 July 1428, the Auld Alliance between France and Scotland was renewed. The Auld Alliance was strenuously tested a few years before when James I fought alongside the English in their war against France. Now that he was firmly in control of Scotland, it was time to mend the relationship. Joan Beaufort is mentioned briefly,

> James, by the grace of God king of Scots… Since the most Christian prince, our most beloved brother, ally and kinsman, Charles [VII], by the grace of God illustrious king of the French, had sent his eminent ambassadors to our presence, … with letters and commissions by the advice of his great council… on the part of the most Christian prince our noble brother, often and earnestly requested us that, on the lines of the treaty, confederation, union and bond that had been entered into by the most Christian princes, the kings of the French, and our ancestors of happy memory, … we have thought fit … to add to the glory and greater prosperity of both kingdoms,…to swear, agree and promise and approve, strengthen and confirm the said treaties and agreements in line with the contents of the letters. …we are anxious to contract and strengthen the joint bond and treaty of unity with which the aforesaid …king of the French, as also their kingdom, were bound together formerly, and will be bound, just as our said ancestors, the kings of Scots from long since have contracted them. … And that all and singular the aforesaid should proceed to be given more firm and secure support by our most beloved

---

1. Joan Stewart, Countess of Morton, is fascinating in her own right. She was deaf and mute and did her best to communicate with sign language. She went on to marry the 1st Earl of Morton and had children. She was referred to as the Muta Domina of Dalkeith or the Mute Lady of Dalkeith.

consort Queen [Joan Beaufort]…personally swore an oath upon the said alliances and bonds on God's Holy Gospels. Given under testimony of our great seal at St John's Town [Perth] on 17 July AD 1428, and in the twenty-third year of our reign.

Stemming from the renewal of the Auld Alliance, Joan's eldest child Margaret was betrothed to Charles VII's son Louis the Prudent, the future King Louis XI of France. At the time of the renewal, Charles VII had not been crowned king of France. Charles's father had signed the Treaty of Troyes back in 1420, declaring Henry VI of England to be the lawful king of France. Hence the ongoing battle between England and France in which James I took part back when James was held captive by the English. Charles was not successfully crowned king until July 1429.

On 16 October 1430, twin boys were born to Joan and James. The infant named Alexander died shortly after birth. The other twin went on to become James II of Scotland. James II was born with a very large, red birthmark that covered almost the entire left side of his face, giving him the epithet "James of the Fiery Face." Joan Beaufort had three more daughters after the birth of her twin sons. They were Eleanor, born in 1433, Mary, born in late 1434 or early 1435, and Annabella, born in 1436.

Joan Intercedes for James I's Subjects

Two accounts relay Joan's efforts to intercede with James I when his subjects were about to be punished. This was a common duty for medieval queens. By interceding with the king on behalf of the wrong doer, the king was afforded an opportunity to be less harsh when administering punishment out of love for the queen.

For instance, a "great nobleman" related to James I slapped another man,

> in the king's hall [at which the man who had been struck complained to the king], the king ordered the same hand as had struck the blow to be stretched out on the dining table, and handing a little knife to the young man who had been slapped, ordered him under pain of death to strike the hand that was pinioned in this way and pierce the palm. On hearing this the queen [Joan Beaufort] and her ladies…prostrated themselves on the floor. They had difficulty for an hour in securing pardon for the culprit, and then only on the basis that the man who had struck the blow was forbidden the court and the king's presence for a time.

Joan and her ladies surely must have made a dramatic impression, especially since they pleaded with James for such a while.

In another account from 1429, Joan interceded on behalf of Alexander of Islay, a distant cousin of James I's. Alexander was the third chief of Clan MacDonald and held the title Lord of the Isles. Alexander at first aided James I upon the latter's return to Scotland in 1424. Unfortunately, by 1426, Alexander was asserting dominion over the earldom of Ross, a royal possession. James invited Alexander and his retainers to meet with James at Inverness in 1428, and subsequently imprisoned them, including Alexander's mother. Diplomatic blunders ensued, ending in James releasing Alexander in late 1428 in exchange for Alexander promising to respect and obey James. That did not last long.

Alexander besieged Inverness in early 1429, hoping to put a grandson of Robert Stewart, Duke of Albany, on the throne. This is the very same Robert Stewart who captured and starved to death James I's brother David some twenty-seven years earlier. Robert's grandson, James Mor Stewart, was known as James the Fat. James the Fat's brothers and father were all executed after a failed rebellion in 1425. James the Fat fled to Ireland but was invited back by Alexander in 1429. Ships were sent to Ireland but did not retrieve James the Fat. It is unknown whether James the Fat died before the ships arrived or lived for another twenty years without returning to Scotland. Either way, Alexander had greatly offended James I. Alexander eventually surrendered to James I at Edinburgh in August 1429.

After his capture, Alexander was brought to Holyrood Abbey, down the Royal Mile from Edinburgh Castle. There, Alexander was forced to wear the clothes of a penitent, which likely included his face being covered, and to go to the high altar. This was Alexander's last chance to ask for forgiveness before being executed. Queen Joan interceded, vigorously and publicly begging James not to kill Alexander. James relented, and instead imprisoned Alexander. Alexander was imprisoned for about two years before being released, although his mother remained a captive of James I's until James died.

Joan's Eldest Child Weds

Joan's eldest daughter, Margaret, left Scotland in late March or early April 1436 for France. The chronicler Bower wrote of eleven-year-old Margaret's journey to France and wedding,

> The English sent one hundred and eighty ships to sea against her with a view of capturing her. As they awaited her arrival opposite the Breton Race at St Matthew of the Havens, a fleet of Flemings suddenly came up

near them, bound for Flanders with a cargo of wine from la Rochelle. The English captured them without a struggle…While this was going on, the dauphiness [Margaret] luckily made her escape and landed at La Rochelle.

Margaret was lodged on French soil with no particular fanfare for a time. Eventually, a French delegation came for her,

> She rested at Nieul Priory which is two leagues from La Rochelle without notice being taken of her until such time as the [arch-] bishop of Rheims [and several other French notables]…welcomed her and lodged her honorably in a splendid palace place for more than two months until the marriage was celebrated at Tours in Touraine.

Margaret met her new husband on 24 June 1436. Twelve-year-old Louis wrapped his arms around Margaret when they met.

The wedding itself took place on 25 June 1436. It was a relatively simple affair, given that Charles VII was effectively broke. The wedding took place at Tours, where it,

> was performed… by the archbishop of Rheims with the greatest possible ceremony, in the presence of the king and queen and also of the queen of Sicily [the mother of the queen of France]. Once the wedding had been formally celebrated, the Scots…were much gratified with various presents and after a safe voyage arrived home.

Despite this successful piece of foreign diplomacy, Joan's husband was not ruling very effectively in Scotland. He was still at war with England, too, and was busy assaulting Roxburgh Castle to wrest it from the English. He failed.

James I's Rule Flounders

James I found himself embroiled in a controversy with Walter Stewart, created Earl of Atholl in 1404. Walter was James's paternal half-uncle through Euphemia de Ross and her husband Robert II of Scotland. Walter was elevated to Earl of Strathearn, and Grand Justiciar of Scotland, in the late 1420s. Strathearn was a very wealthy territory.

Walter exerted a lot of effort in having James returned from England, and Walter's son David went to England as a hostage in 1424 in exchange for the release of James I. Walter's son David died in England in 1434. Walter's only other child and son, Alan, died fighting for James I against the Highlanders in

1431, during the Battle of Inverlochy. Whether Walter hated James I because both of Walter's sons died on James's behalf, or because Walter, as a son of Robert II, wanted to establish his bloodline on the throne of Scotland, James was an enemy in Walter's mind.

James, sensing the delicate nature of his reign, demanded on 15 January 1435 that his nobles renew their fealty to Joan in case something happened to James, "all the lords of parliament, both ecclesiastics and secular men and also the commissioners of the burghs, promised to give their letters of retinue and fealty to our lady, the queen [Joan Beaufort]." Unfortunately, this would later prove insufficient to protect Joan.

Assassination of James I

By early February 1437, Joan and her husband James I were still lodging at the Blackfriars (Dominican) monastery in Perth. They moved there to celebrate Christmastide and decided to stay on well into the new year. On the night of 20 February 1437, things went incredibly wrong for Joan. Walter Stewart's grandson, another Robert, served as James I's chamberlain. That night, when Joan and James were going to dine together, Robert allowed into the monastery a large group of men. There were as many as thirty, and their goal was to murder Joan and her husband.

The exact details of James's death are obscure, but it is certain that he was killed that night and that Joan barely escaped. The chronicler Walter Bower, relating the events of the night some fifty or so years later, wrote,

> This fateful year [of 1437] then smote this kingdom and greatly shook it...I [Walter Bower] am forced to unfold a gloomy account...because the human condition must pay its debts to death...It is said that thus unlucky death for the king was brought about by his paternal uncle [Walter Stewart] the earl of Atholl... According to his confession it was he who ordered his grandson Robert Stewart...and a few other accomplices to kill the king by assassination so that by this means he might imperceptibly take over the government of the kingdom by managing the affairs of the son of the king (who was seven years old) ...
>
> Therefore the said Robert Stewart, grandson of the earl of Atholl, as an intimate attendant, kinsman and member of the king's household... [along with] others, pernicious traitors that they were, cruelly and treacherously killed first the king's young page Walter Straiton, whom the king had sent out of the room to the cellar for some wine, and then the king himself. The queen also was seriously wounded [in the shoulder]. It happened at

night during the holy season of Lent, on 21 February, in the thirty-first year of his reign and forty-fourth year of his life, within the monastery of the friars preacher at Perth.

Joan was in a separate chamber with her ladies when she heard a commotion. Upon investigating, the door lock to Joan's and James's apartments had been broken. It is thought that Robert Stewart is the one who damaged the locks.

James used a fire poker or other similar tool to pull up a couple of floorboards inside the chamber. Underneath the boards was the building's sewer. In the meantime, Joan and her ladies did their best to hold the chamber door shut. From this arises the romantic, most likely untrue, 16th-century might of Kate Barlass, who is identified as either Catherine Douglas or Elizabeth Douglas. The legend goes that, upon discovering that not only were the locks broken, but also the piece of wood used to bar the door was missing, Joan ordered her ladies to sort a way to bar the door. One of her ladies used her arm to bar the door, which was broken by the assassins when they entered the room. By the end of the 16th century, this legendary woman was called "Kate Barlass." Proof of her deed is lacking but is a romantic notion for an otherwise gruesome event.

What is true is that James attempted to exit the monastery through the sewer tunnel, only to find that the exit was barred. The irony is that it was James who ordered that the sewer be barred only days earlier because he enjoyed playing tennis not far from there and kept losing balls in the sewer. He was either murdered in the sewer tunnel, or he turned around and went back into the room, accidentally pulling one of Joan's ladies down into the tunnel. James was stabbed to death.

Joan was injured in the shoulder. Part of a 16th-century account, one that mentions Kate Barlass, describes that a woman was stabbed or injured in the back. Whether this was Joan, and her shoulder was stricken from behind, is not definitive. The injury is attributed to a lady, although as mentioned, Joan herself did receive a serious wound to her shoulder whilst escaping.

Joan's Later Life

Joan managed to quickly have word sent ahead to Edinburgh Castle, where her young son was staying during Joan's time in Perth. Joan went to Edinburgh as quickly as her wounds would let her.

Joan's son was now James II of Scotland. The little boy was crowned on 26 March 1437 at Holyrood Abbey, a break from the centuries-old tradition of crowning the kings of Scotland at Scone. Joan was briefly at the head of her six-year-old son's regency, having been awarded custody of her son and daughters by parliament.

Joan rallied James I's Scots allies, who pursued and captured the assassins, including Walter Stewart. The assassins were brutally tortured in late March, and then executed on 27 March 1437, the day after James II's coronation. Joan was said to have presented a powerful, tragic figure when asking for her husband's supporters to help her find and punish the assassins. Roughly thirty-three years old, injured, and the mother of the king, she appeared brave in her efforts and terrible in her wrath. It is believed that it was none other than Joan who ordered the horrendous torture and executions of the assassins.

Joan lost her hold on the regency by the summer of 1437, although she kept James II in her custody. Archibald Douglas, 5th Earl of Douglas, was appointed Lieutenant General of Scotland and acted as the regent for James II after Joan was removed. James Stewart, the Black Knight of Lorne, was a supporter of his. The Black Knight was a descendant of Alexander Stewart. Presumably, the Black Knight was often in a position to be around Joan at court.

Archibald Douglas died of illness on 26 June 1439. Joan married the Black Knight within a month after the couple received a papal dispensation. One of the new co-regents, Alexander Livingston, was also the Governor of Stirling Castle. Seeing Joan as a threat to his power, Livingston ordered Joan arrested on 3 August 1439, her son James's ninth birthday. Joan was held in Stirling Castle for roughly a month before an agreement was reached, whereby she no longer had custody of her children, but was allowed to freely visit with them. The outcome of the negotiation came to have the rather dull name of the Agreement, and read,

> This appointment made at Stirling on 4 September AD 1439 conveys that it is accorded between a right high and mighty princess Joan, by the grace of God queen of Scotland… and Sir Alexander Livingston of Callander,… [and others], with the advice and consent of the three estates being in the general council held there and gathered, in form and manner following, that is to say:
>
> In the first, touching the declaration of the fame and worship of the foresaid persons for the restriction of the said princess's will and liberty made by them and their assistants, the said princess with her council has fully examined and discussed the causes and the motives by which the said persons were stirred to withdraw the foresaid liberty from her, and has considered and acknowledges that the thing the said persons did in that matter touching her they did from good zeal and motive and from [the] great truth and loyalty that was in them, both to our sovereign lord the king

and his safety, and to the said princess in her worship. And in that matter and all others she reputes, holds and trusts them all, and their assistants therein, both loyal, and true to her, doing that thing as true lieges ought to do for their sovereign lord and her estate and worship, and not otherwise.

This paragraph had the effect of Joan declaring that the instigators had not broken the law, committed treason, or anything else when imprisoning her. They were acting in the interest of her son James II.

Item, touching the declaration of the fame and worship of the said princess, the foresaid Sir Alexander, Sir William, James and John and their foresaid assistants declare and acknowledge in their loyalty that their withdrawal of that liberty from her, and what they did in that matter, was not done in villainy nor for villainy, harm nor slander to her person, nor for any lack, crime or fault that they or any of them were aware of or knew to her womanhood, but only for the safety of our sovereign lord, the worship of her person and the common good of the realm.

Again, this paragraph declares the innocence of the conspirators from any crime against Joan, whether it be speaking poorly of her or assaulting her.

Also, for so much as the said princess, by the occasion of that withdrawal of liberty from her, conceived grief or displeasure against the said Sir Alexander, Sir William, James and John and their assistants, considering that that thing was done from [a] good zeal and motive, as is declared before, she has remitted and removes all the said grief and displeasure that she conceived against them or any of them for the foresaid cause or any other done or said in time bygone.

Here, Joan is affirming that she harbors no ill well against the men who imprisoned her.

And furthermore, that the said princess had full declaration and genuine knowledge of [the] truth and loyalty that was and is in the foresaid Sir Alexander and all the other before written persons. In more open indication of trust and cordiality in the future she has, by the advice of the said three estates, committed to the said Sir Alexander's keeping our said sovereign lord the king, her dearest son, until the time of his age, and lent her castle of Stirling to him for his residence for the said period, and assigned to the said Sir Alexander for the upkeep of our said sovereign lord and his sisters in the foresaid castle until his age, 4,000 merks of the usual money of Scotland, which were assigned to her by the three estates and for the same reason.

Here Joan is being deprived of Stirling Castle until her son comes of age. Of course, the wording is such that she appears to be donating the castle to her son, but that was almost certainly not something she was pleased about doing.

The men had some pity for Joan as a mother, because they included the clause that, "Also the said princess [Joan] shall have access to visit our said sovereign lord [James II] … at her pleasure," of which Joan fully took advantage.

Surely recognizing their precarious position, Joan was forced to agree that she would not take any action against Sir Alexander or his accomplices,

> Item, for greater security, the said princess shall make such lords as are her men and retinue, at the desire of the said Sir …give the foresaid Sir Alexander …under their seals that, if [Joan] acts to the contrary of any [part] … accorded in this writ, that they shall not assist her, nor act to the contrary of him, …but rather with him …in the fulfilling thereof. And the said lords that are men and retinue to her shall be obliged … that they shall neither do nor say to the said Sir Alexander… nor procure to be done nor said to him…shame, villainy nor harm in any way…
>
> Item, if it happens, God forbid, that our said sovereign lord [James II] dies, or that he arrives at his said age, the said Sir Alexander shall receive the foresaid princess [Joan] in her foresaid castle [of Stirling] freely, with many or few at her pleasure, just as he is obliged to her previously by his letters.

No one was legally allowed to support Joan against Sir Alexander. On the contrary, they were to act against her if she ever tried to engage Sir Alexander. Also note that, throughout the Agreement, Joan is referred to as "princess" and not "queen." At least she is promised the return of Stirling Castle once James II outgrows the regency. Additionally, the Agreement went on to say that if Sir Alexander died before the end of the regency, Joan would regain Stirling Castle, "without obstacle or demand, at her desire and request, either by her word or her letters under her seal, so that neither the said Sir Alexander, Sir William, James and John be any nearer to death by means of the said princess, her procuration or servants." Thereafter, Joan, Sir Alexander, and several of the present lords affixed their seals to the Agreement.

After her release from Stirling Castle, Joan went on to have three children with the Black Knight, all sons. Her last child was born in 1443.

Joan's Death

An old rivalry between those who supported Joan as queen and those who did not grew in intensity until war broke out. In late spring 1445, Joan took refuge at Dunbar Castle, one of her properties. Dunbar Castle is little more than a pile of jumbled masonry today. Joan was weak and ill, succumbing to her illness on 15 July 1445. She was later buried in Perth next to her first husband, James I.

As a point of interest, Joan Beaufort is the aunt of Margaret Beaufort. This makes Joan the great-aunt of Henry VII of England, and great-great-aunt of Margaret Tudor.

Chapter 2

Mary of Guelders

Maria van Gelre, known to English speakers as Mary of Guelders, was born around 1432. Her mother, Catherine of Cleves (1417–1476), was the sister of Duke John I of Cleves. Through the siblings Catherine and John, the Stuart monarchs of Scotland, Ireland and England are related to the von der Mark dukes of Cleves. To go a little further, Queen Elizabeth II and King Charles III are twice-over related to the von der Marks by descent from Catherine of Cleves and Sybylla of Cleves (1512–1554), Anna of Cleves's (1515–1557) elder sister. Mary's father, Arnold von Egmond, was a distant relative of Anna of Cleves's mother, Maria of Jülich-Berg.

Mary was the eldest of six children, with two of her brothers dying in childhood. In the end, Mary's surviving brother and two sisters outlived Mary by several years. Mary, and likely her siblings, were raised at the Burgundian court of Philip III of Burgundy. He was known as Philip the Good.

Philip the Good's court was opulent. During her time there, Mary witnessed a multitude of chivalry-themed festivals, jousts, banquets, and the like. Philip the Good was wealthy and had no problem showing it. Items at his various feasts included model buildings and boats, huge pastry pies out of which people would emerge, and a variety of beautiful birds, both natural and fake. Philip founded the Order of the Golden Fleece, a slightly more exclusive order than England's Order of the Garter, with the Order of the Golden Fleece having only twenty-four members at its founding. In contrast, the Order of the Garter had twenty-five.

Philip's court rotated between palaces in Lille, Hesdin, Bruges, and Brussels. Mary presumably went to these palaces during her youth. The palaces were decorated by the finest artists of the day, and Philip hired Jan van Eyck to take Isabella of Portugal's portrait so he could decide whether he wished to marry her. Such was the luxury, concentration of the arts, music, finer things, and wealth to which Mary was exposed in her youth.

Negotiations for Mary's Marriage

Philip the Good and his wife Isabella of Portugal had a strong hand in early marriage negotiations for little Mary. In 1442, when Mary was roughly eight years old, she was first sought as a bride for Count Charles IV of Maine. Charles was about twenty years Mary's senior. He was also the son of Duke Louis II of Anjou. Charles's sister was married to King Charles VII of France, making Charles of Maine a natural supporter of the French king against the English. Ultimately, Mary's father could not find the money to enforce the *de futuro* marriage contract, and negotiations fell through.

A few years later, around 1444, Mary was proposed as a bride for James II of Scotland. While Mary's father Arnold was keen to have one of his daughters wed the Scottish king, he preferred that Mary's younger sister Margaret wed James II. Margaret was born in 1436, four years after Mary. Mary was followed by two brothers, Eduard and Wilhelm, before Margaret arrived. Arnold wished for Mary to wed Duke Albrecht VI of Austria, the younger brother of the Habsburg Holy Roman Emperor Frederick III. Arnold was battling over the succession to the German lands of Jülich-Berg in the 1440s, and so thought that having a powerful Habsburg ally as soon as possible was a good idea. The negotiations for Mary to wed Albrecht VI of Austria never went anywhere, leaving Arnold to fight his battles with Jülich-Berg alone.

Attention turned back to a Scottish match by 1448. Mary was at least fourteen, if not fifteen, in 1448, and thus of an appropriate age by late medieval to early modern standards to safely bear children with her husband. Added to that, both the Scots and the Guelderians were friendly with the French. James II of Scotland reaffirmed the Auld Alliance with Charles VII of France on New Year's Eve, 1448, demonstrating his interest in maintaining ties with France. Mary's aunt Maria of Cleves was already wed to a French nobleman, strengthening the bond between Burgundian-influenced Cleves and France.

On 1 April 1449, a marriage contract was signed between James II of Scotland and Mary of Guelders. Philip the Good promised to pay an enormous dowry of 60,000 gold crowns for Mary, with payment in full due over the next two years. The contract executed and the dowry sufficiently secured, it was time for James II to have Mary retrieved from Burgundy.

Mary's Early Days in Scotland

William Crichton, Chancellor of Scotland, escorted Mary from Sluis in the modern-day Netherlands. A fleet of fourteen ships set sail for Scotland on 9 June 1449. The ships were filled with hundreds of soldiers and several vital nobles.

Before reaching mainland Scotland, Mary stopped at the Isle of May. The Isle of May is at the mouth of the Firth of Forth, or estuary of the river Forth, which flows northwest of Edinburgh. She visited the Chapel of St. Adrian, associated with pregnancy. The chapel was already an ancient site by the time Mary visited. St. Ethernan, whose name evolved into St. Adrian over time, established a monastery on the Isle of May in the late 7th century. Two hundred years later, the monks resident there were slaughtered by Vikings. Another origin story claims that St. Adrian was killed on the island by Vikings in 875. A stone building was erected in the 12th century, probably with the blessing of David I.

One must wonder what the teenager thought of her new home. She was fifteen years old at most, and so very near the country of which she was to be queen. She could see mainland Scotland from the Isle of May, depending on the weather. Whatever Mary felt, she would not see her homeland or siblings again.

Mary's Wedding and Coronation

On 18 June 1449, Mary landed at Leith. At the time, Leith was its own village, not simply a district in Edinburgh. Once unloaded, she stopped at the Convent of St. Anthony to refresh herself. That done, she went to Edinburgh.

A couple of weeks later, on 3 July 1449, Mary celebrated both her marriage and her coronation at Holyrood Abbey. It is thought that the royal apartments within Holyrood Abbey, which were the precursor to Holyrood Palace, were expanded and developed before Mary's arrival. Immediately after the wedding ceremony to Mary's nineteen-year-old husband, Mary was given purple robes to wear. Her coronation ceremony was quickly completed.

Two years later, on 1 July 1451, a charter enumerating the properties given by James II to Mary was recorded. The part which still exists reads,

> James, because he previously granted £5,000 Scots to Mary of Gueldres by reason of a wedding gift... wishing to describe specifically the promise and grant, wishes all to know that he gave...all the earldom of Fife (etc.) with the manor or castle of Falkland and Falkland park; all the lands pertaining to the king by the forfeiture of Walter [*Stewart*] earl of Atholl in the sheriffdom of Fife; the great customs of Cupar; all the earldom of Stirling ...the great customs and burgh fermes of Perth; all the lands of Kinclaven and Methven with Methven Castle; the lordship of Menteith with Doune Castle; all the lands of Strath Gartney, sheriffdom of Perth; the lordship of Brechin, sheriffdom of Forfar; Stirling Castle; the great customs and burgh fermes of Stirling with the office of sheriff of the sheriffdom, with the following lands: Lethbertschel, Sandleth', Skeok, Oldpark [Aldpark], Little Sauchie [Litil Salchy], Roplauch, Queen's Haugh [Quenishalch], Sargeantland [Sergandlande], Skeoch [*sic*], Blargib, the town of Logie, Blairlogie, les Pull', Lubnach, Fossachy, Lossyntrule, a third part of Inverallen, sheriffdom of Stirling; all the barony of Tillycoultry, sheriffdom of Clackmannan; an annual rent of 20 merks from the lands

of Cragorth; the palace or manor of Linlithgow at the loch, with the loch and fishing; the great customs and burgh fermes of Linlithgow, with the office of sheriff of Linlithgow; the following lands: Kincavil, Drumcors'; all our acres on the east and west sides of the said Linlithgow with the sanctuary, crofts, Bonnytoun, the Lochside, Kingsfield, with an annual rent from the orchard croft [orchardcroft] and the Fethelcroft; and £100 Scots from the burgh fermes or water fermes of the burgh of Aberdeen, to be raised annually from the custumars or bailies of the burgh, [all] to be held for the life of the queen our consort. To be held with the usual rights [… … …] [Remainder of charter lost].

Mary was now quite wealthy in her own right. Unfortunately, some of Mary's dower lands were subject to being taken for her husband's political needs.

Part of Mary's property was settled on James Crichton, son of George Crichton after George was imprisoned by his son. George Crichton enjoyed several important positions bestowed upon him by the king. This included George's being created Earl of Caithness in 1452. George did not favor his son, who was likely in his twenties by this point, and made arrangements with his lands such that his son, James Crichton, could not inherit them. After George settled the lands upon King James II in 1453, the young James Crichton thought it best to capture George and shut him up in Blackness Castle. In the end, Mary's husband James II saved George. As part of the negotiations with James Crichton, lands in Perth were settled upon him in July 1454. This included Mary's property of Redgorton,

> James, etc., to all good men, etc. Understands and act or decreet made by the three estates in parliament in the presence of the king in this form:
> On 18 July 1454 in parliament at Edinburgh, in the presence of the king and … with many others from the three estates assembled in parliament, James Crichton, son of George, earl of Caithness, compeared and asked confirmation and approval to be made to him by our lady Mary [of Guelders], queen of Scots, concerning the lands of Strathord in the sheriffdom of Perth, granted to James by the king's charter in a free barony called [Redgorton], and for the queen to resign the said lands of the barony of [Redgorton] from her dowry, according to the tenor of certain letters made thereon. And after James was heard, Queen Mary approved, ratified and confirmed the said donation of the barony made by the king, and promised to resign the lands of the barony of [Redgorton] from her dowry, and promised before the estates that she would make no claim thereto in future, and the king and queen asked for act and witness concerning this to be made to the said James.

Although Mary was overtly wealthy as James II's queen, she did not necessarily have control over her property.

The Births of Mary's Children

By the time Mary's marital properties were settled upon her, she'd already given birth to a child in May 1450. That infant, of unknown name or gender, was born a couple of months prematurely and did not survive. At the time the charter was passed, Mary was very pregnant with her first surviving child. Her baby boy was born on 10 July 1451. He would go on to become James III of Scotland.

Her first daughter, also named Mary, was born 13 May 1453. Her older brother's politics very much dominated baby Mary's life.

Given the gap between the birth of James III and Mary, it is possible that their mother Mary suffered a miscarriage. There is no evidence of that beyond looking at this fertile couple's pattern of births.

A baby boy named Alexander was born in 1454. He survived to adulthood and was created Duke of Albany. When he was around six years old, Alexander was sent to Guelders to visit his maternal grandparents.

Margaret was born after Alexander, but the exact year of her birth is unknown. For a time, she was her eldest brother James's favorite sister. She ran afoul of James by maintaining an affair with William Crichton, 3d Lord Crichton, which resulted in a daughter named Margaret, and possibly a son. Margaret and her brother Alexander rebelled against their brother James during his kingship.

A baby boy, David, was born around 1455 and died as a toddler, in July 1457.

A final child, John, was born around 1456. He, too, eventually crossed his elder brother James. John was imprisoned for using witchcraft against the king and suffered a mysterious death during his imprisonment. He died around 1479.

The Death of Mary's Husband

Not much is known about Mary of Guelders's queenship until James II's dramatic death in 1460. During her entire time as queen, the war between the Lancastrian and Yorkist families in England, called now the Wars of the Roses, simmered in the background, and occasionally spilled into Scotland.

The Scottish royal couple favored supporting their fellow monarchs over the border. Mary's husband took a very active role in supporting Henry VI of England, of the Lancastrian faction, against the rebelling Yorkists. James repeatedly raised his army and ventured to England to assist Henry VI. He experienced enough success to please both the Scots and the English loyal to Henry VI.

James welcomed the English Prince Edward and Queen Margaret, known as Margaret of Anjou, into Scotland in January 1460. Mary went to them at Kinclaven Castle in Perthshire and visited with Margaret and her son for around twelve days. The women discussed marrying Princess Margaret of Scotland to Prince Edward of England.

After achieving some semblance of victory and securing his border, James retired to Scotland at Margaret of Anjou's behest. Margaret's husband Henry VI was suffering from another semi-regular instance of mental incapacitation. In early 1460, the Yorkists began the war anew. James II did his best to seize the castle of Roxburgh, close to modern-day Kelso and the Scottish Borders. The English, then occupying the castle, believed that the real target was nearby Berwick. James was able to besiege the castle on 3 August 1460. During the siege, James was standing near a cannon that misfired, with shrapnel from the explosion striking and killing him. He was buried in Holyrood Abbey. Shortly before James's death, a comet was seen in the sky. It was thought to portend James's death and the bloody battles with the English that year.

The immediate actions Mary took after James II's death are known, although different reports show different timelines. Mary did order that the Scots continue besieging the castle, which met with success on 5 August 1460. Mary, described as having a "stout stomach" and "representing the man-like race" of Guelders, is said to have rushed with seven-year-old James III to Roxburgh. However, a chronicle called *A Short Chronicle of King James II*, written in the mid- to late-16th century, states that Mary did not arrive from Edinburgh until the Friday after James's death, with said Friday being 9 August.

Whenever she arrived, Mary spent her time comforting the nobles who were present when James II died. Shortly after Mary's arrival with her son James, the little boy was crowned James III of Scotland at Kelso.

Mary was appointed one of seven regents to guide little James III until he reached the age of majority. She came to loggerheads with another regent, James Kennedy, Bishop of St. Andrews, a couple of years later. She was accused of trying to take over the entire Scottish government. Fearing civil war, Mary was removed as regent and instead appointed the custodian for James III, his brothers, and his sisters.

In 1461, Henry VI of England asked for safe harbor in Scotland after suffering a defeat by the Yorkists. It was granted, and Henry, his wife Margaret of Anjou, and their son Edward went to Edinburgh Castle. During their time there, Mary and Margaret struck up a close friendship. The two women spoke French as their first language, which helped them communicate effectively. They were pretty close in age, with Margaret being roughly four years older than Mary.

The friendship could not last long. Mary's uncle, Philip the Good of Burgundy, disliked Henry VI of England. Philip allied himself with the Yorkist king of England, Edward IV. Philip disliked Margaret of Anjou's family and likely did not see much use in allying himself with the losing Lancastrians. As a result, Mary could not maintain a friendship with Margaret.

A Tangent about Margaret of Anjou and the English Wars of the Roses

Margaret of Anjou was born to René, Duke of Anjou, and Isabella, daughter of the Duke of Lorraine in Pont-à-Mousson, France on 23 March 1429. Young Margaret spent her early years in the castle of Capua in Naples, Italy, where her father was titular king, and in the castle of Tarascon on the Rhône River. Her well-educated mother tutored Margaret and may have received some lessons from Antoine de la Salle, who tutored Margaret's brothers.

Margaret was betrothed to Henry VI in 1444 and married him on 23 April 1445, one month after Margaret's sixteenth birthday. Margaret was crowned queen consort on 30 May 1445 at Westminster Abbey.

Margaret gave birth to Edward of Westminster on 13 October 1543. After the birth of her son, Margaret retired from London to Greenwich to raise the infant Edward. At this time, Richard, Duke of York, was appointed to the protectorate until Henry VI recovered his sanity. The Duke of York had been heir to the throne until Edward was born. Margaret's conflicts with the Duke of York in 1455 culminated in the start of the Wars of the Roses, with the premier battle of St. Albans resulting in the defeat of the Lancastrian faction.

In 1459, Margaret outlawed the Yorkist leaders to quell the Yorkist faction's agitation toward the throne. Richard, Duke of York died in 1460, leaving his son, the future Edward IV, to take up the Yorkist cause. In her attempts to protect the rights and safety of her husband and son, Margaret fled to Scotland. She returned with the northern army that successfully defeated the Yorkists during the second Battle of St Albans in 1461.

In 1462, with the Wars still raging, Margaret returned to France with her son where she was able to muster a force through the help of her father and King Louis XI. In exchange for granting Calais to Louis XI, Margaret gained a force of 2,000 men, the authority to muster men in Normandy, and 20,000 francs to finance her campaign. Louis XI sent ships to harry the English coast, which put the sitting Edward IV on notice of a Lancastrian invasion. In October 1462, Margaret, Prince Edward, and her force of 2,000 men made for the English coast of Northumberland. Unfortunately, her ships were scattered during a storm, with some lost. The battered Lancastrian force landed near

Alnwick, where they caught wind of an approach by the Yorkist faction with a large force. Margaret's remaining force scattered.

Undeterred by this and other initial setbacks in England, Margaret marched forth and seized or secured several strongholds. These strongholds included Warkworth Castle, Alnwick Castle, and Dunstanburgh Castle. She reinforced Bamburgh Castle with some of her remaining French forces. Margaret was able to recover her husband, as well. Unfortunately, her luck had run out.

The English detested the French garrisons and refused to aid Margaret. Storms thwarted Margaret's attempt at fleeing with her husband and son. Ultimately, her strongholds fell one by one to the Yorkists and Margaret eventually fled to Scotland. She did attempt an invasion to take back the throne, but ultimately, the Lancastrian faction was defeated. Margaret's son died in battle and her husband later died while imprisoned by Edward IV, the Yorkist king.

The end of Margaret's tale is sad: she was imprisoned in England for several years until a ransom was paid for her. She was able to return to France, where she lived the rest of her life in poverty. Margaret finally shuffled off her mortal coil on 25 August 1482.

The Last Years of Mary of Guelder's Life

The last years of Mary's life are a tangled web of virtue and vice. Mary founded Trinity College Church after her husband's death. She took action to found the church in 1460, not long after he died. Mary reached out to Pope Pious II to ask that Soutra Aisle, which was initially founded in the 12th century, be annexed and made part of her planned Trinity College Church. The master of Soutra Aisle, which was then both a friary and a hospital for the poor, had created a scandal and was removed from his post. The vacancy gave Mary the opportunity to found her own religious house. The Pope agreed in October 1460. Mary issued a royal charter for the church on Lady Day 1462.[1]

Mary executed James II's plans for a defensive castle in Ravenscraig, the remains of which can still be seen today. James finished designing the castle shortly before his death, intending for the building to resist cannonballs and other similar artillery. It is of course a great irony that James died due to a misfired cannon, although he could design a fortress to keep Mary safe. Mary wanted the castle built in part as a memorial to James's memory. She and some of her servants moved into Ravenscraig Castle once it was inhabitable, although it was not finished.

---

1. Lady Day, 25 March, was the start of the medieval and early modern fiscal year in Stuart Scotland, Ireland, and England.

After the death of her husband, Mary allegedly took on a lover. Her illicit relationship was frowned upon, and surely did not help Mary's position at court, despite being the dowager queen. Whether or not she indeed took a lover cannot be concretely known. Mary was also rumored to have shared a bed with the king of France, although when she would have had the opportunity is a bit of a mystery.

Mary's fourth surviving son and youngest child, John Stewart, was called illegitimate by her second son, Alexander. John was born in 1459 before Mary's husband died. The thought is that Mary's behavior allowed Alexander to level such allegations at John. On the other hand, Alexander may have leveled the allegations at the young John because John had no one to defend him. Regardless, John died at around age twenty and ceased posing a threat to Alexander, or their older brothers David and James III.

Whatever Mary's behavior after the death of James II, Mary herself did not live long. She died in late November to early December 1463 at Ravenscraig Castle. It is unknown of what she died. Given that she was not yet thirty years old, it seems very possible that she died of disease. While this is pure speculation and further research is needed, Mary could have died from an outbreak of smallpox. Edward IV of England may have contracted smallpox in 1463 because of the Yorkists attacking the Lancastrians in the Scottish Marches. There is only one known source stating that there was an outbreak of smallpox around this time, but if there was indeed an outbreak, perhaps Mary of Guelders became ill and died of the dangerous disease. The plague, which ravaged Europe earlier in the 15th century, occasionally reared its head in autumn and winter and could be another reason for Mary's death. Like so many things about this Stuart queen, it may be impossible ever to know why she died.

It was several months before Mary was buried. Mary's funeral mass was given in June 1464 in Brechin Cathedral, with Brechin being a former royal burgh that is now part of Angus. The building of Trinity College Church was well under way but was not completed to a degree such that Mary could have a swift burial. Winter may have impeded the construction of the church, causing further delay in interring Mary's body. She was eventually buried there. Construction continued on the church, although its final form fell short of what was originally planned. Still, the space was usable for services, and the grounds gained more buildings.

Mary's relatives in Guelders and Burgundy needed to be informed of her passing, as well. While this is speculation, the delay in burying her could be due in part to awaiting instructions from her relatives on the Continent. It was not uncommon during the time period to have an organ, such as the heart, of the deceased buried in their country of origin or in a place special to that person.

It does not appear that any of Mary's body was sent to her Guelderian relatives for burial, leaving it to the Scots to inter their former queen.

Reinterring Mary

Trinity College Church was turned over to the care of the Provost of Edinburgh in 1567. Thereafter, it was used as a parish church for some 300 years. In the 1840s the church had to be moved to make way for warehouses, which eventually gave way to the Waverly train station. It was known that Mary of Guelders was buried in the church, and deemed appropriate for her remains to be moved to Holyrood Abbey. Negotiations between those wishing to preserve the church and the railroad company ensued until a final agreement was reached. It was decided that, before removing the church, an attempt would be made to locate Mary's remains.

Remains of a woman were found in what was likely the mortuary chapel. The skeleton was in an oak coffin. No further inquiry was made, and the skeleton was declared to be Mary of Guelders. A new coffin was made, and the woman's skeleton was buried in the royal vault at Holyrood in July 1847.

The deconstruction of the church, which was carefully taken apart so as to be reassembled elsewhere, began in September 1847. Eventually, the floor where the high altar was had to be removed. Upon so doing, another coffin was discovered about five feet below the modern floor. It was under a slab of concrete, and unknown when the concrete was laid down. Underneath the concrete was found a lead coffin. The body in the coffin was a female skeleton. Water had permeated the lead coffin over the years, rotting away any natural material such as the body, hair, and fabric. No metal items were remarked upon and had presumably rusted away if there were any. To quote the *Edinburgh Evening Chronicle* from 21 September 1847,

> The workmen having, in the course of their excavations on the site of the choir of the church, approached the chancel, where the high altar had once stood… [at which point the architect] gave orders that the utmost vigilance should be employed to discover any remains that might be buried within those sacred limits…as the workmen were…digging in beneath the site of the altar, the end of a wooden coffin was seen.
>
> The first step was to remove the thick and solid mass of concrete in which the coffin was embedded, which having been accomplished with some difficulty, a strong outside frame, formed of fir, was found, the use of which evidently was to protect the coffins enclosed. A coffin, made of oak or elm, was then seen, and within it was a leaden coffin, formed in the

shape of the body, containing the skeleton of a female, the skull of which, upon examination, was found to have been sawed off across the top [as part of the enbalming process], but lying close to the other parts of the head, as if it had undergone some surgical examination. The other bones were lying in the usual position, but the back bone had a strong lateral curve immediately below the shoulder, which must have occasioned some deformity of person. The wood of which the coffins were composed was considerably decayed, but the lead, though to some extent corroded by damp, was in a good state of preservation....

There was no inscription upon the coffin, and, in the absence of the necessary authority, no search was made in it for anything that might indicate the rank of its occupant. Around the bed of the tomb were several rows of stone, wedged together like the causeway of a street, while at the distance of about eighteen inches around was the original earth, which had not apparently been disturbed. The feet of the skeleton lay towards the east, and the head to the west; and it is somewhat remarkable that its position was exactly in the centre of the building.

It is very likely that this second skeleton was that of Mary of Guelders. Given the place of honor at which the woman was buried, she had to be a very high-ranking noblewoman or an important figure within the church. Tradition within the church held that the Mass had to be said at the tomb of the foundress. Mary was, of course, the foundress of the church. A tomb may have existed over top of the coffins, lost to time as the floor was raised, wars came and went, and so on.

The skeleton, left in its original lead coffin, was put inside a wooden box and sent for scientific investigation. Bearing in mind that this was the 19th century, some interesting conclusions were drawn about the skeleton, and thus, Mary of Guelders. The scientific report, dated 2 November 1848, gives the following, at times undignified, information. The scientists were,

of opinion that the female to which [the skeleton] belonged was of a feeble frame; and, more particularly, from the weak and delicate condition of the skeleton generally, but especially of the spine, the long bones of the limbs, and the skull.

It is anyone's guess if the scientists took into consideration that the skeleton itself had deteriorated to a degree. The next bit of the description should be taken with a grain of salt by any 21st-century person and beyond. It is an interesting glimpse into forensic science of the past, from the small, perpendicular, and antero-posterior extent of the frontal region of the head, the very small cerebellar space, the unsymmetrical, contracted, and undeveloped state of the base; the retarded[2] condition of the wisdom teeth [and the skull having been opened, for examination], this female, who was certainly above twenty, but below thirty, years of age, was of feeble or deficient intellect.

How about that? What the modern person can pull from this report is that the age of the skeleton does fit Mary's age at death, that her wisdom teeth were either partially or not at all erupted out of her jaw, and that she might have been petite. It also appears that the woman could have suffered from epilepsy. If so, that is another possible reason for Mary's early death.

This skeleton, too, was reinterred in the ruins of Holyrood Abbey's royal vault.

Mysterious Mary

Extremely little is known about Mary. Her exact age, date of birth, cause of death, and date of death are a mystery. She did not seem to participate in public events very often. If she did, Mary's presence was not regularly recorded. There is no known contemporary portrait of Mary which has survived. Not even her actions after the death of her husband James II are precisely known, making it difficult to truly assess her character. Given the whims and destructive nature of Father Time, Mary will remain a shadowy figure.

---

2. "retarded" here meaning under-developed

Chapter 3

Margaret of Denmark

Margaret of Denmark was the only daughter of King Christian I of Denmark and Norway and his wife, Dorothea of Brandenburg-Kulmbach. The couple's eldest son, Olav, lived for only a year, having been born in 1450 and dying in 1451. The couple's second son, Knut, was born in 1451. He died around the age of four, in 1455. Their next known child, John, was born in 1455. He thankfully survived to adulthood, eventually becoming king of Denmark. Margaret was born on 23 June 1456 in Copenhagen. Their youngest son, Frederick, was born many years later, in 1471. Margaret never met her baby brother.

Nothing is meaningfully known about Margaret's youth. Like so many royal daughters, she was simply an afterthought until she married.

In January 1468, the Scottish Parliament resolved that James would marry the princess of Denmark,

> These following matters are advised, treated and concluded…by the whole of the three estates in the last parliament held earlier in Edinburgh:
>
> Firstly, concerning the marriage of our sovereign lord [James III], it is advised and concluded by all the aforementioned people that an embassy should be sent in all good haste to Denmark and other places seen as expedient between now and next March or April, with full commission to advise and conclude on the marriage of our sovereign lord in a good and profitable place with an appropriate person of noble blood, and to have full power to marry and bring home a queen. And that a prelate, a lord, a knight or a clerk, to be chosen for that purpose by our sovereign lord, should travel in the said embassy with forty honourable and worshipful persons.

Furthermore, Parliament resolved that "concerning the matter of Norway, it is ordained that the embassy traveling for the king's marriage should have instructions in that matter as shall be seen expedient to the king and his council." Effectively, James III would wed Margaret of Denmark as quickly as possible, sight unseen.

Danish Politics in Margaret's Lifetime

Margaret's father was elected as Christian I, King of Denmark in 1448, when he was roughly twenty-two years old. Two years later, he was elected King of Norway. Christian I was the son of Dietrich the Happy of Oldenburg, a territory in Holstein, Germany. The modern federal state of Schleswig-Holstein borders Denmark. Upon his election, Christian became the founder of the Oldenburg dynasty, which endured in Denmark until 1863. Subsequent Stuart spouses from Denmark, such as Anna and George, were descendants of Christian I.

Dorothea of Brandenburg married Christian I in October 1449. Dorothea was married to Christian's predecessor, King Christopher, from the Bavarian noble house of Palatinate-Neumarkt. She did not have any children whatsoever with her first husband, who was unrelated to her second husband. Dorothea was shrewd and efficient, and frequently served as regent when her husband was away. The couple's joint coronation was celebrated after their wedding.

Christian faced multiple difficulties as king, beginning with his desire to be King of Sweden and preserve the Kalmar Union. The Kalmar Union, placing Sweden, Norway, and Denmark under the same crown beginning in 1397, existed with some difficulty until 1523. As mentioned, Christian became King of Norway in 1450, but only after Charles VIII, who was previously elected King of Sweden and Norway, was strong-armed by the Danish-Swedish conflict of 1451 to 1457 into handing over Sweden to Christian. Eventually, Charles was exiled from Sweden in 1457, allowing for Christian to be elected King of Sweden. The Kalmar Union was restored.

Christian's position as King of Sweden did not last long; he was overthrown in 1464 by a group of nobles. Not willing to let go of the prize, Christian fought his way back to the Swedish throne the following year. He was removed from Sweden once and for all in 1467, right before James III's regency counsel sent a deputation to Denmark.

Negotiations for Margaret's Marriage and Her First View of Scottish Politics

In September 1468 when she was fourteen years old and her groom, James III of Scotland, was seventeen, they were betrothed. This was in part to resolve the Scots' failure to comply with the 13th-century Treaty of Perth, which included the term that the Scots were to pay the Danes annually for retaining possession of the Hebrides. In addition, Shetland and Orkney were given to Scotland as part of the marriage treaty and could only be redeemed by the payment of Margaret's rather large dowry to Scotland. Effectively, a mortgage was put on the islands that could only be redeemed by full payment by Denmark of Margaret's dowry.

Margaret arrived in Scotland in the summer of 1469. Upon arrival, Margaret experienced the first hint of trouble that her groom's reign would be uneasy. James's younger sister Mary was married to Thomas Boyd, 1st Earl of Arran, in 1467. She was thirteen at the time and fifteen when Margaret of Denmark arrived in Scotland. Thomas Boyd's birthdate is not known, but it is assumed that he was quite a bit older than Mary Stewart and her brother, James III. Thomas Boyd served on the regency council which saw the removal of Mary of Guelders.

Whilst Boyd was away in Denmark retrieving Margaret, plus negotiating for the return of Shetland and Orkney to Scotland, James III was plotting his revenge against Thomas and Thomas's brother. The Boyd family maintained control of young James III through the regency, which James managed to overthrow whilst Thomas was off in Denmark. On top of that, Thomas's choice to wed Princess Mary Stewart was unpopular, regardless of her reportedly being happy with the match. James III wanted Thomas intercepted when he returned to Scotland with Margaret of Denmark. Thomas heard through Mary of the plot and successfully managed to drop off Margaret of Denmark and sneak out of Scotland without being caught. Unfortunately for Mary Stewart, that gave her brother James the chance to void her marriage to Thomas. Mary was later wed to James, Lord Hamilton. Lord Hamilton was roughly 37 years older than Mary, making him approximately sixty-two when they married, and Mary was roughly twenty-one.

What is so tragic about this series of events, namely what happened to Mary Stewart and what Margaret of Denmark would have witnessed about her new husband, is that these people were all teenagers, "these people" being Margaret, Mary, James III, and enough of their supporters. Having teenagers run a country surely makes for interesting, passionate history. I digress.

Margaret married James III at Holyrood Abbey, the same place where James's parents married. The exact date and details of their wedding are unknown, but it is thought the two married on 13 July 1469. No doubt it was an extravagant affair, especially given that James III had recently taken steps to gain control of his government. It would be the perfect opportunity for the young king to show off his wealth and power.

Margaret went on progress with her husband in 1470. They spent most of their time in northern Scotland, including several weeks at Inverness that summer.

Margaret as Queen

Frustratingly, little is known about Margaret's queenship or her relationship with her husband. Margaret mostly tolerated James III mostly and to engage in sexual activity to fulfill her expectations as a queen. She had to bear children. Margaret respected James in his role as the King of Scots, even if she was otherwise cool toward him.

Margaret was regarded as fashionable. After an unsettling political event, of which there will be more later in this chapter, a chest was made to hold the then-deceased Margaret's remaining possessions. Within the chest were items such as belts made of black damask and cloth of gold, multiple gold beads, a collar with chalcedony, two rubies, two pearls set in gold, a gold chain made with forty knots of gold. She owned an item containing a serpent's tongue and a unicorn's horn, set in gold. Two other notable pieces of jewelry included a small gold chain set with diamonds and an "M" pendant, plus a heart made of gold with a pearl embedded in it.

Beyond expensive, stylish clothing and jewelry, Margaret owned costly items. These included an ostrich feather, a book with leaves of gold, and thirteen pages with gold foil.[1] There were two additional books contained within the chest. She had what appears to be a purple bed cover that had thistles and a unicorn embroidered on it. Remnants of her royal robes were in the chest, too. Margaret much enjoyed the finer things and may have preferred the Scottish unicorn as a design motif.

Margaret was regarded as beautiful and pious. She was popular for having a good disposition and being sensible. Overall, she was a successful queen to the Scottish public.

A Portrait of Margaret

An altarpiece by Hugo van der Goes in the Holy Trinity of Edinburgh shows Margaret and her husband likely not long after they were married. This is also the only extant portrait of a Scottish queen before the fifteenth century. Hugo van der Goes was born between 1430 and 1440, in or around Ghent. He became a master in Ghent's painter's guild in 1467 when Margaret's father was being ousted from Sweden. Hugo started his notable oeuvre in Ghent in 1468 before being called to Bruges to create decorations for the wedding of Margaret of York and Charles the Bold, and their Joyous Entry[2] into Ghent. Known today as the Procession of the Golden Tree, one can still attend the event every five years.

Hugo was exceedingly well connected within the painter's guild. Joos van Wassenhove sponsored Hugo back in 1467. Hugo's cousin went on to marry

---

1. The leaves would be taken out of the book and used to decorate or gild items.
2. A Joyous Entry was the symbolic, peaceful entry of the ruling royal into a city. This was a tradition mostly in the Low Countries, although it was sometimes observed in France and Scotland.

Alexander Bening, whose son Simon Bening and granddaughter Levina Teerlinc went on to serve the English Tudor monarchs in the sixteenth century.

Hugo and his workshop continued their breakneck pace of creating works for important patrons across Europe in the 1460s and 1470s. Most of his work was created for the Burgundian court, with some time spent in Italy or at least, producing works for Florentine patrons. This begs the question as to how on earth Hugo managed to create the altarpiece for Margaret of Denmark and James III between 1469 and 1474 or so. Anglo-Burgundian-Scottish politics were at play.

Margaret of York

While this might seem like an odd place to mention an English princess, Margaret of York's life helps to illustrate some of the machinations of Margaret of Denmark's husband James III, and son, James IV. She is a sufficiently interesting person that it is a crime to relegate her to a mere footnote. With those justifications, this section continues.

On 3 May 1446, the future Edward IV of England and his parents welcomed a baby girl. She was named Margaret, possibly after Margaret of Anjou, who was Queen Consort of England at the time. Margaret of York's life was greatly influenced by her brother Edward IV, and her prominence rose with his. After her marriage and move to Burgundy, Margaret continued to support her family in England and remained an important figure in Burgundy for the rest of her life.

By 1465, Margaret's surviving older brother was King Edward IV of England. Louis XI was King of France, and he offered his four-year-old daughter Anne de Beaujeu to Charles the Bold of Burgundy.[3] Charles and Louis XI were struggling over territory, and the match between Charles and Anne came out of the Treaty of Conflans, which was signed in October 1465. As part of her dowry, Anne would bring the territory of Ponthieu, but Charles was able to gain control of Ponthieu on his own. Not wanting to wait for Anne to come of age, Charles did not make much affirmative noise about the match.

The nineteen-year-old Margaret, a duchess and sister to the King of England was more appealing. Unfortunately, Charles was still bound by treaty. Nevertheless, Charles was interested in marrying Margaret. Edward IV sent an ambassador to Burgundy to negotiate a marriage between Margaret and Charles.

Louis XI of France was vehemently against an Anglo-Burgundian alliance, and there were still the provisions of various treaties with which to contend. Margaret wound up betrothed in 1466 to the rebel would-be-king, Peter,

---

3. Charles was the count of Charolais at the time.

the Constable of Portugal. As a relative of Isabella of Burgundy, Charles's mother, a marriage between Margaret and Peter would have indirectly furthered Anglo-Burgundian interests.

The fetters of a prior treaty obligating Charles to marry a French princess fell away upon the death of Charles's father Philip the Good in 1467.

Margaret of York wed Charles and became Duchess Consort of Burgundy in the summer of 1468. On 26 June 1468 the bride first met with her new mother-in-law, Isabella of Burgundy, and eleven-year-old stepdaughter, Mary of Burgundy, and the three of them remained close the rest of their lives. Margaret and Charles were wed quite early in the morning on 3 July 1468, between 5 a.m and 6 a.m. After her marriage, Margaret became duchess of Burgundy, of Lothringia, of Limburg, of Brabant, of Luxembourg, and of Guelders; countess of Flanders, of Artois, of Hainault, of Holland, of Zeeland, of Namur, of Zutphen, and of Franche Comté; and the lady of Friesland, of Salins, and of Malines.

The ceremony over, the couple left for Bruges, with Margaret a few hours behind Charles, to make their Joyous Entry into Bruges. Margaret's Joyous Entry was sumptuous, to say the least. Though raining, Margaret sparkled in her gilded litter drawn by white horses. The twenty-two-year-old happily waved to the burghers as she passed. Within Bruges, the city was decorated with flowers, torches, artificial trees, the arms of the newly wedded couple, and other carefully planned adornments. The fountains flowed with wine, and both Margaret's and Charles' mottoes were displayed throughout Bruges. Margaret's motto was, *Bien en aviengne* or "May good come of it," and Charles's was, *Je l'ay emprins* or "I have undertaken it."

To honor Margaret of York, Bruges held the aforementioned Procession of the Golden Tree. The inaugural tournament of the Golden Tree was part of a ten-day celebration for Margaret and Charles. Margaret and Charles wore coronets denoting their status. On a fascinating note, Margaret of York's coronet still exists and is held in Aachen. It is one of two English crowns to survive the English Civil War.

As part of the ongoing Wars of the Roses in 1469, Edward IV and the future Richard III fled England for Flanders because of the agitations made by their brother George, Duke of Clarence and Richard Neville, Earl of Warwick. Warwick had instigated a revolt that included signing a treaty with Louis XI, agreeing to eschew any claims by England to the throne of France. Margaret tried her best to reconcile the brothers but was unsuccessful. Furthermore, George was in favor an alliance with France instead of Burgundy. Eventually, Edward managed to regain control of England in 1471 and the good relationship with Burgundy continued.

James III's Political Adventures

James III wanted to capitalize on what he perceived as his Guelderian-granted influence. In 1471, when Charles the Bold of Burgundy and Louis XI of France were bickering over territory and borders, James called a meeting of the Scottish parliament to try and raise taxes. Ideally, he would act as arbiter between the two powerful men. If he were lucky, then James could find a groom for his sister Margaret Stewart. James did not find much purchase there because thirty-seven-year-old Charles the Bold and forty-eight-year-old Louis XI were probably not terribly keen on having twenty-year-old James III mediate between them. Especially since the young man had been in charge of his own country for fewer than two years.

James's next attempt to throw his weight around came the very next year, 1472. His paternal aunt Isabella married the Duke of Brittany. Originally, she was meant to wed Duke John V of Brittany, who was almost forty years older than Isabella. As the Fates would have it, John's thread of life was cut before they could wed. Isabella then married his son, Duke Francis I of Brittany. He was a more manageable ten years or so older than Isabella. Isabella had two daughters with her husband.

Duke Francis of Brittany died in 1450, setting off a succession crisis that saw his brother Peter II, his uncle Arthur III, then a cousin known as Francis II, struggling for control. Effectively, there were four different rulers of Brittany in the 1450s. Francis II managed to survive, but only had daughters, including Anne of Brittany. All that is to say that the succession of Brittany was a mess, which James III believed he could sort. Scottish parliament supported James III in this particular adventure, especially because his aunt Isabella was still residing in Brittany. Additionally, the French decided to invade Brittany, which led to the Scots wishing to uphold the Auld Alliance and support France. The expedition was a failure.

James's next attempt at Continental glory came from his desire to meddle with the messy situation in Guelders. His uncle Adolf of Guelders decided to war against James's maternal grandfather Arnold of Guelders in 1465. Arnold initially succeeded but was later imprisoned by his son in 1471. Arnold reached out to his grandson James in hopes of giving control of Guelders to him. This was never put into effect and Adolf of Guelders' subsequent actions set off a succession crisis that rattled across Central Europe and England throughout the 16th century. James was ineffective in interceding here, too. All his political aspirations on the Continent were non-starters.

Anglo-Scottish Politics

After his multiple impingements in France, Burgundy, Brittany, and Guelders, James III assumed an interest in peace between Scotland and England. Margaret of York, the Burgundian court, and Hugo van der Goes were all effectively tools that could be used by Edward IV of England and James III to reach a peace or alliance between one another. Margaret of York took advantage of having access to one of the most famous artists in Europe at the time, and possibly helped her brother Edward IV woo James III, in part resulting in the Hugo van der Goes altarpiece. Thank goodness for politicking, otherwise, the world may have had to wait longer for a confirmed portrait of a Scottish queen.

James III and Edward IV did eventually reach a truce in 1474. As part of the negotiations, James's heir was pledged to marry Cecily of York, Edward IV's daughter. As part of that, it was agreed that Edward IV would make partial payments of the dowry to James. The scheme was abandoned in the early 1480s, but more on that later. Shortly thereafter, Edward IV died, and a meaningful Anglo-Scottish alliance was not resumed until the reign of Henry VII of England. James's initial alliance with England lasted until the mid-16th century.

Margaret of Denmark and Her Children

Margaret was a devout Catholic, making her more palatable to the Scots than her mother-in-law Mary of Guelders and the latter's ignominious lifestyle as a widow. No evidence of infidelity by either Margaret or her husband has ever been uncovered. Margaret and James had three surviving children together, all sons.

Unfortunately, it did take Margaret and James several years to have a successful pregnancy. As with most things regarding Margaret, there is very little evidence as to why. Whether she suffered multiple miscarriages is unknown, and neither is it known whether she endured any stillbirths. It could be because, as mentioned, Margaret was rather cool toward her husband, only seeking to procreate. Another explanation could be that Margaret was willing to lie with James only when the strict Catholic calendar of feast and holy days allowed for procreation.

Margaret was at Stirling Castle when she victoriously welcomed her first child on 17 March 1473. The little boy was named James. Margaret's husband must have been in high spirits at this time, given that Margaret's father King Christian had failed to fulfill Margaret's dowry, meaning that Shetland and Orkney permanently became part of the Kingdom of Scotland in 1472. Baby James was immediately made the Duke of Rothesay, signifying his position as his father's heir. It is likely that Margaret spent quite a bit of time at Stirling, raising James and his siblings.

As mentioned, the future James IV was originally betrothed to Cecily of York as part of James III's peace treaty with Edward IV of England, the on-again off-again Yorkist king. A formal betrothal was completed by the end of 1474 when Cecily was five years old and James was not quite two. This created an annual dowry payment from England to Scotland.

After James IV's birth, Margaret went on a pilgrimage to Whithorn Priory. The priory was already aged by Margaret's lifetime, having been founded in the mid-12th century. Whithorn was connected with St. Ninian, who is credited with converting the Southern Picts, who lived south of the Mounth region in Scotland. St. Ninian is believed to have lived in the 5th century.

Her second child, another son named James, was born in March of 1476. Amongst other titles, the little boy was created Earl of Ross when he was roughly five years old. James of Ross was his father's favorite. His favoritism of their second son made Margaret uneasy. Most of the reasoning for James of Ross being his father's favorite relies on political favoritism shown to the boy, and Margaret kept out of politics during her husband's lifetime. Margaret's husband did attempt to arrange a marriage between James of Ross and Catherine of York, who was the daughter of Edward IV of England. This favoritism led to a large schism in Margaret's family. A hint of the possible marriage between the two occurred during Margaret's lifetime, but the main overture happened after her death.

Margaret's final child, a boy named John, was born in December 1479 at Dunfermline Palace. When he was six years old, John was created Earl of Mar. He died in March 1503 at the age of twenty-three, unmarried and childless.

James III's Second Set of Bungled Political Wranglings

Despite the 1474 truce with England, the Scots could not keep on their side of the border. James III did try to further strengthen the marital bonds between the Scottish and English royal and sur-royal families by proposing yet another match in 1478. This time, he suggested that Edward IV's brother-in-law wed James's sister Margaret Stewart. One might recall that Margaret, daughter of Mary of Guelders, was engaged to Margaret of Anjou's son until Mary of Guelders ended it. By 1478, Margaret Stewart was already entangled with her illicit lover. That was not a smart proposition by James III.

Glancing over many of the thousand cuts by the Scottish which led to an English invasion of Scotland in 1480, Edward IV declared war. James III asked the French king Louis XI for help in the summer of 1481, harkening to the Auld Alliance. In 1482, James was captured after an English invasion. He was held at Edinburgh Castle and released by the end of the year. After the death of Edward IV, he tried to form a marital alliance with Richard III of England by proposing marriage between his heir James IV, then the Duke of Rothesay, and Richard's niece Anne de la Pole. This came to naught, although James did eventually wind up with an English bride.

Margaret of Denmark was estranged from her husband by this point, staying at Stirling Castle. Margaret became ill in early 1486. It was rumored that Margaret was poisoned by James Ramsay, 1st Lord of Bothwell. There was no proof behind the rumor. She died on 14 July 1486, a few weeks after her thirtieth birthday. Margaret was buried at Cambuskenneth Abbey. The abbey slowly fell into ruin after the Scottish Reformation, and now little more remains besides Margaret's grave and the bell tower.

The Attempted Canonization of Margaret of Denmark

James III was awarded the Golden Rose by Pope Innocent VIII. He received the rose in March of that year, roughly four months before Margaret's death. After her passing, James tried to have Margaret canonized. The Pope was not terribly interested, and thus Margaret of Denmark was not made a saint. The issue has not meaningfully been taken up since that time.

The Death of James III

James III was dreadfully unpopular as a king. A rebellion arose in 1488 with James, Duke of Rothesay, and the heir apparent, as the figurehead. Whether James of Rothesay was interested in the role is uncertain. He was fifteen at the time.

In England, Henry VII was king for about three years after successfully overthrowing Richard III and founding the Tudor dynasty. James III asked Henry VII for help in putting down the rebellion, but none came in time. James III's army met the rebel army of James of Rothesay on 11 June 1488 not far from Stirling Castle. James III died around this time, although his cause of death, whether by slaying or frightened misadventure, is not established.

James III was buried next to Margaret of Denmark. James of Rothesay, now King James IV of Scotland, attended the funeral. This was extremely atypical behavior of a king, and perhaps shows James IV's guilt and repentance over the death of James III. James IV may not have realized that the end goal of the rebellion was his father's death.

Now that James IV was king, he needed a queen. Eager to support the peace between England and Scotland, he looked to Henry VII. The new Tudor king only had a son by 1488, but hopefully a daughter would arrive soon.

Chapter 4

Margaret Tudor

Margaret's Birth and Early Years

Margaret Tudor was the eldest surviving daughter of Henry VII of England and Elizabeth of York. Named after her paternal grandmother, Lady Margaret Beaufort, Princess Margaret was born on 28 November 1489 at the Palace of Westminster, which was initially the primary residence for English monarchs. Her only older sibling, a brother named Arthur, was already three years old by the time she was born. A mere eighteen months after her birth, Margaret's infamous brother Henry VIII of England was born in June 1491. A further three sisters and brother followed, though only Margaret, Henry, and her sister Mary, born in 1496, survived to adulthood.

Margaret spent the first thirteen years of her life in England, where she was surrounded by luxury and beautiful gothic architecture, to which she became accustomed. Margaret was immediately treated to the very best which life as a Tudor princess had to offer. Her cradle was made of oak and lined with ermine.[1] The cradle was adorned with cloth of gold, an expensive fabric made by wrapping silk threads with gold. Margaret's father decreed that cloth of gold could only be worn by royals and high-ranking nobles.

Margaret's education was led by her formidable paternal grandmother Lady Margaret Beaufort. Princess Margaret possessed a solid intellect and zest for life. As a young lady at the English court, Margaret participated in the extravagance of the newly created Tudor pageantry. She was known to enjoy dancing, card games, and archery. Margaret learned to play the lute and clavichord, a stringed instrument with a keyboard, not unlike a piano. Margaret spoke Latin and French, as well. This combination of skills and the relationship with Lady Margaret Beaufort helped shape Margaret as not only an engaging princess but also a strong future queen.

Margaret was betrothed to James IV of Scotland to bring peace and security to Scotland and England. Although James's father, James III, succeeded in establishing peace between Scotland and England during the reign of Edward IV, the proposed marriage between James IV, when he was the Duke of Rothesay,

---

1. The fur from a white stoat, which is a weasel-like animal.

and Cecily of York never came to pass. If Scotland and England could join their royal houses through marriage, then hopefully things would continue to remain calm between the two countries. Before such a marriage could be secured, James IV proved a difficult neighbor to Margaret's father.

A Note on James IV of Scotland

James IV was a complicated personality. He was a model renaissance prince, but he also engaged in behaviors that he likely wished he could forget, such as the rebellion against his father after Margaret of Denmark's death.

James IV was a brilliant and charismatic man, whose country boasted three universities at a time when England had only two. James IV had several poets attending his court, such as William Dunbar, David Lindsay, and Gavin Douglas. Like Margaret's brother Henry VIII, James IV idolized the legendary King Arthur and his chivalric ways.

While king, James secured a papal bull that allowed William Elphinstone, Bishop of Aberdeen, to found the King's College at Aberdeen in 1494. King's College later combined with another university and today forms Aberdeen University. Aberdeen University's coat of arms bears the non-official, differenced version of the King's College and of William Elphinstone.

In 1496, the Education Act was passed, and James made education compulsory for wealthy landowners. The following year, a Chair of Medicine was established at King's College. The Surgeons and Barbers of Edinburgh were incorporated in 1506 and became the Royal College of Surgeons of Edinburgh. By 1507, James allowed for Andrew Myllar and Walter Chapman to set up Scotland's first printing press in Edinburgh.

James's court had Scots Makars there, who were poets. They would hold "flytings," or literary battles, for the court. The Makars are of great cultural importance to this day, as they give us a good snapshot of what life was like during the period. As a point of interest, it should be noted that James spoke at least six languages, including French, German, English, Latin, Flemish, Spanish, and Gaelic.

As a patron of the arts, James displayed tapestries at his palaces of Edinburgh, Stirling, Falkland, and others. He enjoyed music, maintaining several musicians at court. He had an interest in science, too, and sponsored the alchemist John Damian, who most notably conducted experiments in the fields of alchemy and aviation.

James was reasonably skilled in statecraft, having finally brought the Lord of the Isles to heel. He did indulge Perkin Warbeck, the Yorkist Pretender to the throne of England, to exert some sort of control over Henry VII of England.

James was busy with the ladies, as well. He had four different mistresses and at least five illegitimate children, along with the six legitimate children he had with his queen, Margaret Tudor.

Perkin Warbeck

James IV supported Perkin Warbeck when the latter landed in Scotland in 1495. Warbeck convinced Margaret of York, then a wealthy widow of Charles the Bold of Burgundy, that he was her presumed-dead nephew Richard of Shrewsbury, Duke of York. Richard and his brother Edward disappeared very soon after their uncle Richard III proclaimed himself king of England in the 1480s, and it is likely that Margaret of York was quite eager to believe that Warbeck was indeed her nephew. One should note that Margaret left for Burgundy years before either of Edward IV's sons were born, and she never met them in person while Edward IV was alive. Either way, James IV was in favor of supporting Warbeck in his desire to take the English throne.

Warbeck began courting Lady Catherine Gordon almost immediately after his arrival in Scotland, writing her at least one dramatic love letter,

> Most noble lady, it is not without reason that all turn their eyes to you; that all admire love and obey you. For they see your two-fold virtues by which you are so much distinguished above all other mortals. Whilst on the one hand, they admire your riches and immutable prosperity, which secure to you the nobility of your lineage and the loftiness of your rank, they are, on the other hand, struck by your rather divine than human beauty, and believe that you are not born in our days but descended from Heaven.
> All look at your face so bright and serene that it gives splendour to the cloudy sky; all look at your eyes so brilliant as stars which make all pain to be forgotten, and turn despair into delight; all look at your neck which outshines pearls; all look at your fine forehead. Your purple light of youth, your fair hair; in one word at the splendid perfection of your person:—and looking at they cannot choose but admire you; admiring they cannot choose but to love you; loving they cannot choose but to obey you.
> I shall, perhaps, be the happiest of all your admirers, and the happiest man on earth, since I have reason to hope you will think me worthy of your love. If I represent to my mind all your perfections, I am not only compelled to love, to adore, and to worship you, but love makes me your slave. Whether I was waking or sleeping I cannot find rest or happiness except in your affection. All my hopes rest in you, and in you alone.

> Most noble lady, my soul, look mercifully down upon me, your slave; who has ever been devoted to you from the first hour he saw you. Love is not an earthly thing, it is heaven born. Do not think it below yourself to obey love's dictates. Not only kings, but also gods and goddesses have bent their necks beneath its yoke.
>
> I beseech you most noble lady to accept for ever one who in all things will cheerfully do your will as long as his days shall last. Farewell, my soul and consolation. You, the brightest ornament in Scotland, farewell, farewell.

James IV backed the wedding between Warbeck and Lady Gordon, which took place in 1496. Not long after, in September, James IV and Warbeck prepared to invade England.

James IV was in favor of supporting Warbeck if only to scorn the Catholic monarchs Ferdinand of Aragon and Isabella of Castille and Leon. James IV pursued a Scottish-Spanish alliance with them through marriage in 1495, but nothing much came of it. By 1496, when James supported Warbeck's invasion of England, the Catholic Monarchs turned to Henry VII of England to discuss an Anglo-Spanish alliance instead. Whether James really believed that Perkin Warbeck was Richard of Shrewsbury or that he simply wanted to rattle Henry VII's cage is not firmly known.

Warbeck and James IV invaded England in September 1496. They were ultimately unsuccessful. Isabella and Ferdinand asked that their ambassador intercede to promote peace between Scotland and England. Whatever the exact discussions, James IV's support of Warbeck cooled in 1497. The Spanish ambassador Pedro Ayala succeeded in creating a peace treaty between Scotland and England in 1498, known as the Treaty of Ayala after the ambassador.

A Push for Peace

By 1500, James was ready to make peace with the English. Henry VII's eldest daughter, Margaret Tudor, was betrothed to James. The year before, in 1499, Margaret's brother Arthur Tudor celebrated a proxy marriage to Katharine of Aragon. Two years later, Katharine journeyed to England to celebrate her wedding with Arthur and consummate their marriage. Whether they did or not is a subject for a different book. Of these events, the 16th century historian George Buchanan wrote,

> James did not only desire a peace, but [both before and also now] an affinity with Henry and stricter bond of union, and if Henry would bestow his daughter Margaret upon him in marriage, he hoped that the thing would

be for the benefit of both kingdoms. And if Fox, whose authority he knew to be great at home, would but do his endeavour to accomplish the affinity, he did not doubt but it would be soon effected. He freely promised his endeavour, and, coming to the Court of England, acquainted the King with the proposition, and thereupon gave hopes to the Scots embassadors that a peace would easily be accorded betwixt the two Kings. Thus at length, three years after, which was *anno* 1500, even about one and the same time Margaret, Henry's eldest daughter, was betrothed to James the IVth, and also Katharine, daughter to Ferdinand of Spain, to Arthur, Henry's eldest son, and their marriages were celebrated with great pomp the next year. After the marriage all things were quiet, and the Court turned from the study of arms to sports and pastimes, so that there was nothing but masks, shews, feastings, dancings, and balls.

Not a bad arrangement for two usurper kings.

Two Tudor Weddings

Margaret's older brother Arthur was the first of the Tudor children to wed. He married Katharine of Aragon, who was a few months older than him, on 14 November 1501. The wedding was ostentatious and extravagant and must have left an impression on young Margaret. It took place at the old St. Paul's Cathedral in London, with Katharine being escorted by Margaret's little brother Henry. Katharine, wearing cloth of silver embroidered with gold roses, symbolic of the Tudor dynasty, walked down an elevated walkway in St. Paul's that was decorated with a red carpet. Henry, wearing matching fabric, walked with her and gave her away to Arthur Tudor.

Arthur, in white satin, greeted his bride at the high altar. Their wedding mass lasted about three hours, after which they received various blessings from religious officials and Margaret's parents. Upon exiting, the newlyweds were greeted with a "rich mount," an allusion to Henry VII being also the Earl of Richmond. Wine flowed forth from the mountain, amongst other decorative elements.

In the following week, customary jousts and festivities took place to celebrate the wedding. During a tournament at Westminster, Margaret and her sister Mary sat with their new sister-in-law, Katharine. Margaret probably spoke Latin with Katharine, who could not speak English, but was known to correspond with Arthur Tudor in Latin before she came to England. At a dance during the week of celebration, Margaret danced with her brother Henry.

Two months later, in January 1502, James IV of Scotland and Henry VII of England agreed to the terms of a Treaty of Perpetual Peace. Later that year, on 31 October, the treaty was ratified by Henry VII's signature. A month and a half after that, in early December 1502, James swore in Glasgow Cathedral that he would not violate the terms of the Treaty of Perpetual Peace.

In the interim, Arthur Tudor died in April 1502.

The betrothal between Margaret Tudor and James IV was celebrated at Richmond Palace. Margaret married James IV by proxy on 25 January 1503, declaring upon the exchange of vows:

> "I, Margaret, the first begotten daughter of the right excellent, right high and mighty prince and princess, Henry by the Grace of God king of England, and Elizabeth queen of the same, wittingly and of deliberate mind, having twelve years complete in age in the month of November last past, contract matrimony with the right excellent, right high and mighty prince, James king of Scotland, and the person of whom, Patrick earl of Bothwell, procurator of the said prince, represents, and take the said James king of Scotland into and for my husband and spouse, and all other for him forsake, during his and mine lives natural, and thereto I plight and give to him, in your person as procurator aforesaid, my faith and troth."

Thereafter, twelve-year-old Margaret was regularly referred to at court as the "Queen of Scots."

Considering that Margaret was only twelve years old at the time, this speech shows that Margaret had an excellent capacity for public speaking. Although not known for her love of scholarship, it appears that Margaret had a sharp mind and a talent for eloquence, both excellent traits for a queen of the stalwart country of Scotland. She was gifted crimson hangings for her Scottish state bed, along with new clothes.

After the wedding ceremony, Margaret and her mother, Queen Elizabeth of York, sat next to each other on the royal English dais and enjoyed feasting for the next several days.

Margaret Goes to Scotland

Margaret Tudor set out for her new home on 2 July 1503. She briefly visited with her namesake and paternal grandmother, Lady Margaret Beaufort, at Collyweston. An account of Margaret's progress north is given by Tudor citizen Richard Grafton, who recalled that,

> ...this fair lady was conveyed with a great company of lords, ladies, knights, esquires and gentlemen until she came to Berwick and from there to a village called Lambton Kirk in Scotland where the king with the flower

of Scotland was ready to receive her, to whom the earl of Northumberland according to his commission delivered her...

Then this lady was taken to the town of Edinburgh, and there the day after King James IV in the presence of all his nobility married the said princess, and feasted the English lords, and showed them jousts and other pastimes, very honourably, after the fashion of this rude country. When all things were done and finished according to their commission the earl of Surrey with all the English lords and ladies returned to their country, giving more praise to the manhood than to the good manner and nature of Scotland.

After arriving in Scotland, Margaret and James IV were officially wed on 8 August 1503. Their nuptials took place at the chapel of Holyroodhouse. Margaret wore a beautiful gown trimmed in satin, and James IV wore a coordinating outfit of white damask with crimson sleeves. James IV, affectionate from the start, held a magnificent feast until he and Margaret retired for the night.

Margaret Tudor, Queen of Scotland, even inspired a bit of poesy by the resident poets of her new husband's court. A song written about her includes the lyrics:

Sweet lusty lusum [fair] lady clere [bright],
Most myghty kyngis dochter dere,
Borne of a princess most serene,
Welcum of Scotlond to be queen

Margaret enjoyed an warmhearted marriage with James IV and went on to bear six children. Only one survived to adulthood: namely, James V. Life was not to be all easiness and joy for Queen Margaret.

The marriage of James IV, the Thistle, and Margaret Tudor, the Rose, was an attempt by Henry VII to bring peace to the bordering countries. Their marriage was celebrated by the poet William Dunbar, resident of James IV's court, through his poem, "Thistle and the Rose:"

The merle [blackbird] scho [she] sang,
'Haill, Roiss of most delyt,
Haill, of all flouris quene and soverane,'
The lark scho song, 'Haill, Rois, both reid and quhyt [white],
Most plesand flour, of michty cullouris twane;'
The nychtingaill song, 'Haill, naturis suffragene [representative],
In bewty, nurtour and every nobilness,
In riche array, renown, and gentilness.'[2]

---

2. The full poem can be found in the appendix.

Margaret Tudor

The marriage of Queen Margaret facilitated peace between Scotland and England throughout the rest of her father's life. Which does not necessarily say much, given that Henry VII died in 1509. At least he had the comfort of feeling like he succeeded in his political goal with Scotland.

Margaret's Jointure

After James had the Palace at Holyroodhouse built between 1501 and 1504 next to Holyrood Abbey, it was time to grant Margaret her jointure. Margaret's jointure from James the IV was settled on her between 11 and 13 March 1504. In part, the jointure states,

> James, by the grace of God king of Scots, to all good men of all his land, clergy and laymen, greeting. Know that, whereas previously, in contemplation of marriage between ourselves and our dearest wife Margaret, daughter of the most excellent prince and our father Henry, king of England, we have given and granted to our same dearest wife in liferent, by our charter under our great seal… certain earldoms, lordships, lands, possessions, etc., … in this form:
>
> Whereas previously it was agreed…that we should join with the most illustrious Princess Margaret… in lawful matrimony, …and, among other things, it was agreed and concluded in the same covenant and treaty that, before 1 July 1503, we should make, give and grant to the same Lady Margaret, for the term of her life, a marriage gift equivalent in kind and extent to the gift of any queen of Scotland at any time in the past, … and that, around 1 July, we should effectively give… [to] her… full and peaceful possession of the same …sealed under the seals of the commissioners… both of ourself and of our father the king of England, and dated 24 January 1501 [1502], and thereafter approved… our letters patent sealed with our great seal, and signed and subscribed with our own hand…. We, the above James, king of Scots, contemplating in a happy and grateful spirit the solemnization in person of the marriage between us… have given and granted…to the aforesaid Lady Margaret, in perfection and completion of the aforesaid marriage gift, all and sundry the underwritten earldoms, lordships, castles, palaces, towers, fortalices, lands, tenements, rents, fermes, victuals, meadows, woods and pastures, …namely all of our lordship of Ettrick Forest, … in our sheriffdom of Selkirk, likewise the tower, fortalice or manor of Newark in the aforesaid forest; all of our earldom of March, and the lordships of Dunbar and Cockburnspath, …our castle of Dunbar and the keeping of the same specially reserved to ourself and excepted; also

our palace of Linlithgow,… with all of our lordship of Linlithgowshire,… in our sheriffdom of Linlithgow; all of our lordship of Stirlingshire, … and our castle of Stirling…; all of our earldom of Menteith, and the lordship and castle of Doune in our earldom or sheriffdom of Perth; our palace of Methven, and all of our lordship of Methven,… in our sheriffdom of Perth; …of which the rents, issues, profits and proceeds make and constitute £2,000 sterling, English money, which makes and constitutes £6,000 of the money current and having usual course within our realm, beyond all burdens and whatsoever expenses …. Having and holding the said earldoms, lordships, castles, palaces, towers, fortalices and the rest aforesaid, to our dearest above-mentioned Lady Margaret, for the term of her life, …or whatsoever impediment by our heirs or successors, during her natural life, whether the same Lady Margaret should after our death happen to stay within our realm or without it…

And furthermore we confirm and ratify for ourself and our successors to the same Margaret, our wife, with the advice, counsel and deliberation of our three estates of parliament gathered at the said day and place … our lordship of Kilmarnock…by us, as a marriage gift given, granted and promised to our said wife at the time the solemnization of the marriage between ourself and her was performed and completed. Having and holding to the said Margaret for the whole term of her life in the manner of a marriage gift… only during the lifetime of our wife, and that it is not permitted for us or our successors to confer them on others, but that after her death they are to revert, including from any others to whom gift [was made], to the original state of the annexations and unions made formerly. In witness and faith and corroboration of all and sundry the aforesaid things, our great seal, and the seals of the said three estates of our realm [there] present, were appended, at Edinburgh, on the said 13 March 1503 [1504], and in the sixteenth year of our reign.

An extensive number of holdings for the young, fresh Queen of Scots.

Margaret's Coronation and Children with James IV

Margaret was crowned Queen of Scots at Edinburgh in March 1504. She did not give birth to any children until 1507. Thereafter, Margaret gave birth to James, Duke of Rothesay in 1507, a daughter in 1508, and Arthur Stewart, Duke of Rothesay in 1509. None of Margaret's first three children survived infancy. It would be two and a half years before Margaret would have another child.

In April 1512, Margaret welcomed the future James V into the world. Her second daughter was born later in 1512 and passed away shortly after birth. Finally, Alexander Stewart, Duke of Ross, was born in 1514 but also died in infancy. Regardless of the tragedies suffered by the Scottish royal couple, Margaret continued to enjoy a caring relationship with James IV, of whom Desiderius Erasmus commented that "[James IV] had wonderful powers of mind, an astonishing knowledge of everything, an unconquerable magnanimity and the most abundant generosity."

The Scotland that Queen Margaret knew was Catholic. Some of Martin Luther's ideas had begun to trickle into the country. The Chepman and Myllar press was founded in Edinburgh in 1508 due to the patronage of James IV. A Catholic breviary, or priest's handbook, printed by the Chepman and Myllar press exists to this day, showing that at least some form of religious text was being disseminated throughout Scotland while Margaret was queen. James IV also renovated several palaces, including Stirling, Edinburgh, and Linlithgow. Queen Margaret lived at these different castles throughout her time as queen consort. Margaret's husband was known to speak English, Gaelic, German, as mentioned, and other Western European languages. Like Margaret, he could also speak French and Latin. Latin was an international language, much like English is today. One must wonder if Margaret and James IV shared any letters or conversations in French or Latin, like Margaret's brother Henry was known to do with his infamous brunette mistress.

Death of James IV

Henry VII kept up his end of the bargain for the Treaty of Peace, which was signed by Henry VII and James IV in 1502 and included the marriage of Margaret and James IV as a term. When Queen Margaret's younger brother Henry became king of England upon the death of Henry VII in 1509, the young man had little concern for maintaining international peace. Henry VIII swiftly chose to wage war upon France. Scotland and France were allies all the way back to 1295, when the Auld Alliance was constructed through the mutual interests of France and Scotland to keep aggressive England at bay. Henry VIII also declared lordship over Scotland, which was a direct affront to James IV. So far, Henry was proving to be a terrible brother-in-law.

In 1513, Scotland declared war on England to divert the English campaign in France. After a bevy of letters between Henry VIII, James IV, and Pope Leo X, James IV sent his Scottish navy to the assistance of France in the summer of 1513. In response, Leo X ordered the excommunication of James IV. James raised an army of approximately 30,000 men and set out to invade England.

Queen Margaret and King James IV were officially residing at Linlithgow Palace when James IV and the vast Scottish army marched into battle. In what was a tense and devastating time, Queen Margaret awaited news of her husband while she cared for her little son. James IV was killed on 9 September 1513 at the infamous Battle of Flodden, also known as the Battle of Branxton, which took place near the village of Branxton in Northumberland, England. To make matters even more painful, it was Margaret's sister-in-law Katharine of Aragon who guided the English army. Katharine wanted to send Margaret's brother the body of Margaret's husband over in France, but instead sent a piece of James IV's bloodied clothing.

Queen Margaret was bitterly opposed to the war from the start. Now, her toddler son was the new king of Scotland at the age of seventeen months.

Although she may not have known at the time, Margaret was also two months pregnant with her last child conceived between Margaret and James IV. Now queen dowager, Margaret had to act quickly to protect not only herself and family, but also the entire realm of Scotland. Scotland as it was then known was a recently unified country, with the last independent isles of Scotland having submitted to James IV in 1493. Also, there was the current war going on between England and France. The death of Margaret's husband potentially exposed Scotland to civil war on two fronts: first, bitter in-fighting between the Scottish lords over territory and dominance and second, who would hold the regency for the toddler-king James V and be the de facto ruler of Scotland.

Margaret's Regency

Margaret's son was crowned king on 21 September 1513 in the chapel at Stirling Castle, where she and James V were staying while Margaret's husband James IV went to fight the English. Parliament met at Stirling Castle shortly after James IV's death and did confirm Margaret as regent for James V. This made Margaret the most powerful person, man or woman, in Scotland. Unfortunately for Margaret, because she was also sister to the aggressive English king, the Scottish nobility possessed an innate distrust of her.

Plans were being formulated to replace Margaret as regent with John Stewart, Duke of Albany. John Stewart was a descendant of James II of Scotland; John's father, a product of James II's second marriage, had fled Scotland for France. John grew up in France with his French mother, where he was also recognized as Count of Auvergne and Lauraguais. Throughout his life, John was either the heir presumptive or second in line to the Scottish throne. His return to Scotland in spring 1514 at the invitation of parliament almost started a civil war, with Scotland being divided between pro-French and pro-English factions. With the ascension of James V, John was now second in line to throne after Alexander Stewart, Duke of Ross, was born to Margaret on 30 April 1514.

Margaret showed political acumen during her time as regent, assisting in effecting peace between the Auld Alliance and England in 1514. By summer 1514, it was apparent that Margaret, Queen Dowager and Regent of Scotland, was drawing rather close to the Douglas family. In particular, Margaret was fond of Archibald Douglas, 6th Earl of Angus. Archibald had recently inherited his title, as he lost his father at the battle of Flodden. Perhaps Margaret and Archibald were able to bond over their mutual grief from the Battle of Flodden.

On 6 August 1514, Archibald and Margaret were married in secret. A wildly unpopular move, John Stewart, Duke of Albany blockaded Margaret at Stirling Castle. This resulted in Margaret ultimately relenting to John, who became regent and gained custody over James V and the infant Alexander in early 1515. Margaret then fled to London by obtaining permission to travel to Linlithgow Palace. Safely in London by October 1515, Margaret gave birth to the future Countess of Lennox and daughter of Archibald, the Lady Margaret Douglas. Margaret's son Alexander did not survive after she left for England. He died a couple months later in December 1515.

Margaret in England

Henry VIII gave Margaret a warm welcome, lodging her in Scotland Yard, the historic home of Scottish kings. Margaret was granted a letter of safe conduct in November 1516, stating in abstract,

> King James, etc, to all commanders and magistrates by land and sea. Wishing to see his mother's face, and so she can provide him with solace, with the consent of John duke of Albany, ... and the counsel of the three estates, the king grants and permits the queen to enter Scotland with as many Scottish attendants as she wishes, and as many from other countries as Albany and the estates allow to enter. They may remain unmolested in Scotland, and the queen is to be immediately provided with and may enjoy all the rents, profits, rights etc., specified in her dowry, with no exaction extracted. And the queen and her attendants are to be unharmed and unmolested in other ways, providing the queen and her attendants do and procure nothing to the prejudice of the king, Albany or the kingdom.

After a stay of roughly two years, Margaret returned to her adoptive country of Scotland in 1517.

Margaret Returns to Scotland

Once back in Scotland, Margaret learned that Archibald was living off her money and keeping the company of another woman. Margaret did attempt to reconcile with Archibald, but to no avail. She wrote to her brother,

> I am sore troubled with my Lord of Angus since my last coming into Scotland, and every day more and more, so that we have not been together this half year… I am so minded that, and I may by law of God and to my honour, to part with him, for I wit well he loves me not, as he shows me daily.

Margaret would not secure her divorce from Archibald for several years, and not without some help from John Stewart, Duke of Albany.

The regency of James V ended in August 1524, after a bold political move by Margaret. Margaret raised a force in opposition to the regency, which allowed her to press for its termination. John Stewart had recently gone back to France and Margaret organized with other Scottish lords to deliver James V from Stirling Castle to the capital of Edinburgh. In November of that same year, possibly with the encouragement of Margaret, James V proposed a marriage between himself and Margaret's niece, Mary Tudor. In the abstract, the document stated,

> [King James, etc., to all who read the present letters, greeting. Wishing to honour God by avoiding the death brought about by war, and to foster his subjects in just and firm peace, the king proposes to conclude a marriage, the strongest form of alliance and friendship. Therefore he appoints his faithful counsellors … as ambassadors to agree a marriage alliance and peace in the presence of Henry VIII of England, with the consent of the three estates assembled in parliament, and with the counsel of [Queen Margaret Tudor], the king's mother, giving them power to make agreement with King Henry or his commissioners concerning a marriage between King James and the illustrious daughter the heir apparent of King Henry [Princess Mary Tudor], and concerning the payment of the dowry by reason of the marriage, and for exacting sufficient caution until there is a final conclusion of the foregoing. Alternatively for a temporary peace for seven, five or three years, as the ambassadors see fit to conclude. Whatever they agree in the king's name will be held as authoritative and agreeable. Under the great seal at Edinburgh on 18 November 1524, twelfth year of the reign.

This proposal never went far.

In an act that could be seen as revenge, Archibald Douglas, now estranged from Margaret, seized custody of James V in July 1525. James was held as Archibald's prisoner for three years. During that time, Margaret successfully sued for divorce. Her divorce from Archibald was granted by the Pope in March 1527. James V remained in Archibald's custody.

With the assistance of Henry Fitzroy, the illegitimate son of Margaret's brother Henry VIII, James V was finally able to escape the clutches of his stepfather Archibald in 1528. This was six months after Margaret had divorced Archibald. Margaret then protested against or sued Archibald in September 1528 for wasting her property,

> Compeared Master Robert Galbraith, advocate to [Margaret Tudor], the queen's grace, and alleged that [Archibald Douglas], earl of Angus, owed her great sums of money and other goods and, therefore, protested that the process of forfeiture led against him be no hurt or prejudice to her grace regarding the same, but that she may have as much of his lands reserved to her in the said process as will extend to the value and quantity of the sums that she shall happen to obtain from the said earl or any others succeeding in his lands or goods, especially considering that she has him under summons for the said debts.

James V swiftly moved against his former stepfather, finding in Margaret's favor on the same day,

> Our sovereign lord in parliament, with the authority of the three estates of his realm, ratifies and approves this writing underwritten and wills that the same have strength and effect after the form and tenor of the same in all points, of which the tenor follows:
>
> We, moved of filial love due to our dearest mother, [Margaret Tudor], the queen, and also out of equity, having consideration how Archibald, earl of Angus has wrongfully taken over the mails and profits of diverse of her lordships and lands since the sentence of divorce led between them, and diverse other actions which our said dearest mother has and may have against the said earl, as well before the said divorce as since then, therefore we grant and will by these words that all actions and rights to which our said dearest mother has just title and might recover upon the said earl by justice, if he were not forfeited, be excepted and reserved to her in his forfeiture; and by the tenor thereof, we except and reserve the same and give her just interest thereto, commanding and charging our justice or justice clerks to except and reserve the said actions and rights whatsoever

to our dearest mother in the doom of forfeiture to be given upon the said earl in this present parliament, so that what sums of money that may be liquidated and made known that the said earl is owing to our said dearest mother shall be apprised on what lordships and lands that pertained to the said earl as she shall best please to name and choose, and to be assigned to her until she is paid of the same; and wills that this present writ of exception and reservation be registered in the books of council pronounced and admitted in parliament foresaid.

Effectively, properties belonging to the Earl of Angus were seized and otherwise sold off for Margaret's benefit.

Margaret's Third Marriage

A year after officially divorcing Archibald, Margaret entered into what was to be another unhappy marriage, with Henry Stewart, Lord Methven. He was six years her junior. They wed in March 1528. There is some debate over whether Henry Stewart's daughter Dorothea was with Margaret Tudor. It is put forth that Dorothea was born around April 1528, meaning that Margaret was clearly pregnant before she wed Henry Stewart. If Dorothea was Margaret's daughter, it seems she died young, likely in her infancy. Henry Stewart remarried after Margaret Tudor's passing, and had a daughter named Dorothea in the 1540s. That Dorothea lived until at least 1600.

The Scots nobility, and James V, were not inclined toward Margaret's third marriage. The couple were besieged at Stirling Castle, and Henry Stewart was taken into custody by the scorned family of Archibald Douglas. He managed to escape and was later elevated to his position of Lord Methven in July 1528.

Margaret and Henry Stewart did hold influence over James V until approximately 1534, when a meeting Margaret arranged between her son James V, and her brother Henry VIII was frustrated by members of James V's council. That move ultimately led to James V losing trust in his mother.

Margaret found herself unhappy in marriage yet again. She attempted to divorce Henry Stewart in 1537, only to be reconciled to him in approximately 1539. Margaret discovered not long after her reconciliation with Lord Methven that he was keeping a mistress in one of Margaret's castles. That did not sit well with Margaret, who asked her son to grant her a divorce. James did not give in right away, and Nature interceded before he had to make a true decision.

Margaret slipped quietly away from life at Methven Castle on 18 October 1541. During her lifetime, she was not only a queen consort, but also the de facto ruler of Scotland for a time. Margaret was an expert at intrigue and certainly had no fear of standing up against men for what she believed was best for her children and Scotland. Margaret's legacy and initial purpose to attain lasting peace between Scotland and England was achieved through her great-grandson, James VI of Scotland and I of England and Ireland.

Chapter 5

Madeleine de Valois

Madeleine's Childhood

Madeleine de Valois, also called Madeleine of France, was the third daughter and fifth child of her parents, King Francis I of France and Queen Claude. Born on 10 August 1520, her eldest sibling Louise died a couple of years earlier. Her second eldest sibling, Charlotte, died when Madeleine was barely four years old. She outlived her brother Francis, her second oldest sibling, as well. Her brothers Henri and Charles, and sister Margaret, outlived Madeleine.

Madeleine lost her mother from an old tuberculosis infection. The bacteria spread from somewhere else within Claude mere weeks before Madeleine's fourth birthday, in 1524. Claude was noted as having a crooked or bent back during her lifetime. She suffered either from scoliosis or from an earlier tuberculosis infection that eventually went into her spine, causing her back to twist. If it was indeed tuberculosis, the initial infection could have gone from Claude's lungs into the spine. Once in the spine, the tuberculosis bacteria does something similar to arthritis. Visually, it creates a severe bend in a person's back, causing a hunch. It can manifest more like a case of scoliosis. When the infection flared up in 1524, it proved fatal for Claude. Claude's rapid succession of pregnancies arguably weakened her and hastened her death.

The Court of Madeleine's Father

Like her father-in-law, Madeleine's father Francis I of France was considered a model Renaissance prince. Francis was born on 12 September 1494 in Cognac, France. He was the first of five Valois kings from his part of the family. He possessed a chivalrous imagination. This was likely due to the way he was raised by his mother and because he became the heir presumptive of the French throne when he was around four years of age. Francis indulged in the arts and music and appreciated the value of scholarly works.

Francis is to be thanked for bringing da Vinci to France. After Francis's victory at the Battle of Marignano in September 1515, he was invited to dine with the Pope. He spent additional time in Italy and granted a pension to da Vinci, amongst other Italians. Da Vinci traveled with Francis back to France, bringing with him several works of art. Da Vinci passed away in France some years later.

Another significant contribution Francis made to the world of art was establishing the school of Fontainebleau. After another, unsuccessful campaign in Italy in the 1520s, Francis returned to France in 1527 and brought even more talented Italian artists with him. He set about restoring a hunting lodge in the Forest of Bièvre, employing Italian artisans to restore and add to the building. It became the palace of Fontainebleau, a royal residence for Francis. The first Italian artist arrived at Fontainebleau around 1530, with another large group coming along in 1540. The artists developed a specific style, and eventually set about making prints of their work.

After Francis died in 1547, Fontainebleau experienced a lengthy decline until Henri IV became King of France in 1589. This second school of Fontainebleau featured mainly French, not Italian, artists. This second school existed on into the 17th century.

Francis was a patron of music, having established a polyphonic chapel and a monophonic chapel at his court. His court musicians frequently went back and forth between where Francis was holding court and Notre Dame in Paris. This sharing of musicians allowed for developing secular and religious styles to intermix to a degree, creating a unique sound in early modern French music.

Francis's main contributions as a man of the Renaissance live on through the schools of Fontainebleau and through music from the period. A chivalrous romantic, he also embraced the ideals of his time when it came to courting women. Finally, though his Italian campaigns to gain territory may have failed, he gained something far more significant and long-lasting by bringing back many Italian artists and artisans to France.

Madeleine de Valois grew up with the results of her father's visual and auditory opulence as a backdrop to her childhood.

Madeleine's Mother, Claude, Duchess of Brittany

Claude was one of two surviving children, both daughters, of Louis XII of France and Anne, Duchess Regnant of Brittany. Claude was pious and devoted to religion, never taking on the governance of Brittany. She instead let her husband administer Brittany on her behalf. Claude fulfilled her most basic duty of early modern queenship, namely bearing children. Claude gave birth to seven children between August 1515 and June 1523. She lived in the shadow of Francis I's favorite mistress, Françoise de Foix.

The writer Pierre de Bourdeille, seigneur de Brantôme, left extensive memoirs from which trustworthy information about the French court can be gleaned. Brantôme said of Claude,

> I must speak about madame Claude of France, who was very good and very charitable, and very sweet to everyone and never showed displeasure to anybody in her court or of her domains. She was deeply loved by the King Louis and the Queen Anne, her father and mother, and she was always a good daughter to them; after the King took the peaceful Duke of Milan, he made him declare and proclaim her in the Parliament of Paris the Duchess of the two most beautiful Duchies of Christendom, Milan and Brittany, one from the father and the other from the mother. What an heiress! if you please. Both Duchies joined in all good deed to our beautiful kingdom.

A very pleasant, if overly optimistic, view of Claude's legacy.

After Claude's death, the delicate Madeleine was raised by her paternal aunt Marguerite d'Angoulême, Queen of Navarre. Madeleine's father Francis believed the air in Navarre, bordered by France and Spain, would be better for her. Unfortunately, the favorable climate at the Navarrese court would not stop Madeleine from contracting tuberculosis.

Eleonore von Habsburg, a niece of Katharine of Aragon's, became Madeleine's stepmother in 1530. Madeleine was almost ten years old. Madeleine and her little sister Margaret returned to France to live with their new stepmother.

Eleonore von Habsburg, Madeleine's Stepmother

Eleonore, born in 1498, was twenty-three when she was widowed the first time. The eldest of the children between Juana of Castille and Philip von Habsburg, Eleonore went to live at her brother, Charles V's, court in the Low Countries. Charles became Holy Roman Emperor in 1519. Eleonore was an important tool during the ongoing Habsburg-Valois Wars, also known as the Italian Wars. These series of wars began in the 15th century and stemmed from a disagreement over who held claim to the Duchy of Milan.

Eleonore was first betrothed to Charles of Bourbon in 1523, but that was later abandoned. Francis I of France was captured at the Battle of Pavia in 1525. As part of the Ladies' Peace or 1529 Treaty of Cambrai, Eleonore was betrothed to Francis. She later wed him on 4 July 1530. The couple did not have children.

Notwithstanding a very romantic first meeting with the reportedly blonde Spanish beauty in 1526, Francis openly disdained Eleonore. At their introduction,

Eleonore gave Francis her hand, which he kissed and then cheekily stated he should instead kiss her mouth. Eleonore was ready to accept her fate if it meant supporting the Habsburg cause.

Francis, still in Charles V's custody, was forced into signing the Treaty of Madrid in 1526. An arrangement was made that Francis would hand over two of his sons, Madeleine's older brothers, to Charles V. Madeleine's brothers could be ransomed for a large sum of gold. After Francis's release, he initially broke the Treaty of Madrid and thus the engagement, which he was later forced back into in 1529 during the Ladies' Peace.

Eleonore saw Francis again in early July 1530, when she and his sons met Francis after crossing the border river of Bidaossa. They met at Mont-de-Marsan. The wedding between Eleonore and Francis took place quickly after his arrival, in the Capiteux Abbey around two o'clock in the afternoon on 4 July. Francis, Eleonore, and their entourage next sailed to Bordeaux, where Eleonore had her first official, or solemn, entry as Queen Consort of France, and dressed in purple velvet for the occasion.

Francis I respected Eleonore but had no meaningful emotional interest in her. Francis was not present for her coronation in May 1531, and whiled away his time with his mistress Anne de Pisseleu d'Heilly, whom he took up in 1526 after his return from Charles V's captivity. Anne was a Protestant and grew increasingly powerful during the rest of Francis I's life. Francis died in March 1547.

Despite being virtually ignored by her husband, Eleonore was a successful Queen Consort of France. She frequently supported charitable works and took special care in raising her two stepdaughters Madeleine and Margaret. Eleonore was present as Queen of France for all official events, as well. She was, in modern terms, the life of the party at court. She tried her best to secure successful marriages for her stepchildren, and to maintain peace between her husband and brother. Unfortunately, Francis and Charles resumed their battles in 1536, until Pope Paul III acted as intermediary between the two monarchs, creating a ten-year armistice between Francis and Charles in 1538.

James V of Scotland, Madeleine's Husband

James V, son of Margaret Tudor and James IV, was born 10 April 1512. His father died the following year during the Battle of Flodden. James, made King of Scotland at the age of seventeen months, saw his kingdom ruled under the regency of his mother and his half-brother before taking over the rule in 1524, when he was twelve years old.

When James V was seven years old, back in 1517, his regent John Stewart, Duke of Albany and also Count of the French Auvergne and Lauraguais, negotiated a peace between France and Scotland. Known as the 1517 Treaty of Rouen, part of this iteration of the Auld Alliance included that James V would marry a daughter of Francis I of France. Madeleine was not born until three years later in 1520, as mentioned.

In 1534, twenty-two-year-old James began his suit for the hand of fourteen-year-old Madeleine. Francis, nervous for his daughter's ever-delicate health, tried to dissuade James from marrying Madeleine. Mary of Bourbon, daughter of Charles, Duke of Vendôme, was proposed as an alternative, better choice.

Madeleine's aunt, who was caring for the girl, did not like the idea of Madeleine marrying the king of Scots. Marguerite d'Angoulême, Queen Consort of Navarre, injected herself in her brother Francis's politics. She too was not pleased to see her sickly niece head toward the harsher climate of Scotland, but also was not in favor of James V wedding Mary of Bourbon. Mary's father was very close with Holy Roman Emperor Charles V, who at the time was out of favor with both Francis I of France and Henry VIII of England. Marguerite suggested her sister-in-law Isabella of Navarre.

Mary of Bourbon

James V was sent a portrait of Mary of Bourbon, who turned twenty-nine in 1534. James dispatched a letter to Francis in January 1535, reiterating his desire to marry a French princess and thus comport with the terms of the 1517 Treaty of Rouen. James was open to wedding Mary of Bourbon if Francis provided her with a dowry like that of one of Francis's daughters. Although one can never claim to know the mind of a monarch, it seems that James was not terribly interested in Mary or what she brought to a potential marriage. James found another opportunity to dally from the negotiation for Mary of Bourbon after Christina of Denmark, Dowager Duchess of Milan, was widowed in October 1535.

James ultimately decided to continue pursuing Mary of Bourbon. His representatives in France were granted authority in December 1535 to conclude the terms of James's marriage to Mary of Bourbon. A marriage contract was ratified by James V and Francis I in March 1536. James decided he would retrieve his bride from France himself, and so journeyed there. He met Mary in Picardy in September. After meeting her, James went to meet with Francis I at the mountain pass of Col du Pin-Bouchain, by Joux, northwest of Lyon. Francis I was hunting with his family in the area.

King Francis was still melancholy over the death of his eldest son, also named Francis, in August 1536. The young man died of tuberculosis, but it was thought at the time that he was poisoned. Francis's second son, Henri, was the newly created Dauphin of France, the title of the official heir. Henri espied the approach of James V and his company from afar and escorted the Scots party to his father's camp. Delighted with the surprise, Francis ordered that his son Henri treat James as his own brother.

Madeleine Meets James

That evening, Francis, James, and Francis's family retired to a nearby palace. Before retiring to the palace, the chronicler Robert Lindesay of Pitscottie states that,

> the king of Scotland did his due reverence unto the queen of France and her ladies, and especially to the king's daughter Madeleine, who was riding in a chariot because she was sickly and evil-disposed, she might not ride on horse.

Madeleine was a passionate teenager, as teenage girls go, and,

> notwithstanding all her sickness and malady, from the time she saw the king of Scotland and spoke with him she became so enamored with him and loved him so that she would have no man in life but him only, whereof counsel of France and Scotland both liked nothing thereof for they were certified by the medical doctors that no succession would come of her body by reason of her long sickness and malady and that she was not able to travel out of that country [of France] to another, and if she did she would not have long days there unto.

Quite lamentably, the doctors would be proved correct. Knowing full well that Madeleine might not survive, and knowing that James was already promised to Mary of Bourbon, Francis gave his blessing to Madeleine and James because,

> the ardent love that this gentlewoman bore to the king of Scotland caused her father the king of France to consent unto her marriage with the king of Scotland and to the effect desired the king of Scotland to the same consented thereto hastily... and since the gentlewoman [Madeleine] being [the king of France's] eldest daughter it was not good for [James] to refuse that honorable offer of the king of France to have his eldest daughter in marriage with what profit and pleasure the he desired with her.

Young love having triumphed, Francis, James, and the rest returned to Paris to solemnize the marriage between Madeleine and James. Aside from the usual declaration of mutual peace and amity, Francis I was to pay James V 100,000 crowns a year starting a day after the solemnization of Madeleine's marriage to James, which took place on 26 November 1536. The upper nobility of Scotland was requested to come to Paris to observe the wedding ceremony between Madeleine and James. Wishing to wait a year and a day to pay the dowry betrays Francis's doubt that Madeleine would not last long in Scotland.

Madeleine of France, the Summer Queen of Scots

The actual ceremony took place on 1 January 1537,

> the marriage was solemnized at Paris in Notre Dame church at the hour of ten before [noon] with the king of France and queen and their daughter [Madeleine] and counsel and all the hail nobility on the one part, the king of Scotland and his counsel and nobility on the other part, which was such a great multitude on both sides that it was cumbersome and tedious to rehearse.

Rehearse, in this instance, meaning the performance of the wedding. After the wedding,

> there was such jousting and tournaments both on horse and on foot and in burg and land and also upon the sea in ships...set in all parts of France... And also the parties, banqueting, delicate and costly triumph and plays and feasts with pleasant sound of instrument of all kind and also cunning conjurers having the art of illusion to cause things to appear which was as flying dragons in the air [which] shot fire.

After stunning celebrations throughout France, it was time for Madeleine, now recognized as Queen of Scots, to venture to Scotland with her husband. The couple enjoyed the rest of the winter in temperate France, leaving for Scotland in May 1537.

Madeleine's father provided them with two ships, one of which was named the *Salamander*. The salamander was Francis I's personal emblem. Altogether, two Scottish and two French ships were heading from France to Scotland. Additionally, Francis gave to James and Madeleine some of his best horses. Francis gave to the young couple gilded harnesses for the horses, too. Specifically for his daughter, Francis, called on his daughter Madeleine the Queen of Scotland and caused to pass to his wardrobe with her gentlewomen and ladies, and the master of the wardrobe with his command, and take what suits her of cloth of gold, velvet, satin and damask with taffetas and other silks to make her habiliments as she pleased. And also commanded her to take what hangings or tapestry works and bedding of gold and such, as she pleased, or any other jewels that he had in his wardrobe that she pleased; commanded all to be patent to her, take what she would.

Beyond allowing Madeleine to have free rein when choosing what she wished of his textiles, Francis also gifted Madeleine,

chains, tassels, and tablets and rings with rubies and diamonds with sapphires and ilk kind of precious stones that was or might be gotten for gold or silver, for such substance was never seen in Scotland as this young queen brought in it, for there was never the like in no man's time in Scotland.

After showering Madeleine with gifts, it was time for her to depart for Scotland.

The couple sailed for Leith from Calais. The voyage took roughly five days. Once disembarked from the ship, Madeleine knelt on the ground and kissed the earth, thanking God for delivering them safely to Scotland. They arrived on 19 May 1537 at roughly ten o'clock in the morning. Madeleine was already quite ill.

Madeleine and James went to Holyrood Abbey and then into the Palace of Holyroodhouse. They intended to take up residency there whilst preparations were made to celebrate Madeleine's joyous entry into Scotland. They were still there in June 1537, when Madeleine wrote to her father, telling him that she was doing well. Sadly, on 7 July 1537, the summer Queen of Scots died in her husband's arms at Holyrood Palace, aged not quite seventeen years old. Of her death, the chronicler Robert Lindesay of Pitscottie wrote,

their great joy and merriness and triumph hastily was all turned in mourning and dolor for displeasure of the queen for she departed [died]…and therefore all their great blitheness and joy of her coming, farces and plays that should have been made to her, were all turned into solemn masses and dirges, where through their zeal such mourning through the country and lamentation that it was great pity for to hear.

She had suffered from tuberculosis for most of or her entire life. The illness was kept at bay during her time in the mild French climate, but the stress of her new life in Scotland combined with the change in climate aggravated her condition, leading to her death. Madeleine was interred in Holyrood Abbey.

Madeleine's death reopened the possibility that Mary of Bourbon could become the next Queen of Scots. That is, if Mary were not already dead. When James V scorned Mary in favor of Madeleine, Mary "took such displeasure and melancholy for the king of Scotland that she within short while took sickness and died." James's reaction is not known.

James, still young, needed a wife so he could provide Scotland with an heir. Wishing to maintain the Auld Alliance, he once more pursued a French match.

Chapter 6

Marie de Guise

Marie's Birth and Early Years

Marie de Guise, sometimes called Marie of Lorraine, was born 22 November 1515 to Claude of Lorraine, the Duke of Guise, and Antoinette of Bourbon. She was born in the Duchy of Bar, in the independent country of Lorraine. Her family was closely allied with the French monarchy. Marie de Guise's first cousin was Mary of Bourbon, who was jilted by James V of Scotland. She was the eldest of twelve children. All but two of them lived to adulthood, although only Marie's sister Renée of Guise, Abbess of St. Pierre in Reims, outlived their mother.

As a child, Marie was sent to live with her grandmother Philippa of Guelders. Philippa was widowed in 1508 and went to live at the Convent of Poor Clares in Pont-à-Mousson in 1519. Marie went there in roughly 1520 or 1521 when she was five or six years old. Although Marie had a very Catholic upbringing, she was willing to tolerate other religious ideas later in life.

Marie's father Claude of Lorraine was heavily involved in French military ventures during the early years of Marie's life. In September 1515, a couple of months before Marie's birth, Claude was gravely injured at the Battle of Marignano, a triumph for Francis I of France. Claude fought against the English incursion in 1522, leading to Claude gaining prestige. He was also able to increase his wealth, a handy thing for someone with a rapidly growing family.

Marie's mother Antoinette of Bourbon was long-lived, intelligent, and had a good sense of humor. She was the fourth of five children, and the first daughter born to her parents. Antoinette was born on 25 December 1493, eleven and a half months after her brother Louis. Antoinette would outlive all her siblings and eleven of her twelve children, not to mention outliving her husband. Antoinette was adept at administering the Lorraine properties when Claude was away fighting one of his wars. Marie trusted her mother Antoinette tremendously. Antoinette was a devout Catholic and took no issue with the occasional Protestant in her territory being maimed or ending up dead. All in all, a formidable woman.

Turning back to Marie, she grew to be very tall and elegant. When Marie was in her mid-teens, she was brought to Francis I of France's court, where she made quite the impression. She had dark reddish-brown hair, which echoed the royal French children, several of whom had red or reddish hair. Her eyes were reportedly grey. Marie, who made her first appearance at court in 1531 during the celebration of Francis I's and Eleanor von Habsburg's of Austria's wedding, was reportedly charming, too. Marie struck up a friendship with Francis I's daughter Madeleine de Valois.

Between her age, elegance, and charm, it was time for her family to find Marie a suitable husband.

Marie's First Marriage

Marie was first made a wife in 1534 at the age of eighteen when she married the Duke of Longueville, Louis II d'Orléans. They were wed in a suitably decadent style at the Louvre Palace on 30 October 1535. The festivities surrounding the couple's marriage lasted for more than two weeks. Marie's father was, after all, a war hero for the French.

The couple then went to live in the Duchy of Longueville, which is in north-central France, but just outside Paris to the southeast. Francis I of France and his court enjoyed hunting in Longueville, which was heavily forested.

Marie's new husband Louis II was born in early June 1510, making him roughly five years older than Marie. His older brother Claude became Duke of Longueville in 1516 after their father died. Louis' father stood as a proxy for King Louis XII of France during the latter's marriage to Mary Tudor in 1514, which was celebrated at Greenwich Palace in England. Louis' father was ostensibly a prisoner, having been captured during the 1513 Battle of the Spurs. In reality, he was treated as an ambassador.

Louis' mother Johanna of Hachberg-Sausenberg was her father's only heir and showed vigor in administering the county of Neuchâtel. Her husband, Louis II's father, co-ruled the county via *jure uxoris*. Johanna is a slightly shadowy figure, but presumably was involved with the regency of Claude because he was only eight years old when he became Duke of Longueville. Louis became Duke of Longueville in 1524, after the death of his brother Claude.

Marie de Guise was not Duchess of Longueville for too great a length of time. She did have two sons with Louis. Her first child, a son named Francis, was born in October 1535. Louis, who was intellectually inclined, had a reprinted book by the famous humanist Desiderius Erasmus dedicated to the baby in 1536. The book was entitled, *Institutio Principis Christiani*, the *Education of a Christian Prince*, and was originally dedicated to the Holy Roman Emperor Charles V.

Marie's husband Louis died of a fever in June 1537, not long after his twenty-seventh birthday. Marie kept the last letter from Louis for the rest of her life. Their little son Francis was raised by Marie's mother Antoinette. Francis regularly corresponded with Marie throughout his life.

Marie's second son, a boy named Louis after his father, arrived two months after the death of Duke Louis II of Longueville. He lived for roughly four months, from August to December 1537. Marie would become very accustomed to losing children and husbands before their time.

A New Suitor for Marie de Guise

Marie was a popular potential bride, sparking a bit of a rivalry between Henry VIII of England and his nephew, James V of Scotland. The two kings, who were already at odds over the English Reformation, were both searching for a new bride at the same time. Both Henry and James had lost their wives in 1537. Women proposed as possible wives for the kings included Maria of Portugal, Christina of Denmark, and Marie de Guise. Princess Mary, Henry VIII's daughter and James V's cousin through his mother Margaret Tudor, was suggested as a possibility for James.

James V of Scotland's first French bride, Madeleine de Valois, had died in July of 1537. He wanted to marry another French bride as soon as possible, and so wrote to Francis I for his opinion. Another French marriage would bolster the Auld Alliance, too. Marie de Guise, herself a young widow, was the best choice in Francis's opinion. The statuesque young woman, who was roughly five feet and eleven inches tall, had already produced two sons during her first marriage to Louis II, Duke of Longueville. Surely, she would have more boys. Louis died in June 1537, almost exactly a month before Madeleine de Valois. Perhaps it went through Francis's mind that the two could be a source of comfort to each other. Whatever Francis's thought process, he was interested in helping James find another French bride and to do so post haste.

Marie's mother, Duchess Antoinette, was greatly concerned about how quickly Francis expected Marie to take another husband. Writing in January 1538, Antoinette expressed that she did not think the Scottish marriage would be advantageous to Marie or her surviving son. The marriage contract with James V could interfere with Marie's rights as a widow of Longueville and the rights of her son. Antoinette might have also suspected that Marie's son would not be welcomed at the Scottish court, meaning that Marie may never see him again.

James V was not Marie's only potential suitor, as mentioned. In October 1537, Henry VIII of England's third wife Jane Seymour died weeks after giving birth to the couple's only child, the future Edward VI. Given that Henry's only other surviving children were his two daughters, Mary and Elizabeth, who were declared illegitimate after Henry ended his marriages to their respective mothers, Henry very much wanted to remarry and hopefully welcome more sons into the world. Henry's other acknowledged, surviving child, a son named Henry Fitzroy, died in 1536. With the fates of Henry's first three wives, namely the annulment of his over-twenty-year marriage to Katharine of Aragon, the beheading of Anne Boleyn, and the untimely, albeit natural, death of Jane Seymour, chances are that Marie de Guise was not exactly chomping at the bit to become England's next queen.

Marie, her sister Louise, their cousin Anne of Lorraine, and Mary of Bourbon were all potential French brides for Henry VIII. Henry was clearly in competition with his nephew James V, especially given that Mary of Bourbon had been originally negotiating a marriage with James before he scorned her for Madeleine of France. As mentioned in the previous chapter, Mary of Bourbon died in September 1538. Politically speaking, it did not seem that Francis I of France wanted to wed a French princess to Henry VIII of England.

Marie de Guise's sister Louise was the next closest sister to Marie in age. Born in 1520, she was five years younger than Marie. Louise was very involved in the life of her nephew through Marie and the Duke of Longueville, giving the boy attention and care until she married Charles II de Croÿ, Duke of Chimay, in 1541. Louise died in October 1542.

Anne of Lorraine, who was originally promised to William of Cleves when her brother Francis was promised to Anna of Cleves in the 1520s, went on to marry René of Chalon, Prince of Orange, in 1540.

Thankfully, Marie avoided the marriage to James's maternal uncle Henry VIII and went on in May 1538 to marry James by proxy in Paris. She later married him in person after her arrival in Scotland. Marie's proxy marriage took place at the Sainte Chappelle in Châteaudun. The chapel boasted of a wing which had been built by a relative of Marie's first husband, Duke Louis II of Longueville. Upwards of 2,000 Scots were in attendance, with Robert Maxwell, 5th Lord Maxwell, standing as proxy for James V.

Marie brought with her a dowry given by Francis I of France, father of James V's first bride, and it was large enough to be of the same value as a French princess. Of Marie de Guise, Margaret Tudor wrote to her brother Henry VIII, "I trust she will prove a wise Princess. I have been much in her company, and she bears herself very honourably to me, with very good entertaining." Marie would leave behind in France her three-year-old son, who was now the Duke of Longueville.

Marie Goes to Scotland

Marie arrived in Scotland on 16 June 1538. She spent her first night in her new country at Balcomie Castle in Fife. Part of the building in which Marie stayed still exists today. The castle was more of a large manor house, complete with two small towers and a gatehouse. Marie and James had their official meeting, and a few days later, and were wed at St. Andrews Cathedral, also in Fife.

As a point of interest, the nearby castle at St. Andrews was the official home for bishops, and later archbishops, of St. Andrews. The castle fell into disrepair by the end of the 16th century, and eventually parts of it fell into the sea. The remaining ruins of the castle can still be seen.

The couple enjoyed a lengthy wedding celebration of forty days. This would have included pageants, jousts, and feasts. There was also an archery competition. For a bit of what the modern person would recognize as a honeymoon, the new royal couple left on a hunting trip. After their return, Marie prepared for her formal entrance into Edinburgh, which was celebrated on 16 November 1538, with all the attendant pomp and circumstance. Although she was in Scotland for only the last five months, Marie had already made a good impression on the Scots.

Marie was evidently homesick for the familiarity of France. She began adding touches of French influence to buildings in which she lived, such as Falkland Palace, by inviting French stonemasons and the like to decorate and update the buildings. Missing French food, Marie imported boars from France to populate areas for hunting, along with French fruit trees for her Scottish orchards.

Marie's First Two Pregnancies and Coronation

By mid-1539, Marie was not yet pregnant. In hopes of remedying the situation, she and her husband James V decided to sail across the Firth of Forth to the Isle of May. They took three ships for this important excursion, the *Little Unicorn*, the *Mary Willoughby*, and the *Unicorn*. The *Mary Willoughby* was originally one of Henry VIII of England's naval ships. It was named after one of his first wife Katharine of Aragon's ladies-in-waiting, Maria Willoughby, née de Salinas. The Scots captured the ship in 1533, although it was later recaptured by the English in 1547. The other two ships were named after Scotland's national animal, the unicorn, which is a known enemy of the lion, England's national animal.

Marie and James V sought to pray at the shrine of St. Adrian on the Isle of May, asking for the saint's blessing so the couple could conceive. One might recall that Mary of Guelders had stopped at the very same shrine to pray some ninety years before. It seems to have worked because Marie fell pregnant very shortly after their visit to the Isle of May. Planning for Marie's coronation was soon underway, too.

The coronation happened on 22 February 1540. A new crown was made for the occasion, which was set to take place in Holyrood Abbey. Ladies were summoned from all over Scotland to attend. The abbey was hung with tapestries, and items were moved for the occasion from the Palace of Holyroodhouse chapel to Holyrood Abbey. A thirty-gun salute marked the occasion, and fireworks were lit just up the hill at Edinburgh Castle. Marie used a gilded scepter for the coronation, too.

Marie's first child with her new husband was born 22 May 1540 at Stirling Castle. The baby was named James and was immediately recognized as the Duke of Rothesay because he was the heir presumptive to the Scottish throne. He was born in St. Andrews and was baptized there four days after his birth. Marie, still preferring French craftmanship when she could, had a French-style cradle built for her baby prince. Marie's mother-in-law Margaret Tudor was one of the infant prince's godparents.

Parliament at Edinburgh passed legislation on 14 March 1541, stating,

> Item, that the glorious Virgin Mary, mother of our blessed saviour Jesus Christ, be reverently worshipped and honoured over all this realm and that prayers be made to her to make intercession to God almighty, Father, Son and Holy Ghost for the succession, health, welfare and prosperity of the king's grace, his queen [Marie de Guise], our sovereign lady, ~~my lord Prince James VI~~,[1] and their prosperous successes, peace, unity and concord between our said sovereign lord and all Christian princes, and between them all to resist the enemies of the Catholic faith, and between his grace, his estates and lieges; and that his highness and people may remain constantly in the faith and follow the law of God according to the statutes and doctrine of the Holy Kirk received and kept by his predecessors, kings of Scotland, and people in all times bypast since they first received the same; and likewise prayers to be made to all saints, in special and in general, and that worship be had to them.

Marie was heavily pregnant with her second Scottish child at this point.

Marie's baby was born 12 April 1541. He was named Robert. He, too, was born at Stirling Castle. Robert was created the Duke of Albany.

Tragically, both of Marie's sons died on about 20 or 21 April 1541. James, Duke of Rothesay was not quite a year and Robert being only a few days old.

---

1. "my lord Prince James VI" is stricken out here.

Marie's mother Antoinette did her best to console Marie from afar, suggesting reasons for the tragedy and reminding Marie that she and James V could have more children because they were young.

Later that year, 18 October 1541, Marie's mother-in-law Margaret Tudor died at Methven Castle. Along with Margaret died any good will which Henry VIII of England was willing to maintain toward Scotland. By late summer 1542, the Scots were regularly warring with the English. That was the last thing that Marie, or Scotland, needed.

A Birth and a Death for Marie

Marie became pregnant once more in early 1542, roughly a year after her Scottish sons died. Her French son was still alive and well. Over the summer, Marie's husband prepared for war with his uncle Henry. Henry wished to break up the ongoing Auld Alliance between France and Scotland, or otherwise gain control of Scotland. He wanted his nephew to break away from the Catholic Church, too, which James V was unwilling to do. Henry resumed the Anglo-Scottish Wars, which began in 1460 and were fought off and on until late 1542. The last prior battle was fought in 1514, seeing the Scottish achieving an unlikely victory at Hornshole despite the crushing defeat at the Battle of Flodden the year before.

After nearly twenty-eight years of peace between the Scots and the English, the Battle of Hadden Rig, near Kelso, took place on 24 August 1542. The Scots were the victors, suffering very few casualties. One can imagine that Marie was pleased with the outcome. That would change before the end of 1542.

On 24 November 1542, a large Scottish force crossed the border into England. The English met the Scottish force at Solway Moss, a peat bog by what is now the city of Carlisle in Cumbria on the northwestern edge of England. James V was not part of the Battle of Solway Moss, having stayed across the border at Lochmaben Castle, the ruins of which exist today. The Scots took a terrible beating at the battle. Fearing capture, James fled to Falkland Palace, north of Edinburgh and firmly within Scotland. Falkland Palace is roughly 95 miles or 153 kilometers away from Lochmaben Castle. James was reportedly ill.

James V's health was frequently at issue for a decade before his death. He complained of "a sore face," pox, fevers, and other illnesses throughout the 1530s and into 1540. His health was once more poorly, beginning in November 1542 and declining in early December 1542.

On 8 December 1542, Marie's only daughter Mary was born at Linlithgow Palace. Linlithgow Palace is about 33 miles or 53 kilometers southwest of Falkland Palace, making Marie closer to the losing battle site of Solway Moss than her husband the king. The very ill James V was notified of baby Mary's birth, remarking that, "it came in with a lass, and will go out with a lass." James was referring to the beginning of the Scottish Stewart dynasty starting with Marjorie Bruce and her son Robert Stewart, known to history as Robert II, King of Scots.

Marie de Guise was Queen Consort of Scotland for less than five years before her husband died on 14 December 1542. He was buried at Holyrood Abbey next to Madeleine de Valois and his and Marie's two sons. No other Scottish monarch died in Scotland until the passing of Queen Elizabeth II in September 2022.

Marie's six-day-old daughter, Mary, was now the reigning monarch. In the summer of 1543, the Treaty of Greenwich was signed, pledging that Marie's daughter would marry the English Prince Edward. In September 1543, Mary's coronation was celebrated. In December, the Parliament of Scotland revoked the Treaty of Greenwich in favor of maintaining the Auld Alliance, causing Henry VIII of England to resume his campaign against the Scots. This was known as the Rough Wooing. The first major incident, the Burning of Edinburgh, occurred in May 1544.

The pillaging of the Borders continued throughout 1544 and into 1545. Things came to a head at the Battle of Ancrum Moor, also near Kelso, on 27 February 1545. The Scots were successful, and Henry VIII stopped invading Scotland. With the death of Henry VIII of England in January 1547 and the ascension of his son, the boy-king Edward VI, came fresh troubles for Marie, her daughter the queen, and the Scots.

As discussed, Henry VIII of England tried multiple times to arrange a marriage between Marie de Guise's daughter Mary and his son Edward. A true accord was never struck between the two countries. England, which wished to unite Scotland and England, also wished to press the Anglican faith in Scotland. One might recall that Edward VI was the first protestant king of England, and forcibly converting their neighbors to the north would have been an excellent coup.

Battle of Pinkie Cleuch and a Tough Choice for Marie

Lord Protector Edward Seymour, Duke of Somerset and uncle of nine-year-old Edward VI of England, wished to press religious reform upon the Church of Scotland in line with what was being instituted within the Anglican Church. Lord Protector Seymour also wished to secure a marriage between Edward VI and Mary, Queen of Scots, in hopes of undermining the Auld Alliance and bringing Scotland under the thumb of England. James Hamilton, Earl of Arran and heir apparent to the Scottish throne, was acting as regent between 1543 and 1554. One of his agents in England caught wind of the troops there preparing for battle in mid-1547 and sent warning to the earl.

During August to early September 1547, Lord Protector Seymour and a formidable army of over 17,000 made their way along the east coast of England to the Scottish border. By staying near the shoreline, the English army could easily be replenished by the naval fleet that was tracking along with them. A second, much smaller army, made its way through England toward Scotland at the same time as Seymour's main army. Both armies succeeded in capturing and burning minor sites near Scotland. The Earl of Arran raised a larger army near Edinburgh, numbering anywhere between 23,000 and 36,000 men. The Scottish army should have had the advantage based on numbers.

The Battle of Pinkie Cleuch on 10 September 1547 was one of the worst battles in the Rough Wooing. The battle was a sound defeat for the Scottish. The English army included calvary, German mercenaries, arquebusiers, infantry, and more. The day before the main battle, on 9 September, the Scots decided to honor chivalric tradition by approaching the English camp near Falside to engage in a battle with the same number of English. Despite being good military manners, this turned out to be a horrible idea. The Scottish calvary was badly stung and reduced overall by about half, which meant they were not available for the main battle the next day.

Still hoping for a somewhat less violent battle through chivalric tradtion, the Earl of Arran thought he would engage the English in another way. To that end, he asked that Lord Protector Seymour enter into a duel with him to resolve the battle without having their armies fully fight, or, alternatively, for each side to appoint several champions to battle each other. Somerset was not impressed with Arran's ideas and rejected them. Besides, by then, Somerset had could surmise that he was in a stronger position.

The morning of the battle on 10 September saw Somerset trying to position his artillery. Arran approached the English as quickly as he could to try and take out the English artillery before it could be deployed against his forces. It ultimately did not matter. The Scottish were outnumbered and outgunned. An eyewitness account from William Patten describes the battle thusly,

> Soon after this notable strewing of their footmen's weapons, began a pitiful sight of the dead corpses lying dispersed abroad, some their legs off, some but houghed,[2] and left lying half-dead, some thrust quite through the body, others the arms cut off, diverse their necks half asunder, many their

---

2. hamstrung

heads cloven, of sundry the brains [bashed] out, some others again their heads quite off, with other many kinds of killing. After that and further in chase, all for the most part killed either in the head or in the neck, for our horsemen could not well reach the lower [parts of the body] with their swords. And thus with blood and slaughter of the enemy, this chase was continued five miles [eight kilometers] in length westward from the place of their standing, which was in the fallow fields of Inveresk until Edinburgh Park and well nigh to the gates of the town itself and unto Leith, and in breadth nigh 4 miles [6 kilometers], from the Firth sands up toward Dalkeith southward. In all which space, the dead bodies lay as thick as a man may note cattle grazing in a full replenished pasture. The river ran all red with blood, so that in the same chase were counted, as well by some of our men that somewhat diligently did mark it as by some of them taken prisoners, that very much did lament it, to have been slain about 14 thousand. In all this compass of ground what with weapons, arms, hands, legs, heads, blood and dead bodies, their flight might have been easily tracked to every of their three refuges. And for the smallness of our number and the shortness of the time (which was scant five hours, from one to well nigh six) the mortality was so great, as it was thought, the like aforetime not to have been seen.

Marie's daughter was lodged at Inchmahome Priory for three weeks after the battle at the insistence of her guardians. Inchmahome Priory is on an island in Lake of Menteith. The lake is in central Scotland, and sufficiently far enough from the Scottish border to have given Marie some sense of security for her four-year-old daughter. Marie recognized that her daughter was no longer safe in Scotland and made arrangements for toddler Mary to flee to the safety of the French court and Marie's powerful relatives.

The Many Betrothals of Marie's Daughter

Marie's daughter Mary was betrothed multiple times before Marie reached out to Henri II of France for help in 1547. While Henri's father Francis I maintained mild interest in who little Mary would wed, it did not really matter much at the French court. The most important thing to the French was at least to keep the Auld Alliance intact, and at most make sure that neither the widowed Marie nor her daughter allied themselves with the English.

Francis I initially betrothed Mary, Queen of Scots to a French subject in 1543, in hopes of preventing any Anglo-Scots alliance. Three years later, in 1546, Francis tried to arrange a marriage between Mary and one of the three

Danish princes. After the Battle of Pinkie Cleuch, it was imperative for French politics that Mary wed a French subject. The English were showing no sign of letting up on their forceful suit to wed Marie's daughter to the English boy-king Edward VI. For her part, Marie was upset and angry that her family in France had virtually abandoned her and her daughter after the death of Marie's Scottish husband. Marie's displeasure grew to the level of resentment toward her loved ones in France.

An ambassador was sent in November 1547 by Henri II to discuss Mary's future with Marie de Guise. More importantly, the Earl of Arran, who was acting as regent, had to be convinced of a Franco-Scots alliance. Negotiations were successful, and Mary was betrothed to the Dauphin of France.

Around 8 February 1548, the proposed marriage between Marie de Guise's daughter and the future Francis II of France was concluded. Marie sent her daughter to Dumbarton, where Mary arrived on 28 February. Mary was five years old at this point. Mary stayed there for several months before departing for France. In the meantime, Marie de Guise and others at the Scottish court did their best to spread rumors of the little Queen of Scots' demise. Gossip over Mary's serious illness and possible death swirled. When it was quickly ascertained that Mary, Queen of Scots was neither ill nor dead, the next rumor was that she was leaving for France before the end of March 1548. That was also untrue. The English did not want the child to leave the island. To prevent her departure, they were fortifying Haddington, about 17 miles or 27 kilometers east of Edinburgh, close to the mouth of the Firth of Forth. The strategic nearness to Edinburgh would allow the English to intercept Mary if she sailed out of the Firth of Forth. The English would continue to hold Haddington through the summer.

Mary, Queen of Scots is Sent to France

Henri II of France sent a galley and escort to retrieve Mary, Queen of Scots. The small flotilla arrived in the Firth of Forth in summer 1548. Marie was at Elphinstone, roughly 4 miles or 6 kilometers west of Haddington. On 5 July, Marie was informed that things looked favorable to the Scots. She decided to hold counsel there to decide next steps, and ultimately Scottish Parliament was called to negotiate a treaty with the French. Marie de Guise expressed her wish around 7 July, "to be the subject of the French king, by reason of the honor which he has done to the queen my daughter, in desiring to give her to his son. I leave to-morrow, to send her to him as soon as the galleys have made the circuit." The Treaty of Haddington was signed, and Marie's daughter was betrothed to the Dauphin. Marie's grandsons, if she had any from this union, would jointly rule Scotland and France.

The text of the treaty states,

> In the parliament of a most excellent princess Mary, queen of Scots, held at the abbey of Haddington on 7 July 1548, by one noble and mighty prince James [Hamilton], …governor of the realm, and the three estates of the realm being present.
>
> On the which day Monsieur [André de Montalembert, seigneur] d'Essé, lieutenant general of the navy and the army sent by [Henri II], the Most Christian King of France … showed how his master the King of France, having regard to the ancient league and confederation and amity existing between the realm of France and this country, and of the mortal wars, cruelties, depredations and intolerable injuries done by our old enemies of England against our sovereign lady, being of so tender an age…whereby [Henri II], … could do no less but to aid, support, maintain and defend at his power this tender princess, her realm and her lieges as a propitious and helpful brother against all others who would attempt injury against the same, not by words but by way of deed…. Therefore, having consideration of the matters stated above and how that the said Most Christian King has set his whole heart and mind for the defence of this realm, he desires …for the more perfect union and indissolvable bond of perpetual amity, league and confederation, the marriage of our sovereign lady to the effect that the said Most Christian King's eldest son [Francis de Valois], dauphin of France may be joined in matrimony with her grace [Mary, Queen of Scots] to the perpetual honour, pleasure and profit of both realms, observing and keeping this realm and the lieges thereof in the same freedom, liberties and laws as they have been in all the Kings of Scotland's times past, and shall maintain and defend this realm …the same as he does for the realm of France … and, therefore, desires my lord governor and the three estates of parliament to advise herewith and give their determination in this matter if the desire foresaid is reasonable and acceptable or not. [Marie de Guise], the queen's grace, our sovereign lady's most dear mother, being present, my lord governor and the three estates of parliament foresaid, all in one voice, have found and decreed and, by the judgement of parliament, concluded the desire … of the said Most Christian King, … very reasonable and have granted that our said sovereign lady [Mary, Queen of Scots] be married with the said Dauphin at her perfect age, and …that our sovereign lady be married to no other person but to the said Dauphin only.

Word made its way to Mary, Queen of Scots in Dumbarton, across the country from her mother. Mary prepared to leave. On 6 July, Marie de Guise went to Clerkington, a little over a mile and less than two kilometers from Haddington. Not long before, the combined Italian and French troops had torn down a bridge over the River Tyne, which goes past Haddington. On 8 July, the French prepared to besiege Haddington. The siege itself took place on 9 July.

Marie, being so near to the siege at Haddington, wished to behold its progress. Unbeknownst to her, she was too near the English guns. An artillery round landed not far from her, maiming or killing a few of her companions. Marie is said to have fainted from the shock of sudden carnage near her.

The Scots were ultimately victorious after some months of besieging Haddington. After her brush with death, Marie went to visit with her daughter before the latter left for France.

Marie de Guise's Visit to France and Her Regency

Marie joined her daughter at Dumbarton, from which Mary would sail to France. Dumbarton is in western Scotland, west of Glasgow, and on the River Clyde. The plan was to sail west out of the River Clyde, then south out of the Firth of Clyde, turn east around Cornwall, then on to France through the English Channel.

Marie said goodbye to her daughter on 29 July 1548, and headed back to Edinburgh. Marie originally planned to accompany Mary to Whithorn, so that Marie could then go on pilgrimage to Whithorn Priory. One might recall that Margaret Tudor also went to Whithorn Priory after the birth of Marie's husband James V. Marie abandoned the idea of a pilgrimage because she had other important things to tend.

Marie took an active part in planning the siege of Broughty Castle. In February 1550, the Scots and French overpowered the English. Unrest between England against Scotland and France was finally over, and the Treaty of Boulogne was signed in March 1550. Now that there was peace, Marie felt comfortable leaving Scotland so she could visit her homeland.

Poor weather kept Mary in Scottish waters for longer than intended. When Mary finally did arrive in France, she was very well-received. Marie's relations were made part of her daughter's household. For now, Marie's daughter was safe.

Marie left Scotland for France in September 1550. She was reunited with her daughter and her fourteen-year-old son Francis, and the three enjoyed the triumphal entry into Rouen on 1 October 1550 organized by Henri II of France. Rouen's tradition of hosting fabulous entries for monarchs and dukes extends back to the 1300s. Marie brought an entourage of Scottish noblemen, whose behavior was considered rowdy by the French. The processional pathway was covered with sand, and tapestries were hung to decorate the route. Mounted archers were put in place to protect the processional. Marie and her daughter rode together in the processional. The triumphal celebration was awesome in sight and scale, including tableaus, chariots with mythical figures, and elephants.

Marie followed the French court, staying through the Christmas holiday and into 1551. Marie first went to Chartres, and then Blois. In February, she decided to stay at her castle of Châteaudun for a couple of months. As she was making preparations to return to Scotland, she learned that a man hired to poison her daughter Mary had been caught and captured in London. Rattled and extremely distressed, Marie chose to stay on in France a little longer.

During her stay in France, Henri II offered more than once to send someone from his court to be Scotland's regent. Marie was quite welcome at the French court, where she could be near her two surviving children. Marie, perhaps now fond of her home of thirteen years, declined. Henri was four years younger than Marie, and the two could converse more frankly with each other than Marie was able to with Henri's father Francis I. He was disappointed with her decision but could admire Marie's dedication to Scotland.

Marie was finally ready to head back toward Scotland in the late summer of 1551. Unfortunately, her son Francis had taken quite ill. She did her best to take care of him, but he died right around the time she had to leave France. Marie had now outlived all of her children, except for her daughter.

Marie went to Scotland by way of England, landing at Portsmouth in October 1551. She and her entourage were escorted by English gentlemen sent for the purpose by the king. The group slowly made their way to Whitehall Palace, where they met Lady Elizabeth Tudor and Edward VI, Mary's would-be suitor if the Rough Wooing had gone differently. Lady Mary Tudor declined to meet Marie.

Marie was gifted a ring that belonged to Catherine Parr, Henry VIII of England's last wife. It came to her as a gift from the Protestant Edward VI, who was fourteen at this point. The ring, from a quietly Protestant wife of Henry's, was some sort of barb to Catholic Marie is unknown. Marie was having her own difficulties with the Scottish Reformation.

Marie arrived in Scotland in late November and was honored with a multi-gun salute from the walls of Edinburgh Castle. She settled in and resumed her correspondence with foreign officials and heads of government. About eighteen months later, in May 1553, Marie asserted herself against James Hamilton, 2nd Earl of Arran's regency. She thought that her illegitimate stepson James Stewart, 1st Earl of Moray, would do a better job. That idea did not get very far, but Marie herself was made regent on 12 April 1554. Marie's daughter sent her a letter, congratulating Marie.

To the benefit of Marie's preference for Catholicism, Lady Mary Tudor became Mary I of England in July 1553. Mary I of England was famously Catholic, and would hopefully support Mary, Queen of Scots and Marie's regency. Things must have finally felt stable to Marie, for the first time in a decade.

Marie proved to be a strong, effective administrator of Scotland. However, she was not without her dissenters. In June 1555, parliament outlawed speaking ill of Marie or the French,

> Item, forasmuch as diverse seditious persons have, in times past, raised murmurs and slanders amongst the common people, speaking against [Marie de Guise], the queen's grace, sowing evil rumours regarding [Henri II], the Most Christian King of France's subjects sent into this realm for the commonwealth and suppressing of the old enemies out of the same, tending... to steer the hearts of the subjects to hatred against ...[the French and] the Most Christian King of France; ...it is devised, statute and ordained that if any persons in time coming be heard speaking such unreasonable intercourse whereby the people may take occasion of such secret conspiracy against the said prince or sedition against the Most Christian King's subjects foresaid, the same being proven, shall be punished according to the quality of the fault in their bodies and goods at the pleasure of the queen's grace, and in case the hearer thereof does not report the same to the queen's grace or her officers to the effect that the same may be punished as appropriate, that he shall incur the said pains that the principal speaker or raisers of such murmurs deserves.

The extreme penalties for speaking against Henri II, the French, Marie, or her daughter, give an idea of how much anti-French sentiments rose. Tension continued to flair between Marie and her daughter's subjects. This was in part due to the Scottish Reformation, and the desire of the Protestant faction to not be ruled by Catholic women. Thankfully, Mary I of England was Catholic and on the throne, which offered a semblance of a buffer for Marie. A series of events in rapid succession changed the political climate for Marie, starting in 1557.

The marriage between Marie's daughter and the Dauphin of France was nigh in December 1557, with Mary, Queen of Scots having reached her fifteenth birthday. In response, a group of Protestant Scottish nobles formed the Lords of the Congregation. They were against the Queen of Scots' marriage to the Dauphin of France.

Revolts against Marie and her daughter began in 1558 and carried on into 1559. Catholic Mary I of England died in November 1558, leading to the accession of her Protestant half-sister Elizabeth I. The stability which Marie enjoyed died with Mary I. Elizabeth, who had met Marie de Guise a few years earlier, publicly maintained support for Marie. The April 1559 Treaty of Cateau-Cambrésis between Henri II of France and Philip II of Spain, and between Elizabeth I and Henri II, cooled tensions between Scotland and England. Elizabeth's posture with Marie was much different behind the scenes. Elizabeth quietly provided support for the faction that was trying to oust Marie de Guise. Elizabeth's duplicity when it came to Marie was a common theme in Elizabeth's dealings with Mary, Queen of Scots.

Interestingly, Marie de Guise relied on one of her future sons-in-law to help her keep the rebels at bay throughout 1559. James Hepburn, 4th Earl of Bothwell, was appointed the Lord High Admiral of Scotland in 1556. His father and grandfather had held the same position. Bothwell interacted with Marie periodically throughout her time in Scotland, including once hoping to marry her. More on Bothwell in the coming chapters.

Marie negotiated a temporary religious truce with the Lords of the Congregation in July 1559, but it was not enough to stop all the fighting. Elizabeth I of England sent an English army into Scotland to support the Scottish rebels, citing Mary, Queen of Scots' display of the English arms with her own royal Scottish arms as a reason to harass Marie de Guise. Never mind that Elizabeth and other English monarchs continued using French arms as part of the royal English heraldry. Marie refused to back down, but disquiet remained during the rest of 1559 and into 1560.

Marie's Final Illness

Beginning in April 1560, Marie complained of painful swelling in her legs, but she carried on. In May 1560, she met with the Lords of the Congregation. They were tired of so large a French presence within Scottish government. Marie, who was of course French, wished to discuss terms with her French advisors. Any ground gained with the Lords of the Congregation went out the window very quickly.

Marie's legs continued swelling throughout May, as did her belly. Marie, understanding that the battles would continue, saw to it that Edinburgh Castle was fortified once more. She was not willing to allow her health to distract her from her duties.

At some point in late May to early June 1560, Marie was taken ill. It was suspected that she had dropsy, or edema, which is the retention of fluid in one's limbs. In extremely simplified terms, dropsy is evidence that a person's body is shutting down, sometimes from heart or other cardiovascular issues, from kidney failure, or from other causes. Whatever the reason for Marie's dropsy, she faded in and out of conscious reality over a period of little more than a week. On 8 June 1560, she was either well enough to make, or her advisors on her behalf, made Marie's will.

Marie died on 11 June 1560, at the age of forty-four. She passed away at Edinburgh Castle, where she lay in state for roughly nine months after her death. Marie's body was wrapped in cerecloth, a type of fine cloth dipped in wax. She was placed in St. Margaret's Chapel, named after St. Margaret of Scotland. The chapel, a 12th-century building located within the grounds of Edinburgh Castle, is a very intimate space that can still be visited today. The interior of the small chapel was draped completely with black fabric. In March of 1561, Marie's body was sneaked out of the chapel and over to France, where she was buried at Saint-Pierre-les-Dames in Reims. Marie's sister Renée was the abbess there from 1546 until her death in 1602. Unfortunately, Marie's tomb was destroyed in the 18th century during the French Revolution, and very little of the abbey remains.

A Note on the Scottish Reformation and Mary, Queen of Scots

Religious Reform in Europe

Religious reform swept across Europe throughout the 16th century. Although elements pointing to a reformation began appearing in the 15th century, the first marked act occurred with Martin Luther's posting of his *Ninety-Five Theses* in Wittenberg on Halloween 1517. His act of posting the theses was not at all radical, as it was common practice to publicly post items for debate on the castle's chapel door. What made Luther's simple act extraordinary was the reaction of the Saxon government thereafter. In England, Henry VIII was desperate to have a legitimate male heir. He began his campaign to annul his marriage to Katharine of Aragon as early as 1526, formally breaking from Rome in 1534. The French did not have a formal reformation but instead saw the bloody and brutal French Wars of Religion. The Dutch followed a similar approach as the French to religious reformation. The Scots followed their own path when reforming religion within their borders.

There is no exact moment to which one can point as the start of the Scottish Reformation. It can be seen to have started with the Lollards in 14th-century England. The word "lollard" was derogatory, thought to have come from a Dutch word that meant "mumbler." John Wycliffe, a theologian and philosopher at Oxford, began teaching what were viewed as radical theological beliefs. Wycliffe was prosecuted, but not executed, and removed from his position at Oxford.

Once Henry IV of England became king in 1399, things went poorly for the Lollards. They were suppressed in the early 15th century, although maintained a steady following amongst the lower classes. The Lollards saw a revival early in 16th-century England.

The First Scottish Martyr

Patrick Hamilton, born in 1504 and a descendant of James II of Scotland, was the first Scottish Protestant martyr. He spent time in his youth in Leuven, in modern-day Belgium, likely trying to learn more of Desiderius Erasmus's teachings. Upon returning to Scotland, Hamilton, in his position as abbot, began spreading reformist ideas. Unfortunately, he caught the attention of the Archbishop of St. Andrews in early 1527. Hamilton fled to Lutheran Germany that May, but returned in late autumn. He began preaching, renounced his celibacy, and took a wife. He openly taught Martin Luther's ideas. He was eventually arrested for preaching Protestant theology. Thereafter, Hamilton was tried, convicted, and burnt at the stake outside of St. Salvator's Chapel in St. Andrews on 29 February 1528. Everything was done on the same day so there was no time for anyone to intercede on his behalf. With his death, Patrick Hamilton became the first Scottish martyr. His reformist influence had taken hold within Scotland.

A succession of laws were passed throughout the 1530s to try to stop Lutheran teachings from spreading within Scotland. Persecution intensified, and Lutheran books were banned. Foreigners traveling through Scotland, if found with heretical material, were also persecuted. This was an extreme measure for the period. Despite the Scottish church's and government's best attempts, reform had taken hold by 1540. Multiple Scottish nobles favored Luther's teachings, presenting a serious obstacle. Like the English and German Catholic churches, the Scottish Catholic church was desperately in need of improvement. In the 16th century, it was often viewed as morally bankrupt when it suited the church's needs.

The Catholic church within Scotland saw no shortage of critics, even within the monarch's inner circles. Multiple works of Luther's were translated and circulated in Scotland, intensifying the Protestant mood. James V had to slow down his attempts at stamping out Lutheranism in favor of keeping Scotland unified against the English.

During the regency of Mary, Queen of Scots, the Earl of Arran was very much in favor of adopting Lutheran beliefs. With his support, a law was passed granting people permission to read the Bible in either Scot or English in the privacy of their homes. This was a huge step away from Catholicism. Once Arran was removed from the regency, it was advantageous for Mary's mother Marie de Guise, a Catholic, to politely ignore the heresy within her kingdom to protect Scotland from continued English assaults. Once Marie achieved peace through the Treaty of Cateau-Cambrésis in 1559, it was too late to then turn against the pro-reformation Scots.

When Mary, Queen of Scots returned to rule her country, the barely unified kingdom was once more divided.

Mary, Queen of Scots

Although Mary, Queen of Scots is technically not a Stuart consort, her second husband Henry Stewart, Lord Darnley, makes Mary a Stuart spouse. More importantly, Mary's life impacted the lives of five consorts: namely, her mother Marie de Guise, her first husband Francis II of France, her aforementioned second husband Lord Darnley, her third husband James Hepburn, 4th Earl of Bothwell, and to a small extent her daughter-in-law Anna of Denmark. Because of her tumultuous life and all the changes she saw, it is reasonable to briefly discuss Mary.

As seen, Mary was born mere days before her father passed away, leaving her as an infant queen. Mary's accession continued the unwittingly established tradition of Scottish monarchs taking the throne in their childhood if not infancy. Despite being queen for over eighteen years when she returned home, Mary faced a very difficult political landscape. She navigated it poorly, although it would have been troublesome for anyone to navigate the situation successfully.

Mary returned to Scotland in August 1561, a few months shy of her nineteenth birthday. She may have already been considering who her second husband should be. Mary spent her first few years in Scotland as a widow, seeking marital advice from her cousin Elizabeth I of England. She did not know yet that she could not trust Elizabeth. Eventually, Mary married her cousin Henry Stewart in July 1565. Although more detail will be given in subsequent chapters, it is fair to say that Mary's second marriage did not go well. Mary was twenty-two years old when she wed for the second time.

Her only child, a boy whom she named James, was born in June 1566. Eight months later, in February 1567, Mary's second husband died under suspicious circumstances. That summer, in June 1567, Mary married her third and final husband James Hepburn. It is possible that Mary took her third husband under duress. A month later, Mary was forced to abdicate her throne in favor of her one-year-old son. Mary's third husband abandoned her. She was twenty-four years old.

Mary ruled Scotland officially from the time she was six days old until she was twenty-four years, seven months, and three weeks old. Realistically, she actively ruled from August 1561 to July 1567, so for less than six years. Mary died in February 1587. She was unable to overcome the obstacles of her court and the changing tides of the Scottish Kirk (church). Although Mary's mother Marie de Guise was an excellent role model, Mary did not have an opportunity to closely learn from her. Mary, though unsuccessful as a monarch, surely did the best she could as the first queen regnant of the British Isles, and it is important to remember the swirl of difficult circumstances surrounding her when considering her actions, even if it is in the context of how her spouses related to her.

Chapter 7

Francis II of France

Birth and Early Years

Francis de Valois, the future Francis II of France, was born 19 January 1544 at Château de Fontainebleau. He was baptized at Fontainebleau, in the Chapel of the Trinity, a few weeks after birth. Francis was roughly thirteen months younger than his future wife Mary, Queen of Scots. He was the eldest child of Henri II of France and his first wife, Catherine de' Medici. Francis's birth was a source of great joy and relief to his parents and the country.

Henri and Catherine were married in 1533, at a time when Henri was merely a second son. Three years later, in 1536, Henri's elder brother died. Suddenly, Henri and Catherine were the dauphin and dauphine of France. Henri was rather preoccupied with his favorite mistress, Diane de Poitiers, and failed to pay enough attention to Catherine to conceive a child. Allegedly, upon encouragement from Diane, Henri and Catherine finally enjoyed a span of fecundity which produced Francis, three more sons, and five daughters.

Francis's education was overseen by Diane de Poitiers. His primary tutor, Pierre Danés, was born in Paris in 1497. Danés showed a great facility for ancient languages and was appointed in 1530 by Francis II's paternal grandfather Francis I as the first lecturer of Greek in the new Collège de France. In 1535, Danés went to Italy to expand his knowledge. He was back in Paris by the early 1540s. Danés was appointed the ambassador of France to the Council of Trent, which began in 1545. After the death of Francis I, his successor Henri II appointed Danés as Francis II's tutor. Danés remained an important presence in his young charge's life, becoming Francis's personal confessor. Danés passed away in 1577, having outlived Francis II by several years. He was one of the most educated men of his time, although Danés is not known to have written more than a couple of works.

Francis is Betrothed to Mary, Queen of Scots

As discussed in Chapter 6, Mary, Queen of Scots, became queen at only six days old after her father's death. Mary's great-uncle, Henry VIII of England, was very interested in seeing an alliance between Mary and Henry's son Edward VI.

The 1543 Treaty of Greenwich, ratified on 25 August 1543, saw the promise of Mary wedding Edward of England. Scottish Parliament rejected the terms of the Treaty of Greenwich in December of the same year. Thereafter, the English repeatedly raided and attacked the Scottish border and territories just inside of Scotland.

In September 1547, because of the Battle of Pinkie Cleugh, in the very southernmost part of Scotland, was officially occupied by the English. A convention was held at Edinburgh around 16 October 1547, resulting in the Scots asking Henri II of France for help with expelling the English. In return, Marie's daughter would be betrothed to young Francis and sent to France to be raised at court there.

In December, despite the protest from Scottish subjects, Marie de Guise sent a commission to France,

> [Marie of Guise], her grace, the queen regent…understanding that they have directed certain noble men of this realm to pass to France for the completing of the marriage of our sovereign lady with [Francis Valois], my lord dauphin of France, as in their commission, … it …ordained that all and sundry actions, causes and quarrels …shall rest and cease…until their returning within this realm and fourteen days thereafter.

Effectively, the business of marrying Francis to Marie's daughter should not be hindered by the personal shortcomings of the noblemen sent from Scotland to France until two weeks after their return.

English aggression continued throughout spring and summer of 1548, resulting in Mary, Queen of Scots' mother Marie de Guise and parliament completing the marriage negotiations for Francis and Mary through the Treaty of Haddington. Marie de Guise sent Mary to live with her Guise relations in France. Henri II of France welcomed this idea and saw to it that his son Francis was betrothed to Mary. Mary and Francis were brought up together at the French court, and visiting with each other as early as December 1548,

> The king has come to see [Mary] here at St. Germain, where she was with the dauphin [Francis]…[Henri] gave her the best welcome possible, and continues to do so from day to day. He is very happy that she arrived without accident or illness, and considers her no less than his own daughter. I have no doubt that if she and the dauphin were of age, or nearly so, the king would soon carry the project to completion. They are already as friendly as if they were married. Meanwhile he has determined to bring them up together and to make one establishment of their household, so as to accustom them to one another from the beginning.

Mary and Francis could not be more opposite. Where she was intellectually curious, he was aloof. Mary was tall, Francis was stunted. She was charismatic, he was shy. Despite their differences, Mary was in love with Francis. Anne de Montmorency,[1] Marshal and later Constable of France, wrote to Mary's mother Marie de Guise in March 1549 to report of Francis and Mary, "I will assure you that the dauphin pays her little attentions, and is enamoured of her, from which it is easy to judge that God gave them birth the one for the other."

Francis, like other consorts who were overshadowed by a powerful spouse and died young, is another elusive figure. Information and details about Francis, particularly after his accession, are often surrounded by what Mary did or did not do. As such, Francis's short adult life saw some of Mary's political intrigue even before the couple wed.

Two Contracts and a Wedding

Henri II invoked the Auld Alliance, and its mythical Carolingian origins, in the marital alliance between Mary, Queen of Scots and Henri's son Francis de Valois. The marital alliance was for, "the entire and perfect benevolence that is naturally present between the kings and kingdoms of France and Scotland who have reigned until now," treating, "their own affairs as if they were each others'."

Mary, who was all of fifteen at the time, made a secret contract with Henri II on 4 April 1558 that should she die without heirs, Scotland would forever join with and be part of France. The contract was devised with the help of her Guise uncles, and never brought up in Scottish Parliament. Given the current goings-on with revolts and such in 1558 Scotland, becoming part of France would not have found favor with the Scots.

The official wedding contract, if it can be called that, was signed on 19 April 1558. It carefully laid out Scotland's limits and the extent to which France could govern or otherwise influence Scottish politics. Francis and Mary's wedding took place on 24 April 1558 at Notre Dame cathedral in Paris.

A letter from the Ferrarese ambassador Julio Alvarotto to Duke Ercole II written on 25 April 1558 gives a lengthy description of the wedding,

> Yesterday morning [24 April 1558] the marriage took place of the most Serene Dauphin and the most Serene Queen of Scotland. The King [Henri II] with all the Court had gone the night before to sleep at the

---

1. Anne, a man, was named after his godmother Queen Anne of Brittany. Queen Anne married both Charles VII of France and Louis XII of France. Her daughter Claude married Francis I of France and was Francis de Valois's grandmother.

[palace of Eustache du Bellay, Bishop of Paris], which was adorned throughout with very rich tapestries, and in the morning at the hour of Mass, His Majesty [appeared] splendidly attired in a robe of red velvet embroidered with gold and all lined with rich gold, the collar and down to the foot alike. In his company were the most Serene Dauphin, the Grand Duke de Lorraine [Charles of Lorraine], the most Excellent Monsieurs de Guise [Duke Francis of Lorraine], and d'Aumale [Duke Claude d'Aumale, brother of Marie de Guise and the King of Navarre [Antoine de Bourbon]. His Majesty took the Queen of Scotland by the arm, who was royally attired in a dress of silver with a short train, and over this a mantle of purple velvet embroidered with gold, with a train about six yards long, her breast covered with jewels, the crown on her head all of diamonds and pearls, with the "Egg of Naples" hanging there in the middle. [They were] accompanied by the Queen [Catherine de' Medici], and by the [royal] children, by Madame Marguerite [Francis II's paternal aunt], by the Queen of Navarre [Henri's cousin, Jeanne d'Albret, wife of Antoine de Bourbon], by Madame de Nevers [sister of Antoine de Bourbon], by Madame de Guise [Anne d'Este, wife of Francis of Lorraine, second Duke of Guise],…by Madam la Donera [Antoinette de Bourbon, widow of Claude of Lorraine, first Duke of Guise, and also maternal grandmother of Mary, Queen of Scots], by Madame Valentinois [Diane de Poitiers, Duchess de Valentinois], by the Marchioness de Rotbelin [Jacqueline de Rohan, related tenuously to Marie de Guise by marriage], and in short by all the ladies of court, each one so richly dressed that it was dazzling.

This was clearly an important wedding and social event, with the veritable who's who of France in attendance. James Hepburn, Earl of Bothwell, was likely present amongst the Scottish nobles.

[They were also accompanied] by all the nobles and gentlemen of the court, also very richly dressed so that one could see only gold, silver and jewels, by the Most Reverend Grand Cardinals de Lorraine [Charles of Lorraine, Mary's uncle], de Guise [Louis, another uncle of Mary's], [Robert] de Lenoncourt, [Antoine Sanguin] de Medum, by the Legate [Antonio, Cardinal Trivulzio] and by all the ambassadors, to the sound of fifes, trumpets, drums and violins. [The King] conducted her to the bishop's palace along a roadway specially made of wood above the street, and having arrived at the door, the Cardinal [Charles] de Bourbon, in gorgeous vestments, performed the ceremony which is customary in such cases. And this being done, His Majesty turned her round and showed her to the people, and had gold and silver coins thrown [to the crowd].

Mary was seen by her soon-to-be French subjects in her new capacity as the dauphine and future queen consort of France. It must have been exhilarating.

Francis entered Notre Dame with his new bride, whom he had known for almost a decade at this point.

> Then [Francis and Mary] entered the church where Mass was sung. On one side was the King under the cloth of state and the Queen [Catherine de' Medici] behind him; on the other side was the married couple, side by side without any canopy. They went to the offering one after the other. A daughter of Madame de Boglio with others carried the train. When the Mass was over they drew a silver cloth over their heads, which however was suspended and did not touch them at all, and under this the bishop blessed them and then they returned to the palace where they dined in ceremony, and His Excellency Monseigneur de Guise did the office of Grand Master.

A fabulous wedding feast ensued.

> Monseigneur de Nevers [Francis of Cleves, a very distant relative to Henry VIII of England's wife Anna of Cleves] served His Majesty [Henri II] as carver and Signor don Alfonso [d'Este] acted as carver for the Queen [Catherine de' Medici]. The Most Reverend Legate and the ambassadors dined in a room apart, all at one table. After dinner there was dancing and then they retired to rest for a while. Then the two Queens [Catherine de' Medici and Mary, Queen of Scots] stepped into a litter all covered with cloth of silver on a red field, and with all the others on horseback they went to the palace where there is a very large, richly decorated room, with a large buffet which is worth many tens of thousands of ducats, and with an infinite number of lights, where they supped in ceremony as in the morning, with other tables on the sides for the cardinals, for the ambassadors, for the Court of Parliament, Chamber of Accounts, and for the aldermen of the city, that is the "consuls."

A buffet in the 16th century meant a luxurious, sugar-laden dessert display. Often highly decorative, buffets were opulent and commonly held in purpose-built rooms or buildings. One such building, the Banqueting House remaining from England's Whitehall Palace, can be visited today. It replaced in 1622 two prior iterations of banqueting halls at Whitehall. These were grand structures, even if occasionally temporary.

After completing their meals, the entertainment began.

> After supper there were some extremely beautiful masquerades very richly dressed. A chariot pulled by horses appeared, in which was Jupiter with all the gods, attended by six richly caparisoned horses, with the two sons of the King, Monseigneur d'Orleans [the future Charles IX] and Monseigneur d'Angoulême [the future Henri III], the two sons of Monseigneur de Guise and Monseigneur d'Aumale, and two others. They saluted the Queen and sang very well in her praise.
>
> Then, accompanied by six horses all richly adorned, came the chariot of the Muses, and they also sang and played in praise of the Queen. Then came two other cars one after the other, each attended by six horses equally richly caparisoned, with songs in praise of the Queen; and all these things were done at the expense of the King, who was masked along with all these noblemen, except Monseigneur de Guise who had remained [unmasked] to keep everything in order.
>
> After these came six sailing vessels, covered with crimson and yellow satin, which moved (one did not see how), provided at the expense of the Duke de Lorraine, who had spent on them more than six thousand ducats.[2] The sails were all of silver tinsel, very finely and ingeniously made by that Master Barto[lomeo] da Pesaro, who was formerly with the Grand Duke [Guidobaldo della Rovere] in Urbino, on each of which [ships] were two seats side by side, on one of which sat a person masked in Turkish dress. Among these were the King, the King Dauphin as he is now called, and his wife, the Queen Dauphine, the King of Navarre, the Duke de Lorraine, and other nobles. They each had a little ladder for descending and ascending. The Duke de Lorraine who was the first, took up Madame Claude [second daughter of Henri II and future wife of Charles III of Lorraine], who was to be his wife. Then the Queen of Scotland was taken up, Madame Marguerite, the Queen of Navarre, and Madame de Guise. And all of these performed a dance, as if they were all on foot doing the "passo e mezzo," and turning at will; and all was well and cleverly done. And then they retired and accompanied the bridal couple. They say that it is two hundred years since the nuptials of a Dauphin were celebrated in France.

What a lavish, memorable wedding for young Francis!

---

2. For perspective, this is upwards of $900,000 or more than £700,000 in modern money.

Resistance to the Valois-Stuart Match

The Bourbon faction at court did their best to oppose the match between Francis and Mary. Mary's powerful maternal uncle, the Duke of Guise, did an excellent job ingratiating himself at court. This paved the way for the Valois–Stuart marriage instead of Bourbon–Stuart. Over in England, Elizabeth I was not eager for her cousin to cement a relationship with the French monarchy.

As fate would have it, those opposed to the marriage of Francis and Mary would have a chance to seize the frail young man. On 30 June 1559, Francis's father Henri II was gravely injured during a gruesome jousting accident. He died several days later, leaving Francis as the king of France.

Francis II was crowned that September in Reims. He inherited an almost bankrupt kingdom from his father that was tearing at the seams because of religious changes. His fragile mind and body allowed his wife's uncles to swoop in and guide Francis's activities as king. Francis delegated much of his power, first to his mother Catherine de' Medici, and then, as mentioned, to the Guises. This caused further discomfort to a swath of French nobles, including those who disagreed with the Guise family's religious and political policies.

This angered the Bourbon family, who themselves hoped to guide young Francis II. After all, Mary, Queen of Scots' maternal grandmother was from the Bourbon family, who claimed positions at court as *prince* or *princess du sang*. The Bourbons and Valois were both descended from Saint Louis IX of France, making the Guise family mere political upstarts. As a matter of birthright, a *prince du sang* came second only to the French ruling family and had an automatic position within parliament. In hopes of keeping the peace, Louis I de Bourbon, Prince of Condé, was offered in January 1560 the governance of Picardy and a large sum of money. As a second son, Condé had little importance. His brother Antoine de Bourbon had already made an important political wedding match.

The Tumult of Amboise

Francis II's reign saw the run-up the French Wars of Religion, which officially began in 1562 and did not end until 1598. Francis's father Henri II did his best to keep the Huguenots, or French protestants, at bay. After Francis's accession, his wife's uncles did the same. Their actions were met with resistance by the Huguenots. Suspected protestants were imprisoned and, in some instances, executed.

Not long before his deadly jousting accident in 1559, Henri II attended parliament to express his displeasure over the lack of progress at putting down heresy. Anne de Bourg, an educated professor and French magistrate, protested

Henri's position. He and a handful of others were arrested, then tried, and found guilty of heresy. Henri, as mentioned, died in July 1559, leaving the realm to Francis II. It was decided that de Bourg should be executed as a heretic. De Bourg, in hopes of avoiding death, signed a confession of faith on 13 December 1559. Suffering from a crisis of conscience over his soul, he renounced his confession within days. Plans for his execution were made, then carried out on 23 December 1559. De Bourg was executed at the Place de Grève, where only the most public of executions were conducted. He was first strangled, and then burned to death.

Rather than putting any Huguenots on notice that they could expect severe consequences for heresy, it angered them. In the meantime, a group of malcontents conspired to remove the Guises from power and have Francis's cousin-by-marriage, Antoine de Bourbon, King of Navarre *jure uxoris* Jeanne d'Albret, assume the governance and potentially the throne of France. Antoine was not enticed and declined involvement. The conspirators next turned to Louis I de Bourbon, Prince of Condé.

Condé lurked in the shadows of Henri II's reign, having little to no political importance. Marie de Guise and thus, Mary, Queen of Scots were paternal cousins of Condé's. As mentioned, Condé's brother was Antoine de Bourbon and King of Navarre. Condé proved to be a willing figurehead for the Huguenots. Thankfully, whispers of the conspiracy reached the ears of the Guise family in early 1560.

Francis and his court were out hunting in early February 1560 before moving to Amboise. On the way to Amboise, they were intercepted and notified of the conspiracy and intent to have the Duke of Guise arrested. Because of the warning, the Guises were able to safely move Francis II and Mary, Queen of Scots to the castle at Amboise, which was defensible.

On 11 March 1560, a handful of conspirators were discovered and arrested around Amboise. On 15 March, a company of roughly 200 men on horseback wearing white sashes, which was a symbol of the protestant Huguenots, were espied. The Huguenots were attacked until they dispersed. Condé, who remained with Francis's court in hopes of deflecting attention from himself, watched helplessly as the minor rebellion meant to place him, a *prince du sang*, in charge of the government of Francis II, crumbled.

Over the next couple of days, Condé continued to deny his involvement in the tumult. Hundreds more conspirators were arrested. Francis elevated the Duke of Guise even further on 17 March, making him lieutenant-general of France and effectively handing over complete control of the military. More arrests were made, and hundreds were executed. Condé hung around Amboise for a little longer, finally secretly departing to Bordeaux and the safety of the King of Navarre's court. No evidence against Condé was ever found.

Ongoing Uprisings and the Death of Francis II

With the conspirators crushed and Condé's flight, relative peace resumed in the north of France. Leaderless guerrilla armies in the south, originally part of the conspiracy, began looting and rabble-rousing in the summer of 1560. Condé's wider plot was discovered in Lyon in September 1560. With swift action from Francis's government, the threat was ended. Condé was summoned by the Estates-General, arriving in October 1560. His guilt, imprisonment, and execution were a forgone conclusion.

Amid all this, Francis took ill. He fainted on 16 November 1560 after complaining of an ailment with his ear. Like so many others, it is unknown specifically of what Francis II died, although it could have been an ear infection or an abscess related to something within his ear. The famous royal surgeon Ambroise Paré, who wrote multiple medical treatises and an autobiography, was summoned to assist the young king. He briefly considered boring a hole into Francis's head to relieve the pressure and hopefully heal him, but declined. Francis died in Orléans on 5 December 1560. His body was interred at the Basilica of St. Denis, the traditional resting place of the kings of France, on 23 December 1560.

Chapter 8

Henry Stewart, Lord Darnley

Birth and Early Life

Henry Stewart was the son of Margaret Douglas and Matthew Stewart, 4th Earl of Lennox. As might be recalled from Chapter 4, Margaret Douglas was the daughter of Margaret Tudor and her second husband, Archibald Douglas. When Henry was born in 1546, he had a claim to the English throne through his mother Margaret Douglas and maternal grandmother Margaret Tudor, and a claim to the Scottish throne through his father Matthew Stewart's descent from Elizabeth Hamilton, Countess of Lennox. Elizabeth Hamilton was the granddaughter of James II of Scotland on her mother's side, making Henry Stewart James II's great-great-grandson.

Henry's parents wed in 1544, and he was the second of eight children born to the couple. The eldest child, also named Henry, was born in 1545 and was deceased by November 1545. The following year, Henry Stewart was born. A son, Philip Stewart, was born and died in 1556. A fourth son, Charles, was born in 1557. Henry Stewart and his brother Charles both survived to adulthood, and both died before they reached the age of twenty-two. Nothing is known about Henry's four sisters, although it would be reasonable to assume that these sisters were born and died between 1547 and 1555.

Henry was born at Temple Newsam House in Leeds, West Yorkshire. A homestead existed on the site prior to the 1066 Norman Conquest. It passed through several hands before coming to Thomas, Lord Darcy in 1488 during the reign of Henry VII of England. Lord Darcy erected Temple Newsam House between 1500 and 1530. The property was seized from Darcy in 1537 due to his involvement in the Pilgrimage of Grace and later given to Margaret Douglas and her husband on the occasion of their marriage in 1544.

The Intrigues of Henry's Parents

Margaret Douglas raised the ire of her uncle Henry VIII of England by becoming secretly engaged to Lord Thomas Howard in 1535. Howard was a relative of Henry VIII's second wife Anne Boleyn, and Anne's fall necessitated illegitimating both of Henry VIII's young daughters, though the eldest was illegitimated years before. This left Margaret Douglas very high in the line of succession. When Henry discovered the illicit engagement, he threw both Margaret and her secret fiancé in the Tower. Margaret ended the relationship, and her former fiancé died in the Tower in October 1537.

Not satisfied with one secret engagement to a Howard, Margaret allegedly had a secret relationship with Charles Howard in 1540. Charles was the elder brother of Katheryn Howard, Henry VIII's fifth wife. Once the relationship was ended, Margaret's sanctioned marriage needed to be negotiated.

Matthew Stewart, 4th Earl of Lennox maintained a degree of intrigue in his life. He frequently struggled with James Hamilton, 2d Earl of Arran. Arran was by then the Regent of Scotland, having been put into power after the death of Marie de Guise's husband James V. Both Arran and Lennox had claims to the Scottish throne, although Lennox's claim was stronger. This made him a potential threat to Arran. Lennox also hoped to wed Marie de Guise in 1543, although this did not come to pass. Instead, Margaret Douglas was suggested as a possible bride for Lennox. Lennox, now in favor of the Douglas match, took advantage of an opportunity to seize French money and weaponry being sent to Marie de Guise, who was desperately trying to keep the infant Queen of Scots safe. Marie suggested to Lennox that he could wed Mary instead, although Lennox was in his late twenties by this point. Lennox joined sides with Henry VIII and participated in the Rough Wooing. After burning and pillaging several areas in Scotland, Lennox arrived in England on 28 May 1544. He was granted denization in July.

At some point in 1544, Margaret Douglas and the Earl of Lennox married. The Earl of Lennox continued supporting the English cause in Scotland until 1548, when he switched and made several promises to Marie de Guise for the benefit of Mary, Queen of Scots.

Henry Stewart Meets and Weds Mary, Queen of Scots

Elizabeth I of England asked Henry's father to go to Scotland and do his best to influence Mary's search for a husband. Elizabeth did not think or suspect that the Earl of Lennox would dare dangle his son Henry, who had a claim to the English throne as Henry VII of England's great-grandson, as a prospective suitor for Mary, Queen of Scots, herself one of Henry VII's great-grandchildren. Never mind that, in addition to being a possible heir to Elizabeth I, Henry's family was Catholic.

Henry Stewart, Lord Darnley went with his father the Earl of Lennox to Scotland in early 1565. At this point in his young life, Henry was nineteen years old, tall, and handsome. Darnley was at Wemyss Castle in Fife on 17 February

1565 when he and Mary, Queen of Scots first laid eyes on each other. Although it seems likely that the two could have met each other during a visit from Henry to France as part of a Scottish delegation, Mary was not looking for a husband at the time and any prior meeting would not have been remarkable. Henry, not wishing to miss his opportunity and possibly at the instigation of his father, presented himself to Mary at court. He is said to have given Mary a ring, which she at first tried to turn away. What followed was a brief but effective courtship.

Mary was twenty-three years old when she met Henry and had been a widow for over four years. Darnley wrote Mary love poems, which was surely welcomed attention by Mary. Even better for Mary, they were both descended from Margaret Tudor and possible claimants to the English throne. On top of that, Henry was a Catholic, like Mary.

She announced that spring that she would wed Henry, and the Scottish nobles originally took no issue. The children of Henry and Mary would have a very strong claim to the English throne. Single and child-free Elizabeth I of England desired for Mary to wed an Englishman, but not that one. Mary impertinently pointed out that by marrying Henry, she was fulfilling her cousin's wishes. Elizabeth was unimpressed with Mary's response and the behavior of Henry and his father. No one in Scotland paid Elizabeth any mind.

The Wedding and Marriage of Henry Stewart, Lord Darnley and Mary, Queen of Scots

Henry Stewart, Lord Darnley and Mary, Queen of Scots began their journey toward marital bliss with the banns of marriage being read on 22 July 1565 at St. Giles in Edinburgh. Given that Henry and Mary were Catholic, it was unusual that they were announcing their marriage without the papal dispensation necessary for close cousins. Regardless, the banns were read. Afterward, Henry was elevated to Duke of Albany. On 28 July, it was announced in Edinburgh at Mercat Cross, just outside of St. Giles, that Henry and Mary would celebrate their wedding mass the next day. Thereafter, Henry would be recognized as king consort. An English ambassador at the Scots court remarked, "This night very near nine o'clock, my lord Darnley was proclaimed king consort of Scotland by common consent of all the lords present in this town: I know not what this haste means."

The couple arose bright and early on 29 July 1565, a Friday, for their wedding at six o'clock in the morning. The event took place in the chapel of the Palace of Holyroodhouse. By 1565, it was the last remaining bit of the former Holyrood Monastery.

Mary wore her white widow's veil and black widow's dress for the occasion. The dress may have been trimmed with white, as well. John Stewart, 4th Earl of Atholl, a stalwart supporter of Marie de Guise and Mary, and Henry's father the Earl of Lennox, escorted Mary to the chapel for her wedding. John Sinclair, Dean of Restalrig and Bishop of Brechin, performed the wedding ceremony. Henry placed three rings on Mary's finger and kneeled next to her. After the primary portion of the ceremony was performed, Henry kissed Mary. He then left Mary so she could celebrate Mass. Henry went to St. Giles.

In 1566, a rumor was spread at the Italian court that Henry and Mary celebrated their wedding mass well before 29 July. That was based off rumors heard in Scotland. If true, this could explain why Henry left promptly after the main ceremony. Or, more cynically, his act of leaving Mary could be a historical foreshadowing for their relationship.

It is through this royal couple that the spelling of the dynasty's name changed from "Stewart" to the Gallicized "Stuart."

Religious trouble, which had been brewing in Scotland for decades, took Mary's attention later on her wedding day. She was the queen and had work to do. She addressed the General Assembly in writing concerning religion in Scotland. Effectively, Mary refused to abandon Catholicism, and was content to let each person observe Christianity as they chose. The Protestant lords were afraid that Mary and Henry would reinstate Catholicism as the religion in Scotland. Between her hurried marriage to Henry and this displeasing response on the point of religion, Mary had opened the door for rebellion.

Henry, noted by Mary's uncle the Cardinal of Lorraine as, "a young pretty fool," returned later in the day to enjoy the customary wedding feast. By this point, Henry had rapidly ascended from knight to Earl of Ross, to Duke of Albany, and now, King of Scots. The new king and his queen were served their meal in a way that fitted their station. Afterward, there was dancing. Mary, who gently declared Henry king, effectively bypassed parliament. Henry was not the sovereign per se, but he was treated with the same respect as though he were.

Insurrection

Mary's illegitimate half-brother James Stewart, 1st Earl of Moray, had had it with his sister. He switched to the cause of the Protestant Scottish lords and rebelled against Mary. What followed was the Chase-About Raid, which began on 26 August 1565. The Chase-About Raid is so named because Mary and Henry followed her half-brother around Scotland, never directly engaging with him. Henry wore a fancy gilded metal chest plate, whereas the Scots wore a traditional jack of plate made of heavy fabric with metal sown in between the layers. Needless to say, Henry looked like a self-important outsider to his new Scottish subjects.

The Chase-About Raid ended in September 1565 with Mary's half-brother fleeing to England. He arrived at Elizabeth I's court. Despite her displeasure with Mary's marital choices, Elizabeth was outwardly unimpressed with James Stewart's behavior. He remained in England during the winter of 1565 to 1566.

Cracks in the Scottish Marriage

By Christmas 1565, Mary was issuing coinage without Henry's name. Despite their amorous behavior over the summer, Mary was growing tired of her husband. She spent less and less time with him, too.

Mary increasingly found Henry to be arrogant, proud, and immature. Henry seems to have indulged in alcohol rather often, too. During a social event in Edinburgh, a heavily pregnant Mary besought Henry not to overindulge in alcohol. In response, he used sharp, brutish language with her, making her cry.

Henry received significant recognition from the French court over the winter of 1565 to 1566. Mary's former brother-in-law, the current king of France, honored the puffed-up Henry by sending a delegation to confer upon Henry the order of St. Michael. The ceremony included a Catholic Mass. Afterward, those assembled enjoyed a masquerade and a banquet.

At around this time, or perhaps even much before, Henry set his heart on the crown matrimonial. If recognized as king via the crown matrimonial, then he would become a genuine reigning sovereign instead of being a king consort. Most importantly, he would remain king in the event of Mary predeceasing him.

Henry Stewart attended the wedding of James Hepburn, 4th Earl of Bothwell to Lady Jean Gordon in February 1566. There appeared to be a coolness between Henry and Mary, who had been married for not quite seven months.

Henry Grows Paranoid

Mary took into her service a low-born Italian man named David Riccio in around 1562. Riccio originally joined Mary's court as a musician, and next became her secretary in December 1564. Riccio could speak French, which was surely a comfort to the queen. He managed the correspondence between Mary and the Pope, amongst other duties.

Henry, who was all of twenty years old at this time in 1566, grew jealous of Riccio. Riccio was roughly thirty-three years old. He was reportedly unattractive, but Henry convinced himself that Mary was in love with Riccio. Even worse, Henry suspected that his wife was pregnant with Riccio's baby, not his.

Joan Beaufort
and James I,
Forman Armorial.

Euphemia de Ross and
Robert I, Forman Armorial.

Anabella Drummond and Robert II, Forman Armorial.

Mary of Guelders and James II, Forman Armorial.

Margaret of Denmark, from altarpiece attributed to Hugo van der Goes.

Portrait of Margaret Tudor in the Recueil d'Arras (Bibliothèque municipale d'Arras, Ms. 266).

Henry Stuart, Lord Darnley by an anonymous English artist, 1560s.

Madeleine de Valois by Corneille de Lyons.

James V and Marie de Guise by Unknown, 16th century.

Francis II of France c. 1553, attributed to Leonard Limousin. Held by the Louvre, painted enamel on copper. Accession no. N 1253.

James Hepburn, 4th Earl of Bothwell and 1st Duke of Orkney. Artist unknown, 1566. Oil on copper. Held by National Galleries Scotland. Accession no. PG 869.

Anne of Denmark c. 1605 by John de Critz. Oil on canvas. Held by the National Portrait Gallery. Accession no. NPG 6918.

Queen Henrietta Maria by Anthony van Dyck, 1636. Metropolitan Museum of Art.

Henrietta Maria in Mourning, 1650s. Cornelis Janssens van Ceulen. Oil on Canvas.

Elizabeth Bourchier, c. 1653. Robert Walker. Cromwell Museum. Accession no. HUTCM:B2.

Dorothy Maijor, 17th century engraving by unknown English artist.

Catherine of Braganza by Peter Lely, c. 1664. Oil on canvas. Royal Collection. Accession no. RCIN 401214.

Anne Hyde by Peter Lely, c.1662. Oil on canvas. Royal Collection. Accession no. RCIN 405641.

Mary of Modena by Willem Wissing, c. 1676–1685. Oil on canvas. Held by the Museum of London.

Mary II of England by Willem Wissing, c. 1684. Held by the Cultural Heritage Agency of the Netherlands Art Collection.

William III of England after Willem Wissing, c. late 17th–early 18th century. Held by the Rijksmuseum. Accession no. SK-A-879.

Prince George of Denmark and Norway, by Michael Dahl, 1704. Oil on canvas. Royal Collection. Accession no. RCIN 405895.

Even before the Bothwell–Gordon wedding, in early February 1566, Henry reached out to Patrick Ruthven for help against Riccio. Ruthven had remained in contact with the lords exiled by Mary, as well as being friendly with the Protestant faction. The timing could not have been worse for Mary: parliament was about to be called, and it was anticipated that new laws strengthening Catholicism and seizing back property assumed by Scottish lords during Mary's minority were likely to be passed. Within a few months of the Chase-About Raid, Scotland was primed for another pseudo-rebellion. All that is to say, the idea of backing the simple-minded, pompous Henry seemed like a good one to the rebellious Scottish lords.

A confederation of sorts was made between Henry and those connected to his maternal line, the Douglas family, to remove Riccio and capture Mary. Additionally, the lords exiled in England were to do their best to petition Elizabeth I to release Henry's mother Margaret Douglas, and brother Charles. Elizabeth, extremely displeased with her cousin Margaret because of her son's marriage to Mary, Queen of Scots, took out her anger by imprisoning Margaret and her other son Charles in the Tower of London. Finally, it was agreed that Henry would become king if Mary failed to have a child. This sped up Henry's path to kingship. He did not want to wait for Mary to die.

On 7 March 1566, Mary dressed in the finest clothing her pregnancy would allow and rode horseback up along the Royal Mile from the Palace of Holyroodhouse to Edinburgh Castle to open parliament. She did not seem bothered that her husband was absent. Her spirits were high.

Multiple plans were made by Henry to do away with Riccio. First, he wanted to undo Riccio during a visit to Sir George Seton. That did not work. Next, Henry wanted to harm Riccio during a game of balls, but it was feared that too much suspicion would fall on Mary. Finally, Henry got his chance on the night of 9 into 10 March 1566.

A Murder at the Palace

An army of 500 men entered Edinburgh and made their way toward Holyroodhouse. Henry was in his apartments, waiting for Lord Ruthven and other conspirators. They sneaked into the space by going through the palace garden.

The rooms in which the despicable events occurred are largely intact as of this writing, and Mary's apartments can be visited. Henry's apartments were right below Mary's and connected by a discreet private staircase. After entering Mary's bedroom, one can see a door in the north wall behind which is the staircase. To the west of it is a room roughly three-and-a-half meters or twelve feet deep and two-and-a-half meters or eight feet wide, with a fireplace in it. Mary was known to have dinner here with the closest members of her court. The night of 9 March 1566 was no different.

Mary was dining with her half-siblings Robert Stuart, Jane Stuart, and the Earl of Mar, plus her High Steward, her Master of Horse, and Riccio. Henry came up the private stairs and entered the private room. Mary was seated and turned toward Henry when he entered. Henry went over to Mary and put his arm around her waist. Mary was several months pregnant, to the point of her condition being easily noticeable. Next, Lord Ruthven, clad in armor, entered the private room and demanded that Riccio leave. It was no place for the low-born son of a musician.

Upset at this bizarre display of aggression in her private rooms, and surely shocked that Lord Ruthven took the liberty of entering without being summoned or granted permission, Mary commanded Lord Ruthven to leave immediately. As for David Riccio, Mary declared, "we[1] should exhibit the said David before the Lords of Parliament to be punished, if any sort he had offended." Mary's male attendants moved toward Lord Ruthven to seize him. Lord Ruthven brandished a dagger and cried, "Lay no hands on me, for I will not be handled!"

Next, the sound of footsteps rushing up the private staircase floated into the room. Several of Henry's confederates came swooping in, carrying with them torches. A handful of them entered Mary's private room with swords and daggers drawn. So forcefully and chaotically did they enter the room that the dining table was knocked over, with candles and what was left of the meal spilt on the floor. The table hit Mary in the fracas. Her half-sister Jane grabbed a candle, perhaps in a wild attempt to use it as a tool to protect Mary. Lord Ruthven declared that his purpose was not to hurt the queen, but rather, "the villain."

Riccio, who now understood what was happening, scrambled behind Mary for protection, crying, "Madam, I am dead! Justice, Justice!" Henry, still standing next to the queen, viciously pried Riccio's hands from Mary's clothing. One of the conspirators pointed a pistol at Mary's chest. Another grabbed Henry's dagger and plunged it into Riccio, over Mary's shoulder. Henry continued to clutch Mary, who watched in horror as Riccio was dragged from the private room and into her connected bedroom, and on into the next room. Riccio was stabbed fifty-six times until he died in Mary's apartments.

Mary, still in the private room with Henry, wept and cried, "My poor David, my good and faithful servant, God have mercy on thy soul!" Mary later described this scene via letter to her ambassador in Paris,

---

1. Remember that Mary uses the "royal we."

After this deed immediately the said Lord Ruthven, coming again into our presence, declared how they and their accomplices aforesaid were highly offended with our proceedings and tyranny, which was not to them tolerable; how we was [sic] abused by the said David, whom they had actually put to death, namely, in taking his counsel for maintenance of the ancient religion [of Catholicism]; debarring of the lords which were fugitive, and entertaining of amity with foreign princes and nations with whom we were confederate; putting also upon council the lords Bothwell and Huntly, who were traitors, and with whom [Riccio] associated himself.

Lord Ruthven explained that the murder was committed with the king's blessing. Mary turned to Henry, shouting,

"Traitor, son of a traitor, thus you requite her who has done you so great an honor; this is the acknowledgement which you make me for having elevated you to so high a dignity [as king of Scotland]. What injury have I done to you that you have willingly caused me such shame?"

Henry blamed his actions on the cooling of Mary's affections toward him.

Lord Ruthven's account includes the exchange between Mary and Henry, too. Mary asked,

"My lord, why have you caused to do this wicked deed to me; considering that I took you from low estate, and made you my husband? What offence have I given you that you should do me such shame?"

The king answered, "I have good reason for me, for since yonder fellow David came in credit and familiarity with your Majesty, you neither regarded me, entertained me, nor trusted me after your wonted fashion; for every day before dinner you were wont to come to my chamber, and passed the time with me, and this long time you have not done so; and when I came to your Majesty's chamber, you bare me little company except David had been the third person; and after supper your Majesty used to sit up at the cards with the said David till one or two after midnight; and this is the entertainment that I have of you this long time."

Her Majesty answered, "that it was not a gentlewoman's duty to come to her husband's chamber, but rather the husband to come to the wife's."

The king answered, "How came you to my chamber in the beginning, and ever till within these six months, that David fell into familiarity with you?"

Mary reportedly responded,

"My Lord, all the offence that is done me, you have the wite thereof, for the which I shall be your wife no longer, nor lie with you anymore, and shall never like well till I cause you have as sorrowful a heart as I have at this present."

After this exchange, Lord Ruthven knocked and entered Mary's chambers to inform her and Henry that there was fighting outside. Townspeople, including Bothwell, were being led by their provost and went to the palace over fear that something dire had happened to Mary. Mary wanted to address the gathered townspeople to reassure them. Henry and his confederates did not allow Mary so to do and, "in our face declared, if we desired to have spoken to [the crowd], they should cut us to collops and cast us over the walls."

Henry went outside to address the crowd. The provost present asked that Mary appear, to which Henry responded, "Provost, know you not that I am king? I command you to pass home to your houses." And the people did.

The next day, Henry issued two proclamations in his name as king. The first forbade the carrying of weapons within Edinburgh, and the second dissolved parliament, and that those assembled were to leave within three hours of the decree unless Henry had bade them to stay in Edinburgh. Henry had no right to do either. Mary was virtually a prisoner at this point.

Aftermath

Mary invited Henry to overnight with her, possibly as soon as the night after Riccio's murder. Whatever passed that night between Henry and Mary, did, and he slept in the next morning. Henry's disposition toward Mary changed. Mary agreed to a reconciliation with Henry, and Henry outwardly abandoned his pursuit of the crown matrimonial.

The seemingly reconciled couple entered the hall where Henry's men were. Mary agreed to sign whatever the traitors wished that would secure them from punishment. Henry reviewed them and had no qualms. He then directed his confederates to leave the palace and stated that it should be placed back into Mary's care.

The lords left on the Monday afternoon, after agreeing to leave the palace in Henry's custody, not Mary's. Mary was reportedly ill by this time, likely from the tremendous shock and stress she had experienced. However ill she was, a plot was communicated to her by James Hepburn, Earl of Bothwell for her escape. Having escaped over the wall to find waiting horses, Mary and one of her ladies rode through the night to the Castle of Dunbar.

Mary successfully raised an army. She returned to Edinburgh on 19 March 1566, and was well received by her people. After sorting punishment for Henry's conspirators, it was time for Mary to learn more about her husband's involvement in the conspiracy.

Henry was all too happy to give up his accomplices. He formally declared that he had nothing to do with the conspiracy and that he was wrongly accused. Henry's relationship with Mary was clearly at its lowest. Interestingly, the couple's relationship would slightly rebound.

The Birth of Prince James

As Mary prepared for her child's birth, she also necessarily prepared for both of their deaths. Childbirth was a gruesome, dangerous activity, and still is. Mary drafted her testament. A copy was sent to her French relations.

Mary's testament served as an inventory of her jewelry in the summer of 1566. She left all 253 jewels to her child, should the baby survive the birth and Mary not. Mary left 26 items to Henry, including one of her wedding rings from him that was adorned with a diamond.

On 19 June 1566, Mary was safely delivered of a baby boy. Henry was absolutely delighted and took the initiative of having the birth of Prince James announced to the French court as well as at home in Scotland. Henry and Mary were more and more inclined towards each other's company for the rest of the summer. The two even purportedly resumed sleeping together. Mary still harbored negative feelings for Henry and a longing for happier times with him. The first year of their marriage was a whirlwind, with a dramatic murder, two different rebellions, one led by Henry, and the birth of a son.

Decline of Henry's Relationship with Mary

Mary seemed to suffer from depression that autumn. This might have been postpartum depression or a situational depression over the events of March 1566 that was augmented and compounded by postpartum life. Mary reportedly wished herself dead, was outwardly melancholy, and heaved great, despairing sighs rather often.

Mary was largely away in Jedburgh to attend legal courts during October 1566, and into early November. Henry was left to his own devices, including trying to express a greater level of Catholic piety. He was paradoxically upset by the pardoning of his former confederates, who were now quick to turn on him. Henry grew increasingly politically isolated during this time.

Mary spent the better part of November journeying from Jedburgh to Stirling, by way of Berwick-upon-Tweed and Dunbar. Whilst staying at Dunbar, Mary was formally approached regarding separating from Henry. She was willing to consider it.

The idea of prosecuting Henry in Parliament was broached. Henry was the figurehead of the Riccio murder and subsequent rebellion several months before. Given the affection the Scots had shown their queen, it would not be difficult to go after Henry via Parliament and remove him.

Things between Henry and Mary turned sour once again by December 1566. Baby James was baptized at Stirling Castle on 17 December 1566. It was a grand affair, with Elizabeth I of England sending a gold font for the purpose; ambassadors from Savoy and France were present for the occasion. Henry refused to show himself.

Mary comported herself well throughout the festivities. Behind closed doors, she would cry. She also experienced severe pain on one side, which may have been psychosomatic. The queen could easily put on a brave face, but she was despairing and in agony.

Henry lived separate and apart from Mary for several months. In an upset state of mind, Henry considered venturing out of Scotland to Spain, or even France. Around Christmas 1566 and going into New Year 1567, Mary appeared to have a change of heart.

The End for Henry Stuart, Lord Darnley

Henry was in Glasgow with Mary in January 1567. Unfortunately, Henry caught smallpox. Mary was extremely worried for his health and sent her own physician to help him. She wished to return with Henry to Edinburgh as soon as he was well enough. They were able to depart for Edinburgh in late January, arriving in the city on 30 January 1567.

It was suggested that Henry remain at Craigmillar Castle until his health improved and the fear of contagion passed. Mary returned to Holyrood, and Darnley was installed at the parsonage of Kirk o' Fields. The building in which Henry was lodged was two stories tall and had six or seven rooms. Its main door was on the northern side of the building. A second door led down to the cellar. A third door, positioned in the eastern side, led to the garden and the city wall.

The air around Kirk o' Fields was considered healthier than the air around Holyrood because Holyrood was at a lower elevation. This seems somewhat counterintuitive because, being within a churchyard, deceased persons were likely buried nearby. The early modern mind believed air quality to have a huge impact on one's health, so surely being around decay would be of concern. Perhaps this is more a testament to how unhealthy the air within Edinburgh proper was.

Henry was brought furnishings from Holyrood to adorn his area, which included, "a bed of violet velvet, trimmed with lace of gold and silver." Additionally, a dais was erected in one of the other rooms in which Henry could receive guests, if he had any. It was draped in black velvet.

Mary visited Henry as often as she could. She brought along her musicians to cheer Henry. She could be seen walking in the nearby gardens during her visits. She overnighted in Kirk o' Fields a few times, too. The warmth in Henry's and Mary's relationship appeared to be returning.

On 8 February 1567, Henry was warned by Mary's half-brother Robert Stuart, Prior of Holyroodhouse, that Henry was in serious danger. It was imperative that he leave Kirk o' Fields at once for his own safety. Henry sent a message to Mary, who was visiting with friends nearby. She responded with a missive to Robert. He denied having said anything. Thereafter, it is alleged that Henry and Robert may have had a heated, almost violent, discussion. Whether true or not, Henry continued staying at Kirk o' Fields.

Mary visited Henry again on 9 February, sometime in the late evening. She was returning to Holyroodhouse to complete her duties as queen for a wedding ceremony that had taken place earlier that day. Henry and Mary had a mirthful conversation. Mary was pleased to chat about the wedding. She gifted Henry a ring and gave him several kisses throughout her visit. She left at around eleven o'clock that night.

By about one o'clock in the morning on 10 February 1567, the parsonage was blown up, and Henry was dead.

Henry's body, clad only in a linen shift, plus his boots and clothes were found some distance from the explosion. His body reportedly bore no injuries which one would assume should occur if there were an explosion. There was a rumor that he had been suffocated. It is entirely possible that Henry awakened when he heard the men entering the still space of the parsonage, confronted them, and was killed before the explosion, then placed by the wall. Either way, the king was dead through violent means, and Mary was once more a widow.

After lying in state for a couple of days, Henry was interred by torch light in the same vault where Mary's father James V and her brothers were buried inside the Royal Chapel.

Chapter 9

James Hepburn, 4th Earl of Bothwell

Family and Early Years

James Hepburn, 4th Earl of Bothwell, was born in 1536 or 1537. He commonly signed his name as, "James Erle Boithuille." James's father Patrick, who became 3rd Earl of Bothwell after James's grandfather was killed at the 1513 Battle of Flodden, was regarded as haughty and proud in personality with a fair, pale complexion. Patrick was roughly a year old when he was elevated to earl, so this might explain his personality.

Patrick Hepburn had an interesting relationship with morality. In 1529, he concealed robbers, which led to his imprisonment. After his confinement was over, Patrick wasted no time in allying himself with Henry VIII throughout the 1530s and beyond. Given that Patrick was a Scottish earl, this was treason.

Patrick married Agnes Sinclair in 1534. She is an obscure figure. Her father died at the Battle of Flodden as well, and she may have been considerably older than Patrick. The couple had at least two children, the aforementioned James, and a daughter called Janet or Jean. Both Patrick and later, his son James, had designs on marrying a Scottish queen. To that end, Patrick divorced Agnes in 1543. Patrick recorded in his letters that Marie de Guise, "promised faithfully, by her hand writ, at two sundry times, to take the said Earl in marriage." Given Patrick's character, it is difficult to tell how truthful his statement was. Patrick continued engaging in treasonous activity into the early 1550s, at which point he was pardoned by Marie de Guise and welcomed back to Scotland.

Aspiring to marry Scottish queens was something of a tradition for the Hepburns. In the 15th century, the Hepburns of Hales aspired to marry firstly, Joan Beaufort, widow of James I. A subsequent Hepburn tried to woo Mary of Guelders, widow of James II.

James's education and youth are not known in detail. His family possessed books on mathematics and military tactics, and other works. Most of the books were in French, and it is possible that he spent part of his teenage years in France. James's father Patrick died in 1556, and it is noted thereafter that James, "Beginning from his very youth, and first enters to this realm, immediately after the decease of his father." This statement was part of the 1567 instructions for the announcement of Mary, Queen of Scots' marriage presented to the French court.

Given his father's interesting relationship with the English monarchy, he could also have been in England.

More importantly, upon becoming the 4th Earl of Bothwell at the age of twenty, James was automatically an important noble at the Scottish court and had an awesome number of vassals in southern Scotland. Bothwell supported Marie de Guise in the various battles and skirmishes along the Scottish-English border, proving his value as a military leader. He did unfortunately still have a rebellious streak in him, like his father.

Bothwell Ventures to the Continent

In around May 1560, Marie de Guise asked James Hepburn, Earl of Bothwell to go to her daughter Mary's court in France. Bothwell was charged with requesting more military assistance from the French court. Mary, Queen of Scots, was the consort of Francis II of France at this time. Bothwell journeyed to the north of Scotland with a band of five men, ostensibly to find a safe passage to France and out of reach to the English navy. Going to France was possibly a ruse, for instead Bothwell ventured to Denmark by way of the Netherlands.

Bothwell was well received in Denmark. Wanting to go into Germany, Bothwell, "was conducted through Jutland and the duchy [of Holstein, Germany], both by the King and the Duke of Holstein." Thereafter, Bothwell made his way into France by late summer to early autumn of 1560. He was well received at court there, being appointed as a gentleman of the chamber to Francis II and receiving a gift of money.

At some point whilst in Norway, Bothwell married Anna Throndsen. Throndsen's father was a prominent figure at the Danish court, holding the position of Royal Danish Consul in the 1560s. Formerly, he had been a pirate or privateer, depending on whose side observed his behavior.[1] Anna and her sisters were at or around court in Denmark when Bothwell appeared, leading to Anna and Bothwell meeting each other and falling in love.

During his continental adventures, Marie de Guise, who was acting as regent of Scotland, passed away. Swiftly after her June 1560 death, a parliament was illegally called. The illegal parliament banned the hearing of Catholic Mass, amongst other harsh decisions, which disturbed Mary, Queen of Scots. She ordered for several of her Scottish nobles then present in Paris to return to Edinburgh. Bothwell was one of the nobles granted the power by her to call a

---

1. A privateer is a government-sanctioned pirate who is granted a letter of marque to pursue enemy merchant ships. A pirate is either the enemy holding a letter of marque, or a rogue.

new parliament. In November 1560, Bothwell returned to Scotland. He was completely ineffective and instead went back to France.

Mary, Queen of Scots, was widowed by the death of Francis II on 5 December 1560. Bothwell was thereafter present at Mary's French court until her departure for Scotland in August 1561. Mary appointed Bothwell to the privy council which she formed in September, despite Bothwell still being abroad. Bothwell's father Patrick held a place on the privy council during his own lifetime.

Bothwell Returns to Scotland

James Hepburn, 4th Earl of Bothwell was back in Scotland by November 1561. Queen Mary effectively forced Bothwell and his enemies to make peace. Bothwell took up residence with one of Mary's French uncles, René II of Lorraine, Marquis d'Elbeuf, who had accompanied her from France to Scotland and remained on in Edinburgh.

Unfortunately, James Hamilton, 2d Earl of Arran and the very same Earl of Arran who held the regency for a time during the minority of Mary, was bitter enemies with Bothwell. Despite Mary's decree and insistence that Bothwell and his enemies forgive past indiscretions, Arran could not let go of his distaste of Bothwell.

Bothwell's friend the Marquis then stole the affections of a woman possibly named Marguerite Chrestien, daughter of a respectable merchant, from Arran. So enraged was Arran that fights broke out between the Marquis's supporters and Arran's supporters in Edinburgh. The Marquis took part directly, snatching a halberd. He was held back from violence by ten men. Bothwell was presumably present for the excitement.

Mary, trying to gain control of her country, pardoned her uncle the Marquis. He left Scotland in February 1561, leaving behind a pregnant mistress by whom he had an illegitimate son. Bothwell was ordered to leave Edinburgh. Bothwell obliged but then engaged in further mischief.

Bothwell, for whatever reason, decided that kidnapping a nobleman's son was a good idea. John Cockburn, Laird of Ormiston, was out hunting with his wife and son. They were from East Lothian. During their hunting excursion, the family stumbled into Bothwell's neighboring territory. Bothwell thought it wise to kidnap Ormiston's son Alexander, then in his twenties, and imprison him at Bothwell's Crichton Castle. Bothwell later released the young man, who was a follower of the Scottish religious reformer John Knox. Bothwell was a member of the Reformed Kirk, and saw an opportunity for reconciliation with his enemies, such as John Cockburn, via John Knox.

Alexander Cockburn assisted Bothwell in arranging a meeting with John Knox. Knox eagerly accepted the opportunity, no doubt disappointed by the petty shenanigans in which the leaders of the Reformist party engaged. John Cockburn and Bothwell agreed to have their differences settled by Arran. The men met at Kirk o' Field in Edinburgh on 25 March 1562. The 25th of March was known as Lady Day and was the administrative start of the new year during the medieval and early modern periods. Upon Bothwell entering the designated room in Kirk o' Field, Arran greeted him with an embrace. There would not be smooth sailing for Bothwell. On the other hand, Bothwell gained an understanding of the building's layout, if he did not have one already.

More on Anna Throndsen

Anna Throndsen, Bothwell's first wife, and he, married each other in Denmark through a hand-fasting ceremony. A hand-fasting ceremony was legally sufficient in Denmark and Norway to solidify a marriage. Handfasting was viewed as more of an engagement ceremony in Scotland and England, however. Given Bothwell's already sub-legal behavior, he could have very well known the distinction and preferred to keep his options open in Scotland by simply being engaged, even if he were legally married in Denmark, all the way across the North Sea.

Anna was first abandoned by Bothwell in the Netherlands. There, she had to pawn her jewelry and live off what portion of her dowry was in her possession. She appears to have ventured to Scotland in 1563, having received a passport from Mary, Queen of Scots. Anna's activities in Scotland besides having contact with Bothwell are difficult to discern.

Anna and Bothwell may have had a son named William together. Bothwell's mother left everything to him in a testament dated 21 March 1572. For example, the will states, "Item, the said noble Lady left her hail goods, the said debts being paid, to William Hepburn, son natural to James, Earl of Bothwell." If William were the son of Anna, William's being designated as a "son natural" of Bothwell supports the idea that Anna and Bothwell were merely considered as engaged in Scotland.

Anna, who was known at the Danish court as the "Scottish Woman," did not seem to enjoy her time in Scotland. She may have been present at Mary, Queen of Scots' court. If so, Anna's presence was unremarkable.

Alleged Conspiracy

The Earl of Arran lost his mind by the end of March 1562, as recorded by John Knox. Bothwell went to pay his respects to Arran and Arran's father, but

Arran left the castle in the middle of the night. He went to Falkland Palace, where Queen Mary was staying with her half-brother James Stewart, 1st Earl of Moray. Arran arrived on 29 March, claiming that his father, plus Bothwell, and others planned to surprise and capture Mary when she was out hunting around Falkland. Arran even stated that Bothwell himself would reveal the plot to Mary, should Bothwell be brought before her. Knox, having caught wind of this, warned Mary's government that Arran was stricken with mental illness.

Bothwell, oblivious to Arran's accusation, arrived at Falkland on 31 March 1562. He was seized upon by orders of Mary's half-brother James Stewart, Earl of Moray and imprisoned at St. Andrews Castle. At St. Andrews, Bothwell and his alleged accomplices were confronted by Mary and Arran. Arran's insanity became plain when he tried to lay out his accusations against Bothwell, and Arran was taken into custody. Bothwell remained imprisoned over the summer.

Summer 1562 saw the first serious upheaval after Mary, Queen of Scots' return from France in 1561. More street riots broke out in Edinburgh amongst the nobles that summer. Bothwell, tired of being imprisoned and idle, broke out of his cell on 28 August. He had fashioned a rope which, after breaking an iron bar on his window, he lowered and used to escape. Mary did not seem upset over his escape. Afterward, Bothwell saw his position within the Scottish government diminished by Mary's aforementioned half-brother.

Bothwell Returns to France

In the winter of 1562, Bothwell attempted to sail to France. He departed from North Berwick. The North Sea being treacherous on a good day, and especially so in winter, led Bothwell to landing on Holy Island, just south of the Scottish-English border. Bothwell was captured there. He wrote to the Earl of Northumberland, informing the latter that Bothwell had come to English territory because of a storm and not for a nefarious purpose. He even requested Elizabeth I of England's protection against Mary, Queen of Scots.

James Stewart, learning of Bothwell's capture, encouraged the English government to remember that Bothwell was indeed an enemy of the English. It would be safest for him to be imprisoned in England, where he could do no further harm. Elizabeth ordered Bothwell kept in custody throughout 1563. Mary interceded on Bothwell's behalf in early 1564, and he was allowed to leave England for France.

Once in France, Bothwell was awarded with a position in the Scottish Guards. The Scottish Guards were founded in the early 15th century and were comprised of Scotsmen who swore to protect the French monarch. This was a prestigious position to have at court. The Scottish Guard existed until 1791 and had mostly French soldiers by that time.

Bothwell returned to Scotland in March 1565, much to the chagrin of James Stewart. Mary had no quarrel with Bothwell at that point, but she did call him before her to explain the accusations from Arran in 1562, and why he broke out of prison. Bothwell swore to appear before any judicial court she might call. Such a court was called for 2 May 1565.

Bothwell's archenemy James Stewart and Stewart's men were coming to preside over the court. Bothwell knew there was an extremely low chance of acquittal, and so decided to leave Scotland for the Continent again. He successfully left, disembarking in the Netherlands. In the meantime, Mary, Queen of Scots wed Henry Stewart, Lord Darnley, and the Chase-About Raid between Mary and James Stewart began.

Bothwell Re-enters Scotland

Mary recalled Bothwell in late summer 1565, needing his assistance in putting down her half-brother's rebellion. Bothwell was known more for his military prowess than his virtue. He had been pardoned on 5 August 1565 for breaking out of prison.

Bothwell and other Scots lords in France ventured their return to Scotland in September, with Bothwell narrowly escaping capture by the English. He landed at Eyemouth in Scotland on 17 September 1565 and was received by Mary at Holyrood on 20 September. She displayed no ill will toward him and immediately restored him to all the benefices and positions which he had held previously. Mary also designated him commander-in-chief, along with her father-in-law, for the portion of the army that Mary and Henry ventured with during the remaining days of the Chase-About Raid.

The following month, Bothwell had the delight of seeing his enemy James Stewart exiled. At Castlehill by Dumfries on 10 October 1565, the formality occurred. For now, Bothwell could relax a little. He also appreciated the confidence of Mary, who put him in charge of patrolling the border in case any rebellious Scots tried to return.

Bothwell's Second Marriage

At some point during all this excitement, Anna Throndsen returned to Denmark and Norway.

By late 1565 to very early 1566, Bothwell caught the attention of Jean Gordon, daughter of the 4th Earl of Huntly. She was twelve years younger than Bothwell, having been born around 1546. The details of Jean and Bothwell's relationship and whatever courtship they had are waiting to be discovered. Overall, it was a political match for Jean's previously disgraced family.

Jean was a Catholic, which pleased Mary, Queen of Scots. Mary sent Jean cloth of silver and white taffeta for a wedding gown. She hoped that Jean would observe Catholic rites for her wedding ceremony. As per usual, Bothwell had other ideas. The wedding was set for 24 February 1566. Earlier that month, Bothwell eschewed attending Catholic Mass. He chose to have the marriage conducted according to a Protestant ceremony.

Curiously, James Hepburn, 4th Earl of Bothwell's desire to have a Protestant ceremony did not rattle Mary, Queen of Scots. She allowed Bothwell and Jean Gordon to wed in the royal chapel at Holyrood. Two days of feasting and festivities followed the wedding.

The Riccio Murder

Bothwell was honored after a fashion at the next parliament. Parliament was called on 7 March 1566, and Mary, Queen of Scots, expected to use this parliament in part to deal with the exiles. She put Bothwell and his brother-in-law George Gordon, 5th Earl of Huntly in charge of keeping the exiles' threat at bay.

Shortly after receiving such an honor, Bothwell and Huntly, amongst others, rushed to help Mary after her husband Henry Stewart, Lord Darnley had had Riccio murdered. Bothwell and the Earls of Huntly and Atholl were lodged within the palace. Lord Ruthven, who was one of the actors in Riccio's murder, intercepted the band of armed protectors. He attempted to quieten them. Whilst that worked, unfortunately, news already reached Edinburgh, with the ruckus,

> in such manner through the Canongate, that it was said the Queen's Grace was held in captivity and, seigneur David slain, wherethrough the common bell rang in such sort that every man passed to armor, and rushed down with…their provost, to Holyroodhouse, willing to have delivered the Queen's Grace and revenge the cause aforesaid.

Bothwell, along with the others, dispersed after Henry came out and ordered everyone home.

Bothwell and Huntly escaped out a window, with Bothwell recalling that after Riccio's murder, if, "some noblemen and myself, in order to avoid such a peril, had not escaped through a window in the back of the palace [of Holyrood], we should not have received any better treatment [than Riccio], since they had so resolved among themselves, or we had at the least been compelled to approve of an action so very base and detestable." The men descended out of the window and into a garden where Mary kept her lions. Mary recalled of the escape, "Yet, by the providence of God, the Earls of Huntly and Bothwell escaped forth of their chambers in our palace at a back window by some cords." Bothwell and Huntly managed to avoid the lions, too.

Bothwell, not willing to let Queen Mary be held prisoner, secretly communicated to her an escape plan. It went off without a hitch, and soon Mary was at the Castle of Dunbar. Bothwell and Huntly were at Bothwell's Crichton Castle during this time. Mary requested the aid of those loyal to her, and Bothwell came rushing to help. She soon had a strong enough army to re-enter Edinburgh on 19 March 1566, scarcely a week after she had fled Holyroodhouse.

Mary, reflecting on Bothwell's support and ability to raise an army, recalled later, "how suddenly be [Bothwell's] providence not only were we delivered out of the prison, but also that hail company of conspirators dissolved and we recovered our former obedience." Two of the Riccio conspirators were executed, with Bothwell presenting Mary's ring to the provost before the execution of other conspirators could take place. Bothwell informed the provost that any remaining executions for the conspirators were converted to banishment.

Perhaps as a sign of gratitude to Bothwell, Mary left items of her jewelry to him and his wife in her testament. Having drawn up the testament in summer 1566 before her son's birth, Mary left one jewel to Bothwell, and three to his wife Jean Gordon, Lady Huntly.

Bothwell left Edinburgh after the birth of Prince James on 19 June 1566. He made for the Borders, to enforce order there. Things were growing restless there once more, so Bothwell had his work cut out for him.

It seems that Bothwell, or those around him, may have started scheming against Mary's husband Henry Stewart, Lord Darnley as early as mid-August 1566. This could belie the outwardly happy behavior Henry and Mary showed to their courtiers. A letter from the Earl of Bedford hints at a plan, although the plan itself is not described. The Earl of Bedford wrote,

> that there is a plan in contemplation with respect to the Earl of Bothwell, about which I could indeed obtain precise information, but since such things are not addressed to me, I do not wish to hear any more of them. Bothwell has gradually become so detested that matters cannot go on long with him as now.

Bothwell, not known for his looks, began dressing more and more ostentatiously. Reading between the lines, Bothwell was becoming ever bolder because of Mary, Queen of Scots's trust in him.

Autumn Skirmishes

While Bothwell was enforcing the Queen's laws in early October 1566, he was seriously injured. Bothwell came upon an outlaw on 7 October in the woods surrounding the small Hermitage Castle, one of a couple owned by Bothwell. After exchanging words, the outlaw ran away. Bothwell responded by shooting at the outlaw. Bothwell leapt down from his horse and gave chase, stumbling over part of a tree. He fell, winding himself, and lay there for several moments. The outlaw came back and wounded Bothwell with a sword in the latter's hand, torso, and head. Bothwell, recovering himself, quickly stabbed the outlaw twice in the chest. The outlaw stumbled off, bled out, and died. Bothwell passed out, and his servants brought him back to Hermitage Castle to recover.

Mary was in Jedburgh and told of Bothwell's condition. On 16 October, she and a handful of lords quickly made their way to Hermitage Castle to inquire after Bothwell. The land through which they traveled was dangerous and too near the English border, necessitating haste. The loss of Bothwell, an important lord and faithful servant, could have had a potentially devastating impact on Mary's reign, given the two rebellions that had occurred over the past year. After visiting with Bothwell for a couple of hours, Mary and her lords swiftly returned to Jedburgh.

The physical exertion of riding upwards of 50 miles or 80 kilometers in one day took its toll on Mary. She fell ill with a serious fever within the next few days. She was so ill on 26 October 1566 that it was feared she was dead. The reformer John Knox, who was no fan of Mary's specifically, or female rulers overall, noted, "For [Mary] lay two hours long cold dead, as it were without breath, or any sign of life; at length she revived, by reason they had bound small cords about her shackle bones [wrists], her knees, and her great toes." Presumably, the pain or pressure from the cords is what roused her.

Bothwell was present for Prince James's christening that Christmas, once more joined by his brother-in-law the Earl of Huntly. The baptismal ceremony was conducted under Catholic rite, and, "[a]t this time my lords Huntly…and Bothwell… came not within the said chapel, because it was done against the points of their religion." Bothwell had no qualms with outwardly showing his adherence to the Protestant church.

Mary's trust in Bothwell increased during 1566. His family had supported her mother Marie de Guise, and Bothwell himself always came when Mary bade him. He was present at Craigmillar Castle in Dunbar in late November 1566 when Mary was asked to consider separating from Henry. She was willing to discuss it so long as her departure from the marriage was legally sound, and that Prince James's legitimacy and position as heir would not be threatened. Bothwell piped up at this point, reminding the queen that his own parents were divorced. Despite that, Bothwell had no problem asserting his rights as his father's heir.

Bothwell's Marital Relationships Become Complicated

Mary, via the dubious Casket Letters, appears to have started writing Bothwell love letters and sonnets by the end of January 1567. The Casket Letters turned up after the death of Mary's second husband, Henry Stewart, Lord Darnley. The casket itself was covered in silver gilt, with crowned letters "F" decorating it. The box was probably a gift from Mary's first husband Francis II of France. The letters were used as prime evidence of Mary's own complicity in the murder of her second husband. Whether the letters were genuine shall not be discussed here. Importantly to the life of Bothwell and Mary, they were taken as real.

A month later, in February 1567, Bothwell's second marriage to Jean Gordon, Lady Huntly began showing its cracks. Jean fell ill in February 1567, to the point of being presumed dead. She revived, and her brother convinced her to divorce Bothwell. Bothwell's behavior and intrigues during their marriage had become unbearable to the Gordons over the last few months, who themselves were trying to redeem their position at court and regain possessions forfeited to the crown. Jean's marriage to Bothwell lasted for less than fifteen months. The pair never had a child together.

Bothwell Plots a Murder

Bothwell, now on the verge of being or indeed being in the state of free to marry by 9 February 1567, was plotting. He brought barrels of gunpowder from Dunbar Castle. He stored the barrels within the rooms in which he was lodging at Holyrood. Bothwell and his conspirators met for a couple of hours within the same apartments to discuss their plan.

The conspirators knew that Mary would be attending wedding festivities for one of her French servants in the evening. With Mary safely away from Kirk o' Fields, it was time to strike. Both Mary and Bothwell attended an afternoon banquet that day. Bothwell excused himself after darkness fell, venturing out into the wintery evening.

The gunpowder which Bothwell had brought from Dunbar Castle and stored inside Holyroodhouse was discreetly transported outside the city walls of Edinburgh at around ten o'clock that night. The gunpowder, contained within sacks inside the barrels, was removed by Bothwell and his men. The sacks were brought inside the building where Henry was staying.

Mary, who went to visit Henry a couple of hours before, left Kirk o' Fields at around eleven o'clock. She was probably in the building when the gunpowder was placed inside. Bothwell carefully escorted her out of the building, and past the room in which she would stay when overnighting there on account of her husband Henry. What Mary did not know was that inside the room were all the sacks of gunpowder. The room was conveniently below Henry's, making it all the simpler to blow up the current king.

Bothwell appears to have returned to the banquet until around midnight. He then went back to Holyrood to change into simple clothing from his costly, decorated court dress. Other conspirators had come to Holyroodhouse to change their clothes. That done, the band of miscreants donned inconspicuous cloaks, wended through Edinburgh, and back to Kirk o' Fields.

There was a slight hiccup. The men were stopped at Canongate, which was shut for the night. To pass through it, the men told the porter that they were friends of Bothwell, and so should be allowed to pass. They were allowed through Canongate.

Once to the house, Bothwell learned that the fuse in the room with the gunpowder was lit. Impatiently waiting for the explosion, he asked how long it would take for the fuse to ignite the gunpowder. He asked whether there was a way that one could peer into the room, perhaps through a window, to be certain that the fuse had not accidentally burned out. No sooner were the words out of his mouth than a mighty explosion rocked the parsonage and the buildings surrounding it.

Bothwell Takes His Chances

Bothwell managed to return to Holyroodhouse without it being detected that he had left. He was seen viewing the exploded parsonage at daybreak before returning to the palace. Bothwell changed into his bedclothes and feigned shock and horror when he was awakened by the news of the explosion and Henry's gruesome death. Swiftly, he put on his fancy dress from the day before and made his way to Mary's apartments. Mary was informed of Henry's death.

Not long after Henry's death, it was already being bruited that Bothwell was responsible.

The Sheriff of Edinburghshire was called. He had Henry's corpse collected and brought to a house not far from where it was found. There, the body was inspected for injury. Mary came to see Henry's corpse, too. She reportedly regarded him for a long time before departing. She left for Edinburgh Castle, a veritable fortress when compared with the plushness and lack of defenses present at Holyroodhouse. Once there, Mary corresponded with her father-in-law, who was determined to bring the conspirators to justice.

Elizabeth I sent an ambassador straightaway after hearing of the murder. He reported on 8 March 1567, "Her Majesty [Queen Mary is] here in a dark room, so that he could not see her countenance, but by her words she seemed to be very sorrowful." Around 17 March, Mary received a letter from her father-in-law, naming Bothwell and his conspirators. Mary ordered a requiem mass be sung for Henry on 23 March, which was Palm Sunday. A few days before the mass, it was recorded that, "The Queen [Mary] has been for the most part either melancholy or sickly ever since [the death of Henry], especially this week—upon Tuesday and Wednesday often swooned." On Good Friday, 28 March, she and her ladies went to the Royal Chapel to pray for several hours.

Also on Good Friday, it was proclaimed that a Court of Assizes would be held on 12 April. Bothwell would remain out of custody. The meeting of the law court was to be announced in Edinburgh and the major cities nearby, so anyone willing to accuse Bothwell and his conspirators could come forward. Bothwell showed up with a massive train of people, but Henry's father Lord Lennox did not show his face. After passionate arguments in favor of Bothwell's innocence, he was acquitted.

Parliament was dissolved on 19 April 1567. Bothwell, scheming to wed Mary, was complicit in putting together a petition of sorts recommending their marriage. That same day, several Lords of Parliament and other notable men signed the Ainslie Tavern Bond. The Bond declared that the twice-widowed Mary should marry a Scottish subject. This document was then handed to Bothwell. Five days later, 24 April, Bothwell and an escort of 800 armed men intercepted Mary on her way to Linlithgow Palace in Edinburgh. Mary, convinced by Bothwell that danger awaited her in Edinburgh, went with Bothwell to Dunbar. That night, he either sexually assaulted her or Mary consented willingly to Bothwell's advances. Only Mary and Bothwell know what truly happened.

Bothwell was expediently elevated to the position of Duke of Orkney on 12 May 1567. They were married on 15 May 1567. Their wedding was celebrated in the Great Hall at the Palace of Holyroodhouse. Mary reportedly gifted Bothwell a fur-lined nightgown as a wedding present. Curiously, for as devout a Catholic Mary was, the wedding was performed according to the new Protestant fashion. One can speculate that Mary consented to this for a couple of reasons: first, to show she truly did not have any scruples over religion within Scotland, and second, when it came time for an annulment, she could ideally petition the Pope who would not recognize the Protestant ceremony as being valid.

The modern mind might question why Mary would wed someone who possibly sexually assaulted her. It comes down to the mores of the time: there was no precedent for a queen regnant having illegitimate children. A king, certainly, as shown by Mary's father. Mary did fall pregnant with Bothwell's twins, although whether it was from the initial act around 24 April or subsequent acts of amorous congress is anyone's guess.

Battle of Carberry Hill

In June 1567, the Lords previously loyal to Mary declared against Bothwell and the marriage. Similarly, the Lords of Parliament who signed the Bond and were previously against Mary, switched to her side.

From this short description, it can be gleaned that Scottish politics at the time were complicated and quick to change.

The rebellious Lords entered Edinburgh, fully armored and with a force on 11 June. By 15 June, Mary and Bothwell chose to leave the castle of Fa'side, about 3.2 kilometers southeast of Musselburgh, and took position on Carberry Hill. Mary's troops made use of a trench that had been dug for a different battle that took place a couple years before. Her army was equipped with around seven cannons, 300 pikemen, and about 200 trained musket men, for a roughly 2,000-strong army. The opposing force had about 2,000 soldiers, too, but were without cannons and had only a few volunteers from Edinburgh who could use a musket.

The battle began on a rather hot day, with Mary's troops having little to nothing to drink. The parties taunted each other for hours, from late morning until evening. The French ambassador tried unsuccessfully to negotiate a peace, followed by Bothwell firing a cannon at some of the opposition who were trying to spur Mary into action. Eventually, Bothwell agreed to settle things via single combat. Bothwell then summarily dismissed each opposing person willing to take up the challenge, as they were beneath his noble status.

Slowly, members of Bothwell's party began to ride off, some apologizing to the queen. Bothwell himself headed for Dunbar with his guard. Mary chose to surrender to the rebellious lords after Bothwell left. Robert Birrel or Birrell, a citizen of Edinburgh, wrote an account of the event in his diary,

> The 15 day being sonneday, the armies came within view. The one stood upone Carberry Hills, with 4 regiments of shouldiours, and six field-pieces of brasse: the uther armey stoode over against it, messingers going betwixt them all day till neir night; dureing which parley the Duke [Bothwell] fled secretly to Dunbar, and the Queine [Mary] came and randred herself

prisoner to ye Lordis, quho convoyed her to Edinburghe to the Provost's Lodgeing for yat night; Sr. Symeon Prestone of Craigmillar being Provost for ye time.

Mary's dress for the day was recorded by William Drury, Marshall of Berwick, who said of her clothing,

> The Queen's apparel in the field was after the fashion of the women of Edinburgh, in a red petticoat, sleeves tied with points a "partlyte," a velvet hat and muffler. She used great persuasions and encouragements to her people to have tried it by battle. For welcome the Lords showed her the banner with the dead body, which seeing they say that she wished she had never seen him. The banner was hanged out before her window at the Provost's house, wherewith she seemed much offended.

Mary surrendered in dramatic fashion, having changed out of her gorgeous, embroidered black dress with contrasting red cloak and coat, leaving those items with her richly embroidered hat at Fa'side Castle, and choosing to wear what were effectively rags that showed an embarrassing amount of her calves. The Lords took Mary to the aptly named Lochleven Castle, which is on an island in the middle of Loch Leven, where they imprisoned her. Roughly a month later, by 23 July, Mary miscarried twins. The next day, the recovering Mary was forced to abdicate to her one-year-old son, James VI. Mary would spend the next almost twenty years in some form of imprisonment or another, only to die by beheading.

Mary spent her last day of freedom in terrible heat, anxiously waiting with Bothwell, a man who may have killed Mary's second husband and may have raped Mary so he could become king, only to be abandoned by him on the field. One can imagine the range of emotion and brutal thoughts the twenty-four-year-old Mary Stuart endured on her last day as the free Queen of Scots.

Bothwell's Last Days

Bothwell ran off northward to Huntly Castle in Aberdeenshire, an interesting choice considering he had divorced Jean Gordon, Lady Huntly only recently. He could not have expected a warm welcome there. Bothwell was doggedly pursued during his flight.

After Huntly Castle, Bothwell went even farther north to Spynie Palace near Elgin. He next fled to Orkney, and then to Shetland. From Shetland, he was able to take four ships, including one laden with his treasure and moveable goods, north to Unst, on the northernmost portion of the Shetland Islands. Bothwell diverted the ship with his property to another portion of Shetland as he tried to leave the Port of Unst. Bothwell was attacked by his pursuers, which saw one of his remaining ships heavily damaged. Via a storm, Bothwell was pushed toward Norway.

Bothwell was apprehended in the Karmsund Strait, near the Høyevarde lighthouse. It is possible that his ship ran aground during a storm, making it simpler for him to be intercepted near the lighthouse, which did not do its job in this particular instance. One can still visit the lighthouse, although the building that stands today is only about 150 years old. It is thought that Bothwell wanted to reach his friend Frederick II of Denmark's court so that he could recruit an army and possibly a navy. Thereafter, he hoped to return to Scotland and free Mary. That's the romantic spin, at least. It is equally possible that he wished to assert himself as the spouse of the monarch, never mind preserving Mary as Queen of Scots.

Either way, the Norwegian officials took Bothwell into custody. Bothwell did not possess a passport from either Scotland or the joined kingdoms of Denmark and Norway that would allow him to be on the Scandinavian peninsula. His fortunes worsened from there. Anna Throndsen, Bothwell's abandoned first wife to whom he was still legally married under Danish and Norwegian standards, learned that he was once more within Norway and thus, within the jurisdiction of its courts.

Anna launched a complaint against Bothwell for abandoning the marriage. She was still well connected to the administration of Norway and Denmark through her relatives. Her cousin Erik Rosenkrantz was the governor of Bergenhus Fortress when Bothwell reappeared in Norway. The Bergenhus Fortress still stands and is close to the harbor in Bergen, Norway. It bears a building called Rosenkrantz Tower, named after Anna's cousin. This connection made it easy for Bothwell to be seized and tossed into the fortress's dungeon.

Anna, who had been made virtually destitute by Bothwell's abandonment, sought the return of her dowry. The case resolved when Bothwell offered Anna one of his ships, which she accepted. Bothwell was not released from captivity.

Frederick II of Denmark and Norway, who was aware that Bothwell was implicated in the murder of Henry Stewart, Lord Darnley, ordered that he be sent to Copenhagen. From there, Frederick II had Bothwell sent to Malmö Castle, across the Oresund in Sweden, for the next five years. In 1573, Bothwell was moved to Dragsholm Castle in Denmark. Bothwell was chained to a pillar, wearing a groove into the floor from pacing around the cell, until his death in April 1578. He was buried in Fårevejle church, in a crypt in a small chapel on the side of the church. His body was placed in a simple coffin, and he was buried without any regard for his status as an earl, duke, or king of any country.

Chapter 10

Anna of Denmark

Birth and Early Years

Anna von Oldenburg, known to English speakers as Anne of Denmark, was born on 12 December 1574 at Skanderborg Castle. Anna was born the second of seven children and was her parents' second daughter of four. Anna's parents, Sophia of Mecklenburg-Guestrow and Frederick II of Denmark, married in 1572. Sophia was roughly twenty-four years younger than her husband, but the two got on well. Sophia and Frederick II shared a common grandfather, namely, Frederick I of Denmark and Norway.

Anna's mother Sophia was regarded as an intellectual. She and her husband both shared an interest in the astronomer and scientist Tycho Brahe's teachings. She was a good businesswoman, too, managing her estates so well that she lent money to European monarchs later in life.

Anna's father Fredrick II was interested in learning and sought to invite intellectuals to court. Known to have suffered from dyslexia, Frederick was a very bright person with a good memory but struggled greatly with reading and writing. Unfortunately for Frederick, this gave him the inaccurate reputation in his youth of being illiterate and unintelligent.

Rather importantly for the Scots, Frederick was supportive of the country. He showed compassion towards Scottish noblemen when it seemed appropriate, such as James Hepburn, 4th Earl of Bothwell, when he innocently arrived at court in Denmark in 1560. He also showed a firm support toward the Scottish monarchy when required, such as the imprisonment of the very same Bothwell in 1567 until Bothwell's death. Frederick considered wooing Mary, Queen of Scots after her return from France to Scotland in 1561, but as seen, that came to naught.

Frederick II was known to have an aggressive streak, too, beginning his reign with a successful conquest of Schleswig-Holstein, followed by the poorly executed Northern Seven Years' War, which was effectively begun by Frederick II because of his displeasure over the end of the Kalmar Union.[1] Recall that part

---
1. The Kalmar Union was an agreement between Norway, Sweden, and Denmark, made in Kalmar, Sweden in 1397. Denmark and Holstein dominated the union, which was anathema to Sweden. The union, with the occasional interruption, lasted until 1523. A bloody incident under Christian II of Denmark in Sweden was the final straw.

of Margaret of Denmark's dowry back in 1468 included property which was part of the Kalmar Union, namely Shetland and Orkney.

Frederick adored his wife Sophia. The two got on famously, being described as inseparable during their marriage. When Frederick became seriously ill with malaria in 1575, Sophia personally cared for him. All in all, the couple had a very loving, successful marriage.

Life at the Danish Court

Anna and her elder sister Elisabeth were raised in Guestrow, modern-day Mecklenburg-Vorpommern, Germany. Their first language was German. Her maternal grandfather Ulrich III of Mecklenburg-Guestrow replaced the former medieval castle in Guestrow, with construction beginning in 1558. The structure of the medieval castle, which had stood since the late 14th century, had a heavy Slavic influence. It was originally held by the princes of Werle, whose territory extended east. The line was extinguished in the early 15th century, leaving the territory to Ulrich's forbears.

The original castle caught fire in 1557, causing the southern wing to fall into disrepair. Ulrich, who jointly ruled the duchy with his older brother, was perhaps seeking to show off his own wealth at what was a secondary court. Renaissance architecture was introduced to northern Germany by the early 1550s, and as such, Ulrich chose to renovate and update his palace in the west of the family's territory. He succeeded.

Anna and Elisabeth were joined by their younger brother, future king Christian IV in Guestrow. The royal children made frequent trips to their parents' court, watching it evolve out of the Renaissance period and toward the Baroque aesthetic that was popular in European courts beginning in the early 17th century. Anna's father also had a flair for building projects and enjoyed the fine arts. Music and poetry were very popular at the Danish court of Anna's youth, as were masques and pageants. Anna's memories and experiences from such a cultured environment remained with her for the rest of her life.

Death of Anna's Father and Negotiations for Anna's Marriage

Frederick II of Denmark and Norway died 4 April 1588 when he was not quite fifty-four years old. Anna's mother Sophia became Dowager Queen Sophia of Denmark, retiring to her estates granted through her dowager pension. Sophia was quite successful financially and long-lived, surviving until 14 October 1631.

Before the death of Anna's father, a Danish bride for James VI of Scotland was sought. At first, Anna's elder sister Elisabeth was seen as the prime candidate by Scottish ambassadors at the Danish court. Elisabeth was a popular potential bride amongst the German and Imperial aristocracy, leading Frederick II to grant his blessing for her to marry a German prince. To soothe the Scots, Frederick promised that his second daughter Anna would be available for James VI.

Keen was James, but nothing much came of marital negotiations until after the death of Anna's father in 1588, as mentioned. Anna's clever mother Sophia quickly negotiated the Danish-Scots match for her daughter. Sophia pushed through the marriage despite arguing with the Danish regency council over who controlled Anna's minor brother, who was now King Christian IV of Denmark and Norway. Sophia concluded negotiations in July 1589. The terms included that Anna brought with her a dowry of £170,000 Scots, and in return, Anna would receive Falkland and Linlithgow palaces. Anna was allowed to return to Denmark if James predeceased her.

Anna was over the moon with excitement. James was still slightly tepid, even though Anna's family prepared for her coming journey across the North Sea,

> assure the King that great provision is made for the young lady's coming; 12 ships fully furnished, three of them most princely appareled, besides [four] for horses and stuff—16 ships in all. They tell of rich provision of apparel, jewels, furnishing for horses, coaches and women; more than 500 tailors and embroiderers have been at work upon it for three months. The Queen-mother has bought many jewels for her, especially pearls.
>
> Many ladies and noble men are coming with the princess at their own great charge. This forwardness is here thought strange even by the King himself, because there has been no dealing yet that they might assure themselves he would marry there; yet all here rejoice, hoping they will refuse none of the King's demands, and desiring the match to proceed, especially the trade towns.

It is possible that the news of a completed marital contract had not made its way to James yet, but it is unlikely that he was completely in the dark. Gossip can operate faster than diplomatic channels, at times. Whatever the state of information-spreading across the 16th-century North Sea, James sent his betrothed a gift of jewels, including a heart-shaped amethyst.

Anna immediately expressed her devotion to James, whiling away the hours until her wedding and departure for Scotland by embroidering shirts and other items for her future husband. It should be noted that the marriage would be a dynastic success, with her bloodline remaining part of the current monarchy of the United Kingdom.

Emotionally, the marriage would be unfulfilling for Anna. James, for any soft feelings he had toward Anna, may have been more interested in male courtiers. While this is not the appropriate place for a full discussion of James's sexuality, his behavior during adulthood and remarks made by members of his court seem to support that James took a heavy interest in some of the men at his court. If true, could explain at least some of his cool passion towards her.

Turning back to happier early days for Anna, she enjoyed a proxy marriage in Denmark on 20 August 1589. Within a couple of weeks, Anna was ready to sail to her new home, kingdom, and husband. Her fleet prepared to leave on 5 September 1589 from Denmark. In preparation for her arrival,

> As soon as her majesty shall appear in the road, the Earl Bothwell,[2] the Lord Seton, Sir Robert Melville, with some 30 persons of good accompt, are appointed to go aboard, and with them Mr. Peter Yonge to make the harangue in Latin, if her health may permit to hear the same. At her coming to the scaffold upon the shore, the Ladye Marr, principal, and with her the ladies Seton, Boyne, the lady Chancellor, and Diddop, with some 30 persons shall meet her, and upon the scaffold one Mr. James Elphinstone, one of the college of justice, shall make the oration. His Majesty meets her there, and shall convey her to her lodging in Leith, where she is to remain till she shall have well reposed herself. When she shall come to the town of Edinburgh, one Mr. John Russell, advocate, shall make the oration to her entry.

As is typical with best-laid plans, these went awry.

James VI of Scotland, the Romantic Hero

Bad weather cast Anna back to the shores of Norway. After additional attempts, Anna was too seasick and tired of misadventure to retry the voyage. Anna wrote to her husband in French,

> we have already put out to sea four or five times but have always been driven to the ports from which we left by contrary winds and other problems which arose, which is the cause why ... all this company ... [will] make no further attempt at this time but to defer the voyage until the spring.

---

2. Francis Stewart, 5th Earl of Bothwell was an illegitimate cousin of James VI's, descended from a natural son of James V. He was created earl in 1577. Mary, Queen of Scots left him items in her 1565 will.

James was not pleased with this development. At around this time, James wrote the poem, "A Complaint against the Contrary Winds that Hindered the Queen to come to Scotland from Denmark," which is as follows:

> From sacred throne in heaven Empyrick hie[3]
> A breathe divine in poëts breasts does blow
> Wherethrough all things inferior in degree
> As vassals unto them do homage show
> There songs enchants Apollo's self ye know
> And chaste Diana's coach can haste or stay
> Can change the course of planets high or low
> And make the earth obey them every way
> Make rocks to dance, huge hills to skip and play
> Beasts, fouls, and fish to follow them allwhere
> Though thus the heaven, the sea, and earth obey,
> Yet mutins the mid region of the air.
> What hateful Juno, Æolus enticeth
> Whereby contrarious Zephyr thus ariseth.

In the greatest romantic overture of his life, James set sail for Norway to retrieve his bride. His grandfather James V had done the very same when he retrieved Madeleine de Valois from France. James left Scotland for Norway on 22 October 1589. After some delay caused by autumn storms on the North Sea, James arrived in Norway on 19 November 1589.

Anna was surprised when she learned that, not only was James coming in person, but that he already arrived in Norway and was on the way to her. Their first meeting was awkward, but nothing which the couple could not overcome. Anna was a month shy of fifteen years old, and James was twenty-three. Upon learning of his imminent arrival at the Old Bishop's Palace, Anna rushed to the Great Hall to meet James. As soon as he entered, weather-beaten and clad in red, she hurried forward to greet him. James tried to greet Anna with a kiss, a Scottish tradition. This was not customary in Denmark and startled Anna. The two managed to converse in French, as Anna did not speak Scots, English, or Latin, and James did not speak German. He expressed that greeting with a kiss was customary in Scotland. Anna relented, James kissed her, and the two enjoyed a conversation after that.

The next day, James returned to visit with Anna. The couple spent the entire day together. He wore blue velvet for this second meeting. James decided that

---

3. hurry

he preferred to stay in Norway for the winter, rather than returning to Scotland immediately as he promised his lords. Anna was relieved that she did not have to make a sea crossing during tempestuous late-autumn to early-winter weather.

Anna celebrated her marriage with James on 23 November 1589 in Oslo at the Bishop's Palace. The service was given in French in the Great Hall. As a wedding present, James gave Anna Dunfermline lands and abbey.

After their nuptials, the King and Queen of Scots stayed in Norway through Christmastide. Queen Sophia invited Anna and James to spend time with her in Denmark. The wealthy dowager queen sent well-appointed sleds to bring the couple to her home. The horse-drawn sleighs were upholstered with black velvet and gold stitching. They left for Denmark on 7 January 1590 and arrived at Sophia's court around 17 January. Anna must have been overjoyed to see her family once more, especially after saying tearful forever-farewells back in September 1589.

Anna had the good fortune of attending her elder sister Elisabeth's wedding in April 1590. James was able to converse with numerous intellectuals at the Danish court, including the interesting Tycho Brahe, the Danish astronomer who produced a massive body of work during his lifetime. His research propelled forward the science of astronomy. Brahe's work also impacted the understanding of physics. His passions included alchemy and studying medicine. James went on to write at least a couple of poems about Brahe.

Once spring arrived in 1590, the sixteen ships prepared back in the autumn were reappointed for the couple's journey back to Scotland. They arrived at Leith on 1 May 1590 to much fanfare. The royals remained in Leith for several days, in part to await the preparation of Holyroodhouse for their arrival and in part to rest.

Elizabeth I of England approved of Anna as James's wife. Elizabeth sent her a letter in French, welcoming the Danish princess,

> The goodness of our Lord having been so manifested toward you that after many misfortunes you have escaped the mercy of the waves, and it has pleased him at length to bring you safe and sound to the realm of the King your spouse, the news whereof has been very acceptable to us.... Also we would not fail to give you a friendly token thereof by our own letters, and by the same means to let you know how infinitely we rejoice at this nuptial union between the King our good brother and you, deeming his happiness so much the greater.

The country was relieved and joyful to have their new queen and did not hold back when she arrived in Edinburgh. Anna rode alone in a carriage drawn by eight brown horses. She wore white for the occasion. After arriving, she was gifted a purple box with the letter "A" on the lid. The letter was made of diamonds.

Anna's coronation was held on 17 May 1590. It was the first coronation of a queen since September 1543, and the first Protestant coronation for a Queen of Scotland. The Presbyterian minister Robert Bruce performed the ceremony. A bit of oil was poured on her bared right shoulder by him. The crown was placed on her head, and she was handed the scepter. The ceremony and oath were repeated in French for Anna. She was now the queen consort.

Anna, raised a Lutheran, adhered to that religion for a time whilst her husband was a Calvinist. Their religious differences did not cause any issues between the couple in the early years of their lives. The perfidious Scots sometimes believed that the couple had not gone far enough in their religious reforms.

Anna's First Child

Anna's first child, a son named Henry Frederick, was born on 19 February 1594 at Stirling Castle. The Scots, and no doubt Anna's husband, were delighted and relieved by the birth of a healthy son. The people celebrated with dancing in the streets and bonfires. James ordered a mere two days after Henry Frederick's birth that Henry Frederick remain at Stirling Castle to be raised by the Earl of Mar, and that no one may release the prince to Anna without the king's express orders. Anna, by now nineteen years old, was beside herself with frustration. This pattern would be repeated throughout their marriage. James, overly logical, would put something in place. Anna would respond strongly and with great emotion, which James could not manage.

Henry Frederick was baptized that December at great expense to Anna. Most of her dowry was used to pay for the event and surrounding festivities. Anna did not seem to mind, especially since she very much enjoyed pomp and pageantry. Anna never abandoned her Oldenburg roots.

Subsequent Children

Anna became pregnant again around the spring of 1595. She was still utterly distraught over being separated from her baby, even if that was Scottish custom. She miscarried in July that year. It was attributed to her intense feelings about Henry Frederick being kept away at Stirling Castle. On top of that, Anna could not get along with Henry Frederick's caregivers, which left her preferring not to see her son rather than be in their company.

Anna was pregnant again by early 1596 and welcomed her daughter Elizabeth on 19 August 1596 at Dunfermline Palace. James, who was roughly 18 miles or 29 kilometers away at Callendar, got on the road to Dunfermline as soon as he learned of his daughter's birth. Elizabeth was baptized in the royal chapel at Holyroodhouse. She was raised at Linlithgow Palace, which James saw as a compromise with Anna given that Linlithgow was much nearer to both Holyroodhouse and Dunfermline. Anna was still unimpressed, but undoubtedly glad to have her daughter nearby.

Anna was pregnant again in spring 1598 and gave birth to a daughter named Margaret on Christmas Eve that year. Little Margaret was born at Dalkeith. She was baptized in April 1599 at Holyroodhouse, just like her older sister. Margaret was placed with her sister Elizabeth at Linlithgow Palace. Margaret became sick in March 1600 of an unknown illness, passing away that same month. She was buried at Holyrood Abbey by the end of March.

Anna was already pregnant at the time of Margaret's passing, although she may not have been aware. Her fourth child, a boy named Charles, arrived on 19 November 1600. He, too, was born at Dunfermline Palace. Like his siblings, Charles was baptized at the royal chapel in Holyroodhouse, on 23 December 1600.

Anna's last child born on Scottish soil was a little boy named Robert. He came into the world on 18 January 1602 at Dunfermline. Once news reached Edinburgh, where James was at the time, cannons were fired in celebration of the little prince's birth. He was baptized at Dunfermline Abbey, being brought into the building on a purple velvet cushion. He was baptized on 2 May 1602. By the middle of the month, both Robert and Princess Elizabeth were sick. Elizabeth had measles. Having lost half of her children already to either miscarriage or childhood illnesses, Anna remarked to James that she was prepared for God to take one of them. She told James that she felt pregnant again, too. Other than this comment, perhaps said to comfort herself and James, Anna was not in fact pregnant that month. Little Robert passed away on 27 May 1602, but Elizabeth Stuart survived.

The Throne of England

Elizabeth I of England died on 24 March 1603. Once James received the news, he immediately left for London. Anna was pregnant and could not head out so quickly. Besides her delicate state, Anna had a better idea. She would go to Stirling, retrieve Henry Frederick, and travel with him and the other royal Scots children to London. Henry Frederick's keepers did not agree.

The pregnant Anna assembled a group of supportive nobles. She believed that, with James and her son Henry Frederick's keeper gone to England, she could go to Stirling and collect her nine-year-old son. Anna had spent very little time with Henry Frederick over the last few years. Remember that Anna, in response to James's restrictions regarding raising the heir, in a fit of pique declared she would not visit her firstborn anymore.

Anna arrived at Stirling Castle with her nobles, but only two were allowed to accompany her inside. This must have sucked the wind out of Anna's sails. Henry Frederick's caregivers did not wish to violate the order of their king, and Anna left without her son. She had another strong emotional reaction to this defiance, resulting in Anna miscarrying a male child.

Anna, who in the recent past had quietly converted to Catholicism, was accused of staging a coup. The accusations did not go very far, but James reminded her that her main role was to be James's dutiful queen. Anna responded by demanding permission to bring Henry Frederick with her to England, and James finally relented. Anna left for England by mid-May, allegedly with the embalmed body of her miscarried child to show that she was not plotting against James. How that was supposed to show that Anna was not trying to kidnap Henry Frederick and seize the regency of Scotland is a mystery, making this report dubious.

Anna Journeys to England

On 28 May 1603,

> "the queen and prince came from Stirling. There were sundry English ladies and gentlewomen come to give her the convoy. The 30th day, being Tuesday, her M[ajesty] and the prince came to St. Giles' Kirk, well conveyed with coaches, herself and the prince in her own coach, which came with her out of Denmark, and the English gentlewomen in the rest of the coaches. They heard a good sermon in the church, and thereafter road home to Holyroodhouse."

The coach in which they rode might have been the same one Anna used during her entry into Edinburgh. "The 1 June, the queen with the prince [Henry Frederick] took journey to England, and the next day after, the princess [Elizabeth] took journey." Prince Charles remained in Dunfermline because he was recovering from illness.

Anna's progress from Edinburgh to London caused quite a stir. Many people followed the royal train until reaching London. The crowds were deemed unruly. Nobles lined the route to meet her, and there was a huge gathering of England's lords and ladies at Windsor awaiting her arrival.

Anna was the last queen of Scotland to primarily reside in Scotland.

Anna's First Years in England

The coronation festivities kicked off with Henry Frederick being installed as a Knight of the Garter on 2 July 1603. The next couple of weeks were spent preparing for the royal couple's joint coronation. The last coronation in England had been held in 1559 for Elizabeth I.

The coronation was held on 15 July 1603. Anna wore her hair down and was dressed in crimson velvet. A simple gold coronet was on her head. As a secret Catholic, Anna politely refused the Protestant communion. Rumors began that she was Catholic, something which Anna never admitted publicly.

Anna received a new jointure. Most of the property had been given to Katharine of Aragon almost a hundred years before. Anna retained income from her jointure in Scotland, making her a wealthy woman. This income allowed her to become a patron of the arts in England and continue to indulge in her passion for building projects.

Anna was pregnant again by late 1604. Much excitement attended her pregnancy and the birth of Princess Mary on 8 April 1605. Mary was named after her paternal grandmother, and the first royal baby born on English soil since the birth of Edward VI in October 1537.

Anna was advised to go to Greenwich Palace in preparation for her baby's arrival. Anna wanted to be present for and participate in *The Masque of Blackness*, a masque that Anna had commissioned. Illnesses such as measles and smallpox were afflicting courtiers, no doubt making Anna's doctors worried for her safety and the safety of the baby. A couple of Anna's ladies were excused from performing in the masque, held on 6 January 1605, specifically due to illness. The show went on, to very mixed reviews. Thereafter, Anna went to Greenwich.

Mary's birth was celebrated throughout Scotland and England. The people preferred that Mary would have been a boy, but the symbolism of her birth could not be ignored. Church bells rang, and celebratory bonfires were lit.

Mary's baptism was held at Greenwich Palace's chapel. For the occasion, held on 5 May 1605, Mary wore purple velvet with a long train. It was decorated with ermine fur and embroidered with gold thread. After the ceremony, James gifted Anna with jewelry.

A year later, Anna's last baby was born. Sophia, named after her maternal grandmother, was born on 22 June 1606 at Greenwich Palace. It was soon noted that Sophia was a weak infant, and she was quickly baptized. She died on 26 June, a mere four days old. A joust that was to be held in celebration of Sophia's birth was canceled. Anna's brother Christian IV of Denmark was already en route to England, being invited by James to participate in the joust. Christian remained in England for roughly a month but spent very little time with Anna. She was depressed over the loss of baby Sophia and remained at Greenwich throughout the rest of June and all of July.

Sophia's black velvet-covered coffin was sent to Westminster Abbey by barge. She was buried in a tomb that looks like a crib, in Henry VII of England's Lady Chapel. It can still be seen today. To the utter devastation of Anna, Sophia's sister Mary joined her in death in September 1607 after being seized by pneumonia. Perhaps all the more tragic, two-and-a-half-year-old Mary could talk. She allegedly repeated the words, "I go, I go!" in the hours leading up to her death, and faintly whispered them just before she passed.

Mary died on 16 September 1607. Three earls went to Anna to inform her of Mary's death. Anna, perceiving why they'd come, did not want to hear the words. She began grieving and ordered that James be told. She made plans for Mary's burial next to her sister Sophia. Mary's tomb shows the toddler wearing early 17th-century dress, resting on her side, and gazing at her sister Sophia's tomb.

After the deaths of Sophia and Mary, Anna made it plain that she did not want to bear more children. With seventy percent of her pregnancies ending in miscarriage, stillbirth, or premature death, one can understand her reasoning. After this, Anna's and James's independent lifestyles became separate lives.

Anna and James remained friendly to each other but lived almost apart. They had somewhat established that pattern in Scotland, but now each was more dedicated to their own pursuits and courts. James had plenty of time for his male favorites, to whatever degree he wished to enjoy their company. Anna was free to continue as a patron of the arts and regularly treated her courtiers in London to cultural sights and events.

Anna's Lifestyle and Personality

Anna spent exorbitant amounts of money refurbishing and renovating Dunfermline Palace, said to be her favorite residence in Scotland. The palace itself was connected to Dunfermline Abbey by a pend, a passageway through an occupied building. The pend, built into the gatehouse, is medieval in structure. The overall gatehouse took the place of the abbey's former guesthouse.

Malcolm III established a royal residence at Dunfermline in the 11th century. The religious building next to the palace began as a priory founded by Queen, later Saint, Margaret, Malcolm's wife. It was later augmented to an abbey in the early 12th century. Margaret was buried within the abbey, and a shrine built for her.

It is difficult to track the build-works done on Dunfermline Palace because the records have largely not survived. The palace was either renovated or enlarged in around 1429, as evidenced by a purchase of timber. The refectory was targeted in 1560 during the height of the Reformation in Scotland. Several years prior, St. Margaret's body was removed in pieces and sent to the Continent. Marie de Guise is said to have sent parts of St. Margaret's body to France.

James VI ordered the palace renovated in 1587. Months later, the palace was prepared for Anna before her arrival. It was, after all, a wedding gift for his Danish bride. After her arrival, Anna built an entirely new portion of the palace. It was separate from the original palace building. A fire ripped through the complex in 1624. The portion of the palace which Anna commissioned was completely torn down in the 18th century.

Anna spent an unknown amount of money on her favorite palace. She enjoyed having artists, poets, and other creatives present at her court. She spent huge quantities of money on masques, plays, and jewelry. James spent large amounts of money, too. The pair can be recognized as patrons of the arts. With that came large expenditures. The Scots were not impressed with the degree of mirth and merriment that took place at what they believed should have been a dour, serious, Presbyterian court. Anna and James carried on, anyway. Between the two of them, they were in debt to an almost dire degree after ten years of marriage.

James becoming king of England could not have come at a better time, financially. Anna blossomed in some ways at the court in London, where it was common to have the sort of entertainments in which she indulged.

Anna appeared to favor Greenwich Palace as well, birthing her last two children there. She spent money on improving and personalizing the palace. She commissioned the building of the Queen's House at Greenwich in 1616, which was not finished until long after her death.

Anna's personality is a paradox. On the one hand, the Scots' views are that Anna was too serious and almost cold. On the other, she would have serious emotional outbursts, particularly when it came to the care and raising of her children. In 1606, three years after Anna's arrival in England, a Venetian ambassador there commented,

> She is intelligent and prudent; and knows the disorders of the government, in which she has no part, though many hold that as the King is most devoted to her, she might play as large a role as she wished. But she is young and averse to trouble; she sees that those who govern desire to be left alone, and so she professes indifference. All she ever does is to beg a favour for someone. She is full of kindness for those who support her, but on the other hand she is terrible, proud, unendurable to those she dislikes.

It seems that either a person liked Anna or did not. She was either charming or rude, depending on with whom she interacted.

Anna's Later Years

In 1612, it was time for fourteen-year-old Elizabeth Stuart to marry. She had no shortage of suitors. Anna's preference was for Elizabeth to marry a prince or king, especially because Anna herself was the daughter, sister, and wife of kings, and would become the mother of a king. From James's perspective, Elizabeth could only marry someone who was of the Protestant faith. To Anna's disappointment but Elizabeth's delight, Frederick V, Count Palatine of the Rhine, was chosen for Elizabeth. Frederick arrived in England in October 1612. It is possible that Elizabeth spoke some German already given that Anna was a German speaker. This would have enabled Elizabeth and Frederick to get to know each other easily. A February wedding in England was planned.

Unfortunately, tragedy struck Anna and the courts of England and Scotland in November 1612. Prince Henry Frederick was afflicted with typhoid fever and died. He was buried with impressive pomp and circumstance on 7 December 1612. Anna was tremendously sorrowful over the death of her eldest son. At the age of not quite thirty-eight, Anna survived eight of her ten children.

At around this time, Anna's health very slowly began to fail. She was pained by gout beginning around 1612. She experienced serious pain in her feet starting in 1614. She removed herself from court by 1615, after struggling with dropsy. Her gout worsened throughout 1615. She removed to Somerset House in January 1616, thereafter, taking little care of her appearance.

Anna spent time at both Oatlands and Greenwich Palace later in 1616 and failed to accompany James on a visit to Scotland. She did occasionally rally but was reckoned to be in quite poor health by the end of 1617. The year 1618 was not much better for Anna. She removed to Hampton Court Palace, where she was joined by her son Charles. Anna's body was shutting down by late February 1619, including her losing her eyesight. She died on 2 March 1619, with her son Charles at her side. After her passing, James wrote Anna one last poem,

> So did my Queen from hence her court remove
> And left off earth to be enthroned above.
> She's changed, not dead, for sure no good prince dies,
> But, as the sun, sets, only for to rise.

Two months after her death, Anna was buried in Henry VII's Lady Chapel. A simple engraving in the floor marks her resting place.

Chapter 11

Henriette Marie of France

Early Life

Henriette Marie de Bourbon, frequently called Henrietta Maria of France by English speakers, was born 25 or 26 November 1609. Born at the Louvre Palace, she was the youngest child of Marie de' Medici and Henri IV of France. She was part of the newly founded Bourbon dynasty, after the Valois line failed with the deaths of Henri II's and Catherine de' Medici's sons.

Tragedy struck when she was less than six months old. Henriette's father Henri was assassinated on 14 May 1610 during the coronation of his queen. Henriette's mother Maria, who wed Henriette's father in October 1600, had to wait almost ten years for her coronation. Maria's coronation ceremony was finally held on 13 May 1610. Henri decided it was time, it seems, because he wished to involve himself in the Jülich Feud, a war which broke out after Duke Johann Wilhelm of Jülich-Cleves-Berg died without heirs.[1] If Henri died whilst engaging in battle or negotiation amongst Johann Wilhelm's relatives, then Marie was recognized formally as queen. That would pave the way for her to hold the regency for their son, the future Louis XIII. Unfortunately for the family, this would come to pass all too quickly.

After the coronation festivities, Henri was traveling in a coach when it was stopped due to traffic congestion. A mentally ill religious fanatic, a devout Catholic[2] named François Ravaillac, took hold of the opportunity and attacked Henri with a knife. Henri was stabbed between the second and third ribs, passing away that same day. Henriette's mother was appointed regent, and Henriette's life was changed irrevocably.

Henriette and her siblings were raised by a governess named Françoise de Montglat. Françoise held the position from roughly 1600 to 1615. All the royal children, legitimate and illegitimate, were raised together under Françoise's watchful eye. Françoise's daughter Jeanne, thirty years older than

---

1. Johann Wilhelm was a fraternal nephew of Anna of Cleves, Henry VIII of England's fourth wife and the first German queen of England. He was the last von der Mark duke.
2. This by no means implies that Catholics in particular or those who observe religion in general are mentally ill, but this particular person showed a pattern of behavior which appears to illustrate severe mental disturbance.

Henriette's oldest sibling Louis XIII of France, served the royal children too. The children call the women "Mamangat" and "Mamie", respectively, even into their adulthoods. Jeanne was appointed as lady-in-waiting to Henriette and her older sister Christine.

Henriette received an education befitting her station. She learned to read and write, although she was not particularly interested in either skill. She was exposed to the glittering French court, taking part in plays. She was taught to dance and sing, necessary skills for a French princess. She also learned practical skills, such as how to ride a horse.

Henriette spent most of her early years with her brother Gaston. He was closest to her in age of her legitimate siblings. The two were baptized at the same time on 15 June 1614 at the Queen's Chapel in the Louvre Palace.

Henriette was raised as a Catholic, adhering to the religion throughout her life. Carmelite nuns were a frequent presence at court. The nuns had their primary residence in Vannes, modern Brittany, living at the monastery of the Three Marys. Henriette grew to have personality traits and interests like her mother. Both women were pious and enjoyed the fine arts.

Henriette's mother, who was very involved in the regency of Henriette's brother Louis XIII, would not loosen her grip on power even after Louis came of age. Several coups were staged against her, although none was more successful than Louis's own plan to overthrow his mother in April 1617 and seize back the kingdom. After capturing and killing Marie de' Medici's main supporter in court, Marie was exiled to Blois and politely imprisoned there for several years. Henriette, only six years old, had now suffered the loss of her father and separation from her mother.

Marie escaped from Blois in February 1619, was taken across the bridge, and escorted by supporters to the Château d'Angoulême. From there, Marie launched what was referred to as the "war of mother and son." Henriette's brother Louis XIII repeatedly tried to keep their mother Marie in exile whilst negotiating peace with her. He realized that, so long as Marie was exiled, she and disgruntled nobles would not stop challenging him. She was allowed to return to court by 1621 and was formally involved in the French government by the end of 1621.

Although she could not have guessed it, the internal upheaval at the French court may have prepared Henriette for her own future troubles. By the time her mother was completely welcomed back at court, Henriette was around thirteen years old and would have been aware of the conflict between her mother and brother. If Henriette were not overtly aware at that young age, she likely would have grown to understand it.

A Marriage for Henriette

In 1622, James VI & I of Scotland, Ireland and England was negotiating with Spain for a bride for Charles Stuart, the future Charles I. Maria Anna of Spain's brother Philip IV had come to the Spanish throne in 1621 and was eager to shore up alliances. He approached James, no doubt hopeful that he could also bring the kingdoms back into the Catholic fold by marrying his devout sister to the heir of the Scottish and English crowns.

Things moved forward, and a papal dispensation for the marriage was granted. It was decided in early 1623 that Charles would travel to Spain to meet Maria Anna. On the way there, he stopped at the French court, where Henriette and Charles met for the first time. He left an impression on her before continuing his journey to Spain.

Charles was not on his best behavior in Madrid. His carousing put the Spanish royal family on edge and made them doubt whether he would be a suitable match for Maria Anna. Maria Anna insisted that Charles convert to Catholicism, which he refused to do. The match was abandoned, and Charles went home single. By the end of 1623, it was decided that a French bride be sought for Charles.

The following year, in February 1624, a diplomat was sent to the French court to see whether Henriette was available to marry, and whether her brother Louis XIII favored a match between the then Prince of Wales and Louis's youngest sibling. The diplomat was in Paris by 25 February 1624.

In honor of carnival and the impending French-Anglo alliance, a ballet was performed that very same night on 25 February 1624. It was commissioned by Anne of Austria, Louis XIII's wife. The ballet was called *Ballet de la reine, dansé par les nymphes des jardins*, or *Ballet of the Queen, Danced by the Nymphs of the Gardens*. Henriette, who performed in ballets commissioned by Anne of Austria in 1621 and 1623, participated in this production as well. The story of the ballet opens with Mercury, the messenger god, welcoming the Gods of the Gardens after winter. The gods arriving included Spring, Flora, Vertumnus, Zephyrus, and Pomona. Venus makes an appearance too, and brings springtime's nymphs with her to the mortal realm. It is likely that Henriette participated as one of the nymphs, who were all dressed in costumes resembling flowers. As such, it is usually assumed that she played the role of Iris.

The English diplomat had an opportunity to espy Henriette whilst people were preparing for the ballet. He had nothing but a glowing review of her,

> [Henriette] is a lovely, sweet, young creature. Her growth is not great yet, but her shape is perfect, and they all swear, that her sister the Princess

[Christine] (who is now grown a tall goodly lady) was not taller than she is at her age.

The day after Henriette's performance in the ballet,[3] the diplomat sent a letter to Charles, Prince of Wales. He encouraged Charles to match with Henriette,

> Sir, if your intentions proceed this way…you will find a lady of much loveliness and sweetness to deserve your affection, as any creature under heaven can do. And Sir, by all her fashions since my being here, and by what I hear from the ladies, it is most visible to me, her infinite value, and respect unto you…the impressions I had of her were but ordinary, but the amazement extraordinary to find her…the sweetest creature in France. Her growth is very little, short for her age; and her wisdom infinitely beyond it. I heard her discourse with her Mother [Dowager Queen Marie de' Medici], and the ladies about her, with extraordinary discretion, and quickness. She dances…as well as ever I saw any creature; they say she sings most sweetly, I am sure she looks so.

Quite the glowing review. Later in her life, Henriette was described as having uneven shoulders, a pretty face, but protruding teeth. One cannot have everything.

Henriette did have at least one speaking part in the ballet. It should be noted that a ballet at the French court in the 17th century was analogous to an English masque. During the ballet, Henriette, the most eligible bachelorette in France, addressed her mother,

> Today when I [Henriette] appear so beautiful,
> Shining in a splendor without equal:
> If I am a new flower;
> I am one of the Sunflowers,
> As soon as I see you appear,
> I turn in all directions
> Toward your celestial beauties,
> Great Sun who gave birth to me.

Lovely words for any mother to hear. Henriette was the only person given spoken lines other than her sister-in-law Queen Anne. This surely drew the attention of the English ambassador.

---

3. No original livrets from the ballet exist, so it is unknown which part Henriette played.

Whatever Charles's developing intentions for Henriette were, there was still the pesky issue of his marriage contract with Maria Anna of Spain. Making matters more complicated, Maria Anna was a niece of Anne of Austria, Queen Consort of France. The English and the French had to craftily break off the Spanish match to make way for the Anglo-French.

Marie de' Medici, Henriette's mother, subtly communicated with the English ambassador about her support for the match with Charles. It was effective, and the marriage contract was drafted. Henriette's future father-in-law James VI & I died in March 1625, a couple of months before Henriette's proxy marriage took place in front of Notre Dame de Paris on 1 May 1625. Charles's Protestant representatives were present. After the proxy marriage, Henriette and her Catholic company processed into the cathedral to hear Mass, whilst Charles's men remained outside. Henriette was fifteen years old, and Charles was twenty-four.

Once married, she was duly shipped off to England to begin her new life as a queen consort. It would prove to be a difficult role for her.

Henriette's First Years in England

Henriette did not speak English, was a Catholic, and did not get along well with Charles. She met with her new husband on 13 June 1625 in Canterbury. The couple soon consummated their relationship. Leading up to her marriage with Charles, he caused several blunders in Parliament which later came back to haunt him. Henriette of course had no idea.

Henriette, as a French princess from the Bourbon dynasty, was not trained on how to be a foreign consort, and especially not one at a Protestant court. She had only learned to speak, read, and write French, and would have picked up some Latin from attending mass. Before Charles came calling, it was assumed that she would wed a French noble to strengthen support for her brother. On top of all this, the Pope himself tasked Henriette with assisting the Catholics in her new realm.

Henriette arrived with a large French retinue, many of whom stayed on at her court. Of course, she brought with her several Catholic priests. Her new English subjects did not appreciate the presence of the priests, and it's likely that the Scottish subjects did not like it either.

A coronation for Charles was held on 2 February 1626 at Westminster Abbey. Henriette did not participate because she was Catholic and would only allow a Catholic priest to perform the important parts of her coronation service. Henriette was allowed to watch the coronation, and great care was taken to prepare a space suitable for her to observe her husband's literal crowning moment. She declined attending the opening of Charles's first post-coronation opening of parliament for the same religious reasons.

Charles dismissed many of Henriette's French retinue, including her priests, that summer. She flagrantly violated English laws in place since the reign of Henry VIII by engaging in a pilgrimage. Added to that, the pilgrimage in which she engaged was to Tyburn, the site of the gallows where Henry VIII executed the primary actors in the 1537 Pilgrimage of Grace.

It took a few years for Henriette to conceive with Charles. This was due to Henriette's strict Catholic training, meaning that she could lie with her husband on certain days only. She had to withhold her favors on days prescribed by her strict adherence to Catholicism. After the arrival of their first child, the couple had eight children in eleven years, and a ninth child after a four-year pause.

Their first baby, a boy named Charles James, was born and died on 13 May 1629. Their second child, a son named Charles, was born on 29 May 1630. Next came Mary Henrietta, born on 4 November 1631. She went on to wed William II, Prince of Orange, with whom she had a son named William. A boy named James arrived on 14 October 1633. Next came Elizabeth on 28 June 1635, who was intelligent and thoughtful, but sickly. Little Anne came on 17 March 1637. She contracted tuberculosis. The disease killed her in November 1640. She was buried near her oldest brother Charles James in Westminster Abbey. Catherine was born and died on 29 June 1639. Henry was born on 8 July 1640, and survived to adulthood. The last child, Henrietta, was born on 16 June 1644.

With Henriette's obstetric history out of the way, attention can be turned to her artistic pursuits. Henriette never lost her passion for masques. The royal couple hosted them each year during Christmastide and carnival, beginning in 1630. Themes were frequently religious. The masques were a good way to show unity amongst the royal couple, too. The most devout Christians at the English court, the Puritans, skewered the performances.

Rumblings in the Kingdoms

Charles I carried on with making poor choices in the administration of his kingdom during the 1630s. Henriette continued alienating her subjects by breaking the law when it came to religion. She had not forgotten her mission, per the Pope. She began reestablishing Catholic chapels in her properties in 1632, and earnestly converting the women at her court, including creating a female religious house. A representative from the Pope was sent to England in 1634, too. He helped Henriette convert even more women. Her mother Marie de' Medici, who never saw an intrigue against her son Louis XIII that did not interest her, again plotted against him. He removed her from court, and Marie decided to visit various courts around Europe. This included a three-year visit to her daughter Henriette in England from around 1638 to 1641, which could not have made the anti-Catholic faction at court happy.

Things continued to worsen for Charles's and Henriette's relationship with their subjects. Charles decided in late 1640 to strengthen his overseas alliances by wedding his daughter Mary Henrietta to a foreign Dutch prince. At the time, William II of Orange was a suitably eligible bachelor in the Netherlands. By 10 February 1641, the engagement between Mary Henrietta and William II of Orange was in place. Charles concluded the negotiations without mentioning it to parliament until it was a done deal, exacerbating the political strife in England even more.

Mary Henrietta, who was nine years old, enjoyed a small Protestant wedding ceremony at Whitehall Palace's Chapel Royal. Henriette did not attend because it was not a Catholic ceremony. Unlike her husband's coronation, Henriette did observe the entire ceremony from afar. The wedding was a non-event to Londoners, who had grown tired of their popish queen and arrogant king.

Mary Henrietta and her new husband received small gifts from the courtiers and attendants who did come to the wedding. Mary Henrietta was supposed to stay in England until she was twelve years old. She would be allowed to follow the teachings of the Church of England and would not be forced to convert to observing the teachings of the Dutch Reformed Church.

A change in politics for the Stuarts necessitated Mary Henrietta leaving England much sooner.

Civil War

The reasons for and events leading up to the English Civil War are complex and will be only briefly reviewed here. The bottom line was that enough people were tired of Charles I's theory of personal rule. Henriette's unrelenting Catholicism did not help the situation. The English Civil War was a part of the overall Wars of the Three Kingdoms, which included the Scottish Bishop's War that was short-lived between 1639 and 1640, the two English Civil Wars, the Irish Confederate Wars, and additional wars in Scotland and Ireland. Charles's religious policies in Scotland made him unpopular there, on top of his grating against the government in England. The stage was set for tragedy.

Sensing that something serious was happening, the royal family removed to Hampton Court Palace, leaving London proper on 10 January 1642. The couple decided that Henriette would escort Princess Mary Henrietta to the Netherlands in February. The excuse was convenient enough: Henriette and Charles could reason that it made sense for Mary Henrietta to begin life in her new country and learn Dutch sooner rather than later. It also gave Henriette the opportunity to ask the Dutch for military assistance, should things continue souring in the three kingdoms.

Off went Henriette and Mary Henrietta on 23 February 1642 for the Netherlands. The Dutch sent a fleet of over a dozen ships to bring their new princess consort home. Just before leaving for the Netherlands, Charles I created a new honorary title for Mary Henrietta. The title was an homage to the French tradition of Henriette's family. Mary Henrietta was designated as Princess Royal.

After arriving at The Hague roughly two weeks after departing England, Henriette set to work drumming up support for Charles. She did her best to convince Christian IV of Denmark, Charles's maternal uncle, and Mary Henrietta's new father-in-law Frederick Henry, Prince of Orange, that they should help Charles. Henriette creatively tried to obtain cold, hard cash by selling off some of the royal jewelry. Not many sought to buy due to Henriette's dubious ownership of the jewels, as opposed to the jewels being properly owned by England or Scotland.

Henriette had some success in gaining support and money for Charles. She left for England in January 1643, while experiencing a nagging cough and poor health. After a dangerous initial expedition toward England, Henriette had to turn back to the Netherlands because the seas were too rough. She took advantage of her unforeseen return to agitate Frederick Henry that a ship filled with guns for Charles should be released and sent as part of her fleet. England's parliament asked that the Dutch hold onto the ship for the time being. Fredrick Henry relented, and Henriette was bound for England once more.

She left the Netherlands for England again in February 1643. Her fleet managed to avoid a Parliamentarian navy that sought to prevent arms and munitions from reaching Charles I and the Royalist faction. Henriette landed in Yorkshire on 22 February 1643. Her fleet was attacked in the harbor by the Parliamentary navy, causing Henriette to flee.

Henriette was an avid dog lover. Her servants accidentally forgot to grab, or could not find, her dog Mitte. Henriette simply could not bear leaving her pet in mortal danger, and so returned herself to retrieve Mitte. Henriette and her pup found each other, and she was able to save her dog.

After successfully rescuing her dog, Henriette boldly led her accompanying army to Oxford, where Charles I was. The English capital for purposes of the Royalists was now in Oxford instead of London. In fact, back in London, Henriette's chapels and religious imagery were being destroyed by Parliamentarians. It took Henriette several months to safely navigate to Oxford through the Midlands, but she maintained a cheery countenance.

Henriette finally reunited with Charles, staying with him for the rest of 1643. It was during this time that her final child, Henrietta, was conceived. Henriette tried her best to keep the Oxford court happy and vivacious, despite it being a shadow of what the couple enjoyed in London. Unfortunately, despite Henriette's courageous and successful efforts to bring Charles and the Royalists fresh troops and provisions, the Royalists were not powerful enough to repulse Parliamentarian advances toward Oxford. Now heavily pregnant, Henriette fled to Exeter, a distance of roughly 136 miles or 219 kilometers. She arrived on 1 May 1644.

Catching wind of pregnant Henriette's flight to Exeter, the Parliamentarians plotted to capture her. Henriette experienced a trying birth, but she and baby Henrietta, who was nicknamed Minette, survived. As mentioned, Minette was born on 16 June 1644. Henriette, in poor condition from the birth, learned that Parliamentarian forces were just outside Exeter. She left as soon as she could walk, abandoning Henrietta for the infant's own safety. Henriette planned on returning to France, and Minette was too frail as a newborn to make the treacherous sea journey.

Exile

Henriette boarded a ship at Falmouth, reaching Brest in July 1644 despite being assailed by a Parliamentarian ship. By arriving across the English Channel at Brest, Henriette reached a haven with her French family. She was allowed to stay in Paris for the next several years, where she set up a sort of shadow court.

Minette, still in England, met her father on 26 July 1644, a few days after she was baptized. She was later moved to a palace outside of London.

Henriette's remaining children tried making their way to either her side in France, or to the court of her daughter Mary of Orange in the Netherlands. Minette was smuggled to France in June 1646, and able to stay with Henriette in apartments at the Louvre. Charles, her eldest, followed a similar route to France in spring 1646. Charles stayed with Henriette in Paris for a couple of years before he moved to The Hague in 1648. James fled to The Hague in 1648 as well.

Henriette's husband was captured by the Parliamentarians in January 1647, to oversimplify things.

Henriette's children Elizabeth and Henry had a difficult time of it. Elizabeth and her brother Henry had been in the custody of Parliament since 1643, with no hope of release. Elizabeth's household was dissolved in 1648. Henry was likely supposed to flee when his brother James did, but it is thought that Elizabeth refused to let her young brother make the journey, so James left without him.

Henriette's husband remained a prisoner during this time. He was frequently moved around the country in 1648. He was charged with treason in January 1549 and brought to London. Charles was tried at Westminster Hall on 20 January 1649, with the trial lasting five days. Charles was taken away from the trial after the first three days and confined at St. James's Palace, in a room behind the Chapel Royal's altar. Charles was found guilty and sentenced to death. The day before his execution, Elizabeth and Henry visited him. Charles's head was separated from his body around two o'clock in the afternoon on 30 January 1649.

Grieving the horrendous death of her husband Charles I, Henriette wrote to their son Charles that she, "should have had the consolation of accompanying him to prison and to the horrors of death, and our spirits, so united in life, would have mutually rejoiced to pass united to another life." Henriette was now reduced to the status of a widowed refugee in France.

A Cromwellian Interlude
Elizabeth Bourchier and Dorothy Maijor

After the execution of Henriette Marie's husband, the English Council of State was put in place by the February 1649 Rump Parliament. In this iteration, "rump" referred to the remaining members of the Long Parliament who were not antithesis to Charles I's downfall. Oliver Cromwell was appointed as chair of the Rump Parliament. The Rump Parliament was dissolved in April 1653. A few months later, in December 1653, Cromwell was sworn in as Lord Protector. After Cromwell's death in September 1658, Cromwell was succeeded by his son Richard Cromwell. Richard held the Protectorate until May 1659, at which point he resigned, allowing Henriette Marie's son Charles II to return to England and rule.

Both Oliver and Richard Cromwell married and had children. Despite being upstarts and rebels, and decidedly neither monarchs nor Stuarts, their wives held a place in history and so shall briefly be discussed here.

Elizabeth Bourchier, Wife of Oliver Cromwell

Elizabeth Bourchier was born around 1598 as her parents' first child. Her precise date of birth is unknown, but it is assumed that she was close in age to her future husband, Oliver Cromwell, who was born in 1599. Eleven siblings came after Elizabeth. Elizabeth's father Sir James Bourchier was a wealthy leather merchant. Elizabeth was not regarded as a beauty and may have suffered from a malformation or other noticeable issue with one of her eyes.

On 22 August 1620, Elizabeth and Oliver Cromwell were married. The ceremony took place at St. Giles-without-Cripplegate in London, the name of the church stating that when it was built, St. Giles was outside the city wall near Cripplegate. On 25 August 1620, Oliver Cromwell signed a document pertaining to Elizabeth's jointure. Elizabeth was awarded the parsonage house at Hartford, the county of Huntingdon, and related tithes.

Curiously, Cromwell was noted in the jointure document as having the alias of "Williams." It is assumed that this alludes to the family's original name, with Oliver's paternal great-grandfather Richard Williams being a maternal nephew of Thomas Cromwell, who served Henry VIII and was responsible for the Dissolution of the Monasteries in the 1530s. The Welsh Williams family's descent comes through Katherine Cromwell, Thomas's elder sister.

Turning back to Elizabeth Bourchier, she enjoyed a successful marriage with her husband, even if she was not comfortable with her husband's change of career. They first lived at Oliver Cromwell's family estate of Huntingdon.

Elizabeth's Children

Elizabeth was frequently pregnant the first nine years or so of her marriage. Her first six children were born before 1630, and her last three born between 1632 and 1638. This number excludes any miscarriages which she may have suffered.

The exact dates of birth of Elizabeth and Oliver's children are unknown, but their baptisms were recorded at the local parish, which was Felstead Church. Elizabeth's eldest child, a son named Robert, was baptized 13 October 1621. Robert died before his eighteenth birthday and was described as being quite pious despite his youth. He was quickly followed by another boy named Oliver, baptized on 6 February 1623. Oliver served in the army of the Earl of Essex, dying from smallpox at the age of roughly twenty-one in 1644. Elizabeth's first daughter Bridget was baptized on 4 August 1624. She married Henry Ireton in 1646. The couple went to Ireland in 1651, but Bridget did not stay. Her husband was dead by the end of the year. She married for a second time in 1652 to Charles Fleetwood. Both men were supporters of her father. Bridget had seven children from her two marriages that survived her. She died in June 1662.

Elizabeth's son Richard came on 4 October 1626 and would follow in his father's footsteps, becoming Lord Protector. Henry arrived on 20 January 1628 and went on to become Lord Deputy of Ireland. Possessed of an irritable, sensitive nature, Henry died in March 1674 leaving behind seven children. The last of this first spate of children, a daughter named Elizabeth, was nicknamed "Bettie" by her parents. Bettie was reportedly Oliver Cromwell's favorite child. Bettie's family supported Elizabeth later in her life.

The family moved to St. Ives in the early 1630s. Elizabeth's husband sold the estate in Huntingdon in May 1631 and used the money to lease farmland. Due to the sale of the Huntingdon estate, Elizabeth gave up her jointure in 1632.

After roughly five years in St. Ives, the family moved to Ely. Oliver took over his uncle's farming work. Their last three children were born during this time. James was born in 1632 and died that same year. Mary was baptized on 9 February 1637, and likely baptized at St. Mary's Church in Ely. She married her husband Thomas Belasyse, 1st Earl Fauconberg, at Hampton Court in November 1657. Mary lived until 1713.

Elizabeth's last child, a daughter named Frances, was baptized at St. Mary's Church in Ely on 6 December 1638. She was rumored to be a possible match for the future Charles II of England, but if true, nothing came of it. Frances married firstly Robert Rich, 2d Earl of Warwick, on 11 November 1657. He died at Whitehall three months later, on 16 February 1658. Frances wed secondly Sir John Russell in May 1663, with whom Frances had two daughters and three sons. Frances's second husband passed away in March 1669, and Frances went to live with her sister Mary and Mary's family. Frances outlived her parents and siblings by a wide margin, passing away in January 1720 at the age of eighty-one.

After the births of her last three children, Elizabeth's husband became interested in Puritanism. He represented Cambridge in parliament and served in the military with his eldest surviving son Oliver during the early 1640s. The Cromwells were present for multiple key battles of the English Civil War. After his elevation to Lord Protector, Elizabeth and her family were known to reside at Whitehall Palace and Hampton Court Palace. Elizabeth felt uncomfortable when the family first moved to Whitehall, which was her husband's decision, and not that of the government.

Elizabeth's Personality

The truth about Elizabeth's personality and proclivities is difficult to discern. When she is brought into public life by virtue of being married to her husband, society is divided as to whether they are pro-commonwealth or pro-monarchy. Elizabeth was treated to mean-spirited rumors and publications just as much as her husband. This can make it challenging to gain a genuine understanding of what Elizabeth was like as a person.

Elizabeth was regarded as thrifty, although that was a negative aspersion. During her time as Protectress, entertainment and banqueting were both minimal. A condescending pamphlet published about Elizabeth remarked that she had but one male servant who occupied multiple positions, rather than a separate servant for each task. The servant acted as the driver of her second-hand coach, too. There seem to be some echoes of truth to the pamphlet, which referred to her as "Mrs. Joan Cromwell." The name Joan, in the mid-17th century, held an unpleasant connotation.[1] Elizabeth was not possessed of an unpleasing personality.

Elizabeth took her duties as Protectress seriously, being very supportive of her husband. She was uncomfortable when the family moved into the former

---

1. "Joans" were to mid-17th-century England what "Karens" are to early 21st-century UK, US, etc.

royal palace. Elizabeth recognized that she was not a queen and bristled at the change in station. This could explain why Elizabeth remained thrifty during her life. She was sometimes blamed and at other times praised for advising her husband regarding military affairs when he was in those leadership positions. She was likewise blamed for her husband's choices when he was Lord Protector.

What was Elizabeth Bourchier's true personality? She dedicated herself to her domestic duties and raising the couple's children. She was spirited but in a quiet way. Even if Elizabeth did advise her husband behind closed doors, there are no reputable accounts of her so doing. Of course, that is the nature of things behind closed doors and without witnesses, but it shows that Elizabeth would have possessed a sense of discretion when it came to her husband's public service.

Elizabeth was very dedicated to the family, exhibiting modest behavior that pleased Oliver. Oliver Cromwell was rather stern and observed to have respected Elizabeth for being the mother of his children, and not for her involvement in governance. Elizabeth did not overtly or outwardly object to the Puritanical lifestyle which her husband preferred. She was self-conscious and careful about her behavior in public, not wishing to be the basis for rumors about her family. There were reports by royalists of Elizabeth being a drunkard, but it seems unlikely that Oliver would have tolerated such behavior.

A tale about Elizabeth relates that, not long after moving into Whitehall, she was approached by Elizabeth Murray, Countess of Dysart. Not long before, Charles II sent an offer for a carte blanche to Oliver and his family if they capitulated to the monarchy being restored. Aware of this, the Countess of Dysart besought Elizabeth to encourage her husband to abandon the Protectorate and reinstall the monarchy. Moved by the Countess of Dysart, Elizabeth decided to approach Oliver early one morning before breakfast. Oliver effectively called her a fool for thinking that Charles II would do anything other than execute the lot of them for killing Charles I.

Elizabeth did not try to dissuade her husband from his path again. She did prefer that the governance of England be returned to the Stuarts and might have favored the 1657 proposal that the monarchy be restored. None of Elizabeth's children shared her view. If they did, it was out of their father's earshot.

Elizabeth's level of education is a mystery. She was trained in domestic arts such as embroidery. She could read and write, although her handwriting was not the best from the examples that survive.

Elizabeth's Widowhood and Death

Summer 1658 was a very unhealthy one. A disease which caused fever tore through England, grasping Elizabeth's daughter Bettie and killing her on

6 August 1658. Oliver was already sickly, and tending to his ill favorite child did not help matters. He developed a tertian ague, which could have been malaria. Oliver took to his bed at around the same time that Bettie died. He was seen toward the end of August out riding in the grounds of Hampton Court but looked exceedingly unwell. He moved from Hampton Court to Whitehall. He died at Whitehall on 3 September 1658. He was originally buried in Henry VII's lady chapel in Westminster Abbey. Oliver's corpse saw an interesting treatment thereafter, being moved and buried in multiple places.

Elizabeth survived her husband for several years. She was granted the residence of St James's Palace and an annuity, but the arrangement lasted for maybe a year before she was forced to leave.

Elizabeth's and Oliver's son Richard became the next Lord Protector but held the position for a mere eight months. Realizing that the monarchy might be returning, and finding herself facing impoverishment, Elizabeth spirited away a large amount of gold and several pieces of valuable, moveable possessions that belonged to the royal family. She moved them in May 1660 to a fruiterer's warehouse on Thames Street with the ambition of exporting them to a different country. It was rumored that Elizabeth spent time in Switzerland after her husband's death, so that was a possible end point for the items. It should be noted that there is no proof that she ever went to Switzerland.

Elizabeth went to Wales whilst the monarchy was being restored. She eventually went to live in Northamptonshire with her former son-in-law John Claypole, widowed husband of Bettie.

Elizabeth died 19 November 1665.

Dorothy Maijor, Wife of Richard Cromwell

Not much is known about the first Protectress, Elizabeth Bourchier Cromwell, and even less is known about her daughter-in-law, Dorothy Maijor Cromwell. Not even her true first name is known, with some accounts given it as Dorothea, and others as Dorothy. For purposes of this book, she will be referred to as Dorothy. It is believed that Dorothy was born around 1620, making her roughly six years older than her husband Richard.

Dorothy married Richard Cromwell in 1649. The couple lived on her father's estate for the first roughly ten years of their marriage. Dorothy bore at least seven children, with some sources stating that she had as many as nine. Of her known seven children, Dorothy had six daughters and one son. Three daughters, Elizabeth, Anna, and Dorothy, survived to adulthood, as did her only son Oliver. Elizabeth, born in 1650, lived until 1731, thereby outliving everyone in her immediate family. Anna lived from 1659 to 1727, and Dorothy from 1660 to 1681. Oliver lived from 1656 to 1705.

Richard became Lord Protector on 3 September 1658, immediately after the death of his father. The family presumably was already living in London, given that Richard was being groomed for the position of Lord Protector beginning in 1657. Dorothy's final known child, also named Dorothy, was likely born in London. Dorothy Maijor might have been styled as the Protectress, but her time in this position was too short for any meaningful objets d'arts or other items to be made, memorializing her title.

Richard was not a good fit for the role of Lord Protector and was asked to step aside in April 1659. Richard acquiesced, and completely removed himself from government by May 1659. Richard, and likely Dorothy and the children, continued to live at Whitehall until July. The family was forced to return to Dorothy's father's land in Hursley thereafter.

Dorothy's father died in April 1660, leaving her son Oliver as owner of Hursley Park and Lodge. Dorothy and her children were abandoned by Richard Cromwell in July 1660. He initially went to France, then went on something of a European tour for the next twenty years or so. He faithfully wrote letters to Dorothy and their children, even if he could not be bothered to return.

Dorothy died on 5 January 1675 at around the age of fifty-five, waiting for her husband to come home.

Richard outlived his son Oliver, who died in 1705. As a result, Richard wished to claim Dorothy's father's manor of Hursley. Richard wanted his surviving daughters Anna and Elizabeth to take possession of the property, and then turn it over to him for his retirement. Anna, the younger daughter, arrived at Hursley first. She utterly refused to give her father the property, possibly recalling to mind Richard's abandonment of their mother Dorothy and themselves. After all, Anna was a baby when Richard chose to begin his European adventure, not returning until she was in her twenties. Richard petitioned the courts for Hursley to be turned over to him, which it eventually was. He died in July 1712, aged eighty-six. Dorothy and Richard's daughters Anna and Elizabeth sold off Hursley after their father's death.

Chapter 12

Catherine of Braganza

Return of the Stuarts

Charles II was forced to flee England in 1646 when he was around sixteen years old. Following, Dear Reader, is a very simplified retelling of his next steps. His mother Henriette was already at her brother's court in France. Charles moved to Den Haag, or The Hague, Netherlands, in 1648 after an invitation from his sister Mary Henrietta. He ventured to Scotland in June 1650, where he enjoyed a coronation at Scone Abbey on 1 January 1651. Oliver Cromwell's forces attempted to capture Charles in late summer 1651, but he successfully fled to Normandy. France and the Netherlands turned their backs on Charles by the mid-1650s, so he ventured to Spain. Cromwell's troops followed him there in 1658. As mentioned before, Oliver died in September 1658.

Charles returned to the Netherlands. After some negotiation with the English Parliament, the Declaration of Breda was ratified. Charles was clear to return home. He arrived in London on his thirtieth birthday of 29 May 1660, restored to the rule of England, Scotland, Ireland and Wales. Charles's coronation was held eleven months later, on 23 April 1661. It was now time for Charles to find his queen.

During the 1640s, Charles's father had negotiated with Queen Luisa of Portugal for a bride for Charles. Wars of the Three Kingdoms, Charles I's execution, and the establishment of the Protectorate made it a little difficult for negotiations to continue. Now that Charles II was securely on the throne, he could renew the effort with Portugal.

Catherine of Braganza

Queen Luisa of Portugal, a shrewd and ambitious woman, resumed negotiating for her daughter Catherine's marriage to Charles II almost immediately. Catarina Henriqueta de Bragança, or to English speakers, Catherine of Braganza, was born 25 November 1638. She was the fourth of seven children born to her parents John IV of Portugal and Luisa de Guzman, Queen of Portugal. An older sister and younger brother died in infancy.

Catherine was born in Vila Viçosa at the Ducal Palace. Her father became king of Portugal when she was two years old. She was raised in Lisbon, spending a considerable amount of her time being cared for at a convent. Her mother, now Queen Luisa, was very protective of her children. As a result, young Catherine grew to be pious and kind, but unworldly.

Upon reaching adolescence, Catherine had no shortage of suitors. Portugal was an imperial power by this time, and a marriage with Catherine meant the might of Portugal would in theory be available to aid whatever territory Catherine was involved with through marriage. Her elder and only sister Joanna died at the age of seventeen in 1653, increasing Catherine's international appeal on the marriage market. Joanna reportedly suffered from a very lengthy illness. Portuguese princesses were in short supply.

Catherine's father John IV of Portugal died in 1656, leaving her mother Queen Luisa as regent. Luisa wasted no time in finding a husband for Catherine and agreed to Charles II of England's overtures. Charles II's mother Henriette was surely delighted that her son found a Catholic bride.

Henriette Returns, Leaves, and Passes Away

Henriette, Charles II's mother, never lost hope that her family would be restored in England. She also never lost her faith, founding a convent in Chaillot in 1651.

Henriette did everything she could during her time in exile to support the claims of her son, now Charles II. She visited him in London toward the end of 1660. Henriette and her children experienced a series of very emotional highs and lows in 1660. On the one hand, Charles II was restored to the throne and Minette was betrothed to her French cousin. On the other, two of Henriette's children, Mary, Princess of Orange, and Henry, died of smallpox in the autumn of 1660. The marriage of Minette and the coronation of Charles II, in March and April 1661, respectively, restored some of the joy to Henriette.

Henriette returned to France for a year to eighteen months before coming back to London with her household in August 1662, just before her son Charles's marriage to Catherine the following month. No one in London was very happy that Henriette was back. Henriette did not let that bother her and got on with greeting her new daughter-in-law.

Henriette was plagued with severe bronchitis in 1665 and thought that returning to France would help her. Her health never really returned, and she began experiencing pain. She spent time with her newlywed daughter Minette, even meeting her granddaughter Anne Marie d'Orléans in 1669.

Henriette, overburdened by pain, was recommended by her physician to consume an awesome quantity of opiates. She did, overdosed, and died on 10 September 1669, a couple of months shy of her sixtieth birthday. Her body was buried in the Basilica of St. Denis. Henriette's heart, at her request, was removed, placed in a silver casket, and buried in the convent she had founded in Chaillot.

Catherine Arrives in England

The marriage contract between Catherine and Charles II was signed on 23 June 1661. Her dowry included jewels, money, sugar, and Bombay, now known as Mumbai, and Tangier, which is a Moroccan port in the Strait of Gibraltar. She came with a dowry of £300,000 to bolster the restored monarchy's coffers. The fledgling royal house of Braganza achieved victory in allying itself with the ancient Stuarts of Scotland, and since 1603, England, Ireland, and Wales. It also renewed an alliance between the countries which first began in 1373.

Ten months later, on 23 April 1662, Catherine departed from Lisbon for England. This being a grand adventure for anyone, it was even more so for the very sheltered Catherine. She stayed in Queen Luisa's apartments the night before boarding the English ship that awaited her. Catherine's brothers escorted her to the ship after she hugged their mother goodbye. Catherine's journey was delayed for a couple of days due to poor weather, so the festivities surrounding her departure continued. The English grew impatient and set off on the third day, despite rain and wind.

Catherine, "scarce ever was out of the palace door before." Catherine and her dozens of Portuguese ladies were sea-sick for the bulk of the journey, with it being remarked of Catherine, "how recluse the Queen hath ever been and all the voyage never came upon the deck, nor put her head out of her cabin." At least she had a comfortable cabin, specially decorated for her. The furnishings in her cabin were upholstered with crimson velvet, trimmed in gold. Her bed had a beautiful white covering. Heavy, expensive fabric covered the windows in her room. There was also something of a throne room prepared in her cabin. She was, after all, the queen consort of England, Scotland, and Ireland. She spent almost two weeks in the cabin, enduring the unrelenting bad weather on her journey from Portugal to England.

Twenty-three-year-old Catherine landed at Portsmouth in mid-May 1662. She was greeted by her brother-in-law James, whom she invited on board her boat. She wore English dress for the occasion. Catherine and James greeted each other formally in their respective languages of Portuguese and English. They availed themselves of translators for their formal meeting. Once the introductions and requisite obeisance were out of the way, the two chatted in Spanish. Catherine left a good impression on James.

Charles II arrived in Portsmouth on 20 May. Catherine was sickly, and so she met her husband for the first time while she was still abed. The couple enjoyed their wedding ceremonies on 21 May. Catherine rallied for the afternoon so they could have their formal wedding. They first had a private, secret Catholic ceremony, per the marriage contract which allowed Catherine to continue observing the religion of her choice. Their second, Anglican service was celebrated in public.

The newlyweds enjoyed their summer together before entering London. Charles's mother Henriette, as mentioned, came from France, arriving in August 1662. The royal couple joyfully entered London with great pomp and circumstance on 30 September 1662. Henriette, now recognized as Queen Mother, was delighted with Catherine and with her son's affection toward Catherine. Even with a pleasant beginning in England, Catherine's time as queen consort was lackluster.

Catherine's Queenship

Catherine of Braganza had a brilliant temperament for being queen. She was shy, meek, abstemious in disposition, and respectful of and devoted to her husband. Despite her exemplary character, she never fulfilled her main duty as queen consort. She experienced three miscarriages in quick succession, and ultimately never had a successful pregnancy. On top of her infertility, she was yet another Catholic queen in a Protestant country. Catherine kept several Portuguese priests in her retinue and established a religious house that was built by 1667. She had difficulty learning English.

Cultural clashes abounded, too. Catherine's style of dress was thought unfashionable. Although she dressed in a style popular to the Iberian Peninsula, it was considered outdated. In reality, Catherine was dressed as fashionably and up to date as one might expect, but her clothes were very different from French styles that were popular in England. Her Portuguese musicians played strange instruments, including Portuguese-style bagpipes. Portuguese music never really caught on at Catherine's court.

Charles II was always respectful, in a sense, of Catherine. When the subject of divorcing her was occasionally brought up, he outright refused. Despite his seeming devotion to her, in reality he entertained a succession of mistresses who completely eclipsed Catherine at court. He had at least seven long-term mistresses. Between the seven, he had fourteen illegitimate children, most of whom he recognized. Catherine weathered his series of infidelities as gracefully as she could.

Catherine used portraits of herself as political tools. She was known to hire talented, Catholic Italian artists. A portrait painted of her as St. Catherine of Alexandria, who was purportedly a princess, was widely circulated in England as an engraving. Catherine commissioned portraits of herself where she is in English dress, as well.

Although Catherine adhered to Catholicism throughout her life, she did not behave as her mother-in-law Henriette did. Catherine's Catholicism was no secret, but she was more discreet in her support of the religion than was Henriette. Despite her less notorious behavior, Catherine and her Catholicism were always a sore subject.

Catherine's character changed during her time as a Stuart queen. After arriving as a shy, sheltered young woman, Catherine learned how to stand up for herself and how to relax. She utilized patronage of the arts to remain popular, and perhaps relevant, at court. Both the English and Portuguese courts favored Italian opera, and so Catherine sought to support the artform at court. As an added allure for her, Catholics abounded in Italy and thus she could recruit Catholic artists. Additionally, focusing on musical art forms allowed her to keep her Portuguese musicians active in her court.

Embracing Italian artistic forms and art helped diminish the French influence on culture at the Stuart court. Henriette's influence and elements of the now-defunct Auld Alliance were strong, but Catherine now had the chance to weaken them.

One of the main ways she may have accomplished this was through introducing tea drinking as a common beverage at court. Tea was certainly not unknown in England but was more of a drink that gentlewomen enjoyed in private with their friends. Catherine took her tea publicly at court. She was able to show the ladies at court how to properly brew tea as well, which added to the appeal. Brewing tea was special knowledge in a time when the leaves were green and not as processed as now, necessitating careful brewing to avoid an overly bitter and unpleasant taste. Adding to it the elegant porcelain which Catherine used to prepare and serve tea, it quickly became viewed as a refined beverage. Catherine's elegant consumption of tea in public popularized it, and her influence echoes to this day.

Death of Charles II and Time as Queen Dowager in England

Catherine remained quietly at court, respected by her husband, but in the shadow of his numerous mistresses throughout her queenship. Charles II's bedroom exploits will not be recited here. Catherine's presence in England persists to this day, even if during her own lifetime she remained in the background.

Charles II suffered from what was believed to be a hemorrhagic stroke on 2 February 1685, possibly brought on by the manifestation of a kidney disorder. He died on 6 February 1685 after converting to Catholicism on his deathbed.

How coherent Charles was at the time is dubious. He did reportedly apologize to Catherine for his womanizing. Catherine, a heroically dutiful wife to a lackluster man, was very much aggrieved over Charles's death.

Catherine's brother-in-law became James II of England and Ireland, and James VII of Scotland after Charles II's death. James was a Catholic, which might have brought Catherine a sense of relief. She got along well with Maria of Modena, who was James II's wife when he ascended the throne. Maria was a Catholic, too, from a foreign country. As an Italian, she may have appreciated Catherine's cultivation of Italian artists and art forms.

Unfortunately, James II did not remain king for long, and was replaced by his daughter Mary II and Mary's husband, a Stuart cousin, William III. Mary II and William III were Protestants, the first fully Protestant monarchy since the death of Elizabeth I in 1603. Catherine, ever a Catholic, was no longer appreciated at court. Aside from that, Mary II never took a liking to her aunt Catherine.

Catherine finally returned to Portugal in early 1692, when she was fifty-three years old.

Catherine's Last Years in Portugal

Catherine, who had been home to Portugal only twice since 1662, was a changed woman when she returned to her native country for good. She was more openly fun-loving and had fully adopted English-style dress. The English continued to have a heavy French influence on clothing, meaning that more skin was on display at the English court than at the Portuguese court. Catherine's dress was no doubt a salacious shock to the very conservative court of her Portuguese brother.

Catherine's brother Pedro II had been king of Portugal since September 1683. He deposed his and Catherine's mentally and physically incapable brother Afonso in 1668. Pedro ruled as prince regent until Afonso's death. By the time Catherine arrived back in Portugal, Pedro was on his second wife, having initially married Afonso's wife after Afonso's marriage to her ended. Pedro's second wife, Maria Sofia of Neuburg, was in her mid-twenties when Catherine came to reside at the Portuguese court. The women had met back in 1688 when James II invited the Portuguese royal couple to England to celebrate their nuptials.

Catherine's new sense of etiquette and matters vexed her brother King Pedro. To resolve the issue, the queen dowager of England purchased an estate near the main palace in Lisbon shortly after arriving. She had what is now known as Bemposta Palace built and made certain that a chapel was included within the structure because one had been there since 1501. Construction started in 1694, and Catherine used it as her permanent primary residence beginning in

1702. The royal chapel was completed in 1706. While Catherine waited for her palace to be built, she lodged with different aristocratic families near Lisbon.

Catherine's personal wealth allowed her to keep her own court, filled with faithful English and Portuguese servants. Having lived in England for three decades, Catherine had a keen sense of the political atmosphere there, even if she did not directly involve herself. She had also learned English games and her musicians learned English music. Manners at the Portuguese court were restrictive during Catherine's youth, especially because she had grown up virtually confined to a convent. As mentioned, things grew even more restrictive under her brother's rule. Catherine's lax, English-infused manners were wholly inappropriate in Portugal. Her English-friendly court caused Catherine to be termed an Anglophile, certainly a derogatory term for her.

Catherine had an overt impact on the Portuguese court, and fairly quickly, which she had not had in England. Catherine's sister-in-law Maria Sofia was accustomed to wearing the austere, sober clothing of the still-influential Spanish court. Maria Sofia petitioned for her and her ladies to wear clothing like Catherine's and was eventually successful. Although Maria Sofia admired Catherine's fashion, Catherine and Maria Sofia did not necessarily get along. Catherine's habits had taken on an English flair, whereas Maria Sofia possessed her German sensibilities that were only harshened by her husband's court. A conflict arose between the two women that lasted for seven years, ending with Maria Sofia's death in 1699. With Maria Sofia's death, Catherine became the main royal woman in Portugal.

As the premier woman of the House of Braganza, Catherine was given an important non-political role. At least in theory, the role was non-political. She was granted the *Casa de Rainhas*, which was not a physical space but rather a collection of properties and sources of income that the queen consort, who ideally became a queen mother, would use to fund her activities. The *Casa* had its own separate administration and tax authority separate from the crown. It also had influence over the *Casa do Infantado*, a similar body created by Catherine's father to support her brother Pedro when Pedro was a second son and not the king. Despite the *Casa de Rainhas* not being a political body, it had awesome financial authority when administered properly.

Toward the end of her life, Catherine stepped in to assist her brother when he began showing symptoms of his final illness. Pedro appointed Catherine as his regent in 1701. A faction at the Portuguese court would neither respect nor listen to Catherine, fearing that she was too pro-English to genuinely care about Portugal. Pedro was able to rally for a period before an infection in his throat began getting the better of him. Pedro was still willing to personally go to the battlefield, which he did from 1704 to 1705. Catherine was once more appointed as his regent.

Catherine of Braganza was at Bemposta Palace when she passed away. She died on 31 December 1705 at around ten o'clock in the evening. She had fallen ill a few days before, and her brother came for a brief visit. He needed to officially end her regency before she died. Her funeral took place on the afternoon of 3 January 1706. Catherine's face was left visible during the ceremony. She was entombed next to her oldest brother, Teodósio, in the church belonging to the Brotherhood of Misericordia. Some 150 years later, Catherine and her relatives were moved to the newly constructed Pantheon of the House of Braganza in the Convent of St. Vincente de Fora, where her body is still entombed today.

Chapter 13

Anne Hyde and Maria of Modena

Anne Hyde was never a Stuart consort. As the mother of two queens regnant and wife of a royal heir, she deserves to be considered. She was, after all, a Stuart spouse. Her successor, Maria of Modena, queen consort to James VII & II, will be discussed in this chapter as well.

Anne Hyde's Early Years

Anne Hyde was born on 12 March 1637 at Cranbourne Lodge in Windsor. Curiously, she was named after her father's first wife. Anne's father Edward Hyde married Anne Ayliffe, who became ill with smallpox a few months into their marriage. She was pregnant at the time and subsequently miscarried. Her body could not handle both the smallpox and the miscarriage, and she died soon after. On 10 July 1634, Edward married his second wife, Frances Aylesbury. Anne Hyde was their first child and first daughter. The couple had two daughters and four sons in total, with all their children surviving to adulthood.

In 1649, when Anne was about twelve years old, Anne and her family fled to Breda in the Netherlands. Anne's father was supportive of King Charles I. As tension mounted and the English Civil War came on, Anne's father was part of the party that escorted the future Charles II to the Netherlands so that he could escape danger and the Stuarts could live on. Mary of Orange, Charles I's eldest daughter, harbored a multitude of English refugees. Mary had moved to the Netherlands in 1642, when she was roughly ten years old, to live with her husband Prince William II of Orange. Originally, Mary was supposed to stay in England until she was twelve, but the political unrest forced her to leave her home country early. Mary of Orange's only child, a boy named William, became a Stuart spouse in his turn.

Anne Hyde entered Mary of Orange's service and was generally well-received at Mary's court in the Netherlands. Mary was rejected by the Dutch public, particularly after the death of Mary's husband in 1647. She was also at loggerheads with her mother-in-law over the care and keeping of little William. As a result, Mary bore ill will towards the Dutch and would only hire English people for her court.

Henriette, dowager queen-in-exile of England, Scotland, and Ireland, did not approve of Anne Hyde. She was displeased that her daughter Mary employed Anne. Just imagine how upset Henriette was when her son James began delighting in Anne's favors.

The Lovely Anne

Anne had plenty of male attention at Mary of Orange's court. She was beautiful and did her best to be fashionable. She caught the attention of Henry Jermyn, who tried to woo Anne's employer Mary of Orange after the latter was widowed. It was mere rumor, but Charles II did not like what he had heard. On top of that, Jermyn also held amorous congress with women about court who knew Charles II's bed.

Anne's dalliance with the womanizing Jermyn did not last for too long before she caught the eye of James Stuart. He was the Duke of York at the time, whatever that meant for a deposed royal family. The two struck up a relationship, and within a couple of years, in November 1659, James promised to marry Anne. The story goes that both James's mother Henriette and Anne's father loathed the idea of the two marrying, to the point that Anne's father virtually imprisoned her and suggested that Charles II do away with her. Whether true or not, Anne and James did marry.

Return to England and Life as Duchess of York

After the Restoration of the Monarchy, James and Anne left the Netherlands for England. Anne was pregnant by this time, and her pregnancy became visible not long after arriving back in England. Out of decency, Anne and James had to marry each other. They celebrated their marriage on 3 September 1660 late at night at Worcester House. Anne's father owned the property.

Anne's marriage to James was just as controversial as she was. On the one hand, Anne was regarded as attractive, intelligent, and having a strong personality. On the other, she was despised at court in part because of her low birth. Anne and James engaged in what were over-wrought public displays of affection at court, but James kept a string of mistresses, much like his brother Charles II.

Children

The couple welcomed eight children between October 1660 and February 1671. Their first, Charles, styled Duke of Cambridge, was born on 22 October 1660 at Worcester House. He died on 5 May 1661 from smallpox. Anne was pregnant by the end of the year and welcomed her daughter Mary on 30 April 1662 at St. James's Palace. Mary went on to become queen regnant of England, Scotland, and Ireland, and is discussed in the next chapter. The following year, on 12 July 1663, Anne and James welcomed another son. He was named James and was created Duke of Cambridge and Baron of Dauntsey. He fell ill, dying on 20 June 1667 after being sick for almost two months with either smallpox or bubonic plague, or possibly even one right after the other.

A second daughter, named Anne, was born 6 February 1665, again at St. James's Palace. She went on to become queen regnant of Great Britain and Ireland. Eighteen months later, Anne and James welcomed another boy on 4 July 1666, whom they also named Charles. He, too, was born at St. James's Palace. Charles was styled Duke of Kendal. He died on 22 May 1667, a month before his older brother James, Duke of Cambridge, who is mentioned above.

Edgar, Duke of Cambridge, lived longer than any of Anne's and James's other sons. He was born 14 September 1667, at the couple's favored residence of St. James's Palace. He was created Duke of Cambridge and Baron of Dauntsey, since his older brother James left the titles vacant upon his passing earlier that summer. Anne's pregnancy with and the birth of Edgar led to her having poor health for the rest of her life. It is possible that the succession of six pregnancies in seven years weakened her. Anne went on to have two more children with James.

On 13 January 1669, Anne and James welcomed a little girl whom they named Henrietta. This was no doubt in honor of James's mother Henriette Marie, who was still alive at the time of Henrietta's birth. Given Henriette's great distaste for Anne, she probably had mixed feelings about her new Stuart namesake. Unfortunately, Henrietta died on 15 November 1669. A final child, named Catherine in honor of Catherine of Braganza, was born on 9 February 1671.

Anne, exhausted and depleted from such a succession of children, died on 31 March 1671. It is thought that she may have had breast cancer. On her deathbed, she received the Catholic rite. When Anne died, she had four living children, namely, Mary, Anne, Edgar, and Catherine. By the end of 1671, only Mary and Anne were alive. Edgar, who died 8 June 1671, was buried in a coffin placed on top of his mother within Mary, Queen of Scots's tomb at Westminster Abbey. Catherine died in December 1671.

Mary of Modena's Early Years

Maria Beatrice Eleonora Anna Margherita Isabella d'Este was born on 5 October 1658 under the New Style,[1] at the Ducal Palace in Modena, Italy. Known to English speakers as Mary of Modena, she was the second of three children born to her parents. She may have been born prematurely. Maria's older brother, Francesco, died six months before her birth. He was only five months old. Her younger brother, also named Francesco, was born 6 March 1660 and roughly seventeen months younger than her.

Maria's father Alfonso IV d'Este was Duke of Modena and Reggio. He married Maria's mother Laura Martinozzi in 1655. Alfonso struggled with poor health throughout his life and died in 1662 at the age of twenty-seven. Maria was four years old when her father passed. Maria's mother Laura Martinozzi acted as regent for Maria's brother Francesco.

Laura Martinozzi was well-connected with the French court and had an excellent education. Her maternal uncle was Cardinal Jules Mazarin, an important figure at the French court. After the death of Laura's father, Laura, her sister, and her mother were invited to France by Cardinal Mazarin. There they were raised, and Laura was married off to Alfonso IV d'Este, Duke of Modena.

An English Proposal

In 1673, when Maria was roughly fourteen years old, her mother was approached by Charles II of England's ambassadors. His younger brother James, whose low-born wife died in 1671, needed another bride. This one surely had to be born to a noble family, young enough to bear children, and ideally for James, Catholic. He converted to Catholicism roughly five years before. Maria preferred to become a nun instead of a wife, or at least that was the rumor James had heard.

Maria was not a first choice for James, either. There were several German, perfectly Protestant princesses available. A Protestant German princess would have helped the Stuart royal family maintain the façade of protecting the Anglican church. The favored woman for the task as of February 1673 was Claudia Felicitas of Austria, a member of both the Habsburg and Medici families. She was vivacious, beautiful, intelligent, and about to turn twenty years old. She had also caught the eye of her second cousin Holy Roman Emperor

---

1. This is under the Gregorian calendar, then being used by parts of Italy and France. England, Scotland, and other Protestant-leaning countries continued to use the old style, or Julian calendar, of dating, which was behind the Gregorian calendar by ten days. Thus, whilst it was 5 October 1658 when Maria was born in Italy, it was 25 September in England.

Leopold I, resulting in James's overtures going nowhere. There was mention of him marrying a distant Guise relation, but James was firmly disinterested.

Maria was already a possibility in early 1673, but quickly became a prime candidate after pursuing a German princess lost its luster. James must have been pleased with a report from Modena that,

> The Princess of Modena, Mary of Este, His Lordship could not see; but by means of a Scotch gentleman that had been conversant in the House of Conti...he was introduced into the palace of that Prince, whose wife had been one of the young Princess of Modena's nearest relations, and there he saw her pictures, that had been lately sent thither from that Court. It bore the appearance of a young Creature about Fourteen years of Age; but such a light of Beauty, such Characters of Ingenuity and Goodness as it surprised [him], and fixt upon his Phancy that he had found his Mistress, and the Fortune of England.

Maria was attractive, tall, and of a good countenance. She had a facility for languages, arriving in England already knowing Italian, French, and plenty of Latin. Maria did not have much knowledge or awareness of countries and territories outside of Modena. She never heard of the Stuarts generally, nor James specifically. She knew nothing of England.

Despite her mother Laura's hesitation and Maria's wishes to enter a convent, Laura acquiesced to the English marriage. There had been some chatter of wedding Maria to Charles II of Spain, which came to naught. Charles II, known as the Bewitched, was afflicted with multiple genetic defects which manifested through generations of Habsburgs closely intermarrying. His parents were uncle and niece. He was visibly physically deformed. Reports of Charles's poor health and physical appearance, plus his being a few years younger than Maria, may have caused James Stuart to look like a better husband for Maria. It was agreed by the end of July 1673 that Maria and James would wed, but Maria refused with all the might accorded a fourteen-year-old girl.

A letter from Pope Clement X in September 1673, supporting Maria's match with James, helped things along. Written to Maria in Latin, the letter said in part,

> Dear daughter in Christ, noble Damsel, greeting etc. Since the design of the Duke of York to contract alliance with you Nobility reached our ears, We return thanks to the Father of Mercies who...is preparing for us in the Kingdom of England an ample harvest of joy. Considering...the influence of your virtues, We easily conceived a firm hope that an end might come to the persecution still smouldering in that kingdom and that the orthodox

faith, reinstated by you in a place of honor might recover the… security of former days, an effect…which might become due to the victory of your piety…. You can therefore easily understand, dear daughter in Christ, the anxiety which filled Us when We were informed of your repugnance for marriage…We therefore…earnestly exhort you by these presents to place before your eyes the great profit which may accrue to the Catholic faith in the above-named kingdom through your marriage…We send your Nobility, from the depth of our heart, our Apostolic Benediction.

Maria capitulated to the match.

Maria celebrated her marriage to James by proxy on 30 September 1673 in Modena. Maria turned fifteen only a few days before. She was finally eager to be married and Maria, "did venture upon frank disobedience, and has caused the marriage to be solemnized without giving the Court of Rome any further satisfaction." Maria was credited for, "her own merit, for she is really an extraordinary woman, has a great deal of wit, and spirit, and…wants not good humor if she were in a place where it was the custom to make use of it." After the proxy ceremony, Maria was declared the Duchess of York. Her mother the Duchess regent and her step-grandmother the Duchess Dowager made obeisance to Maria as the highest-ranking lady then present in Modena.

The day after the wedding, 1 October 1673, a procession and banquet were held in honor of Maria,

> At break of day…which happened to be Sunday, began preparations for the Cavalcade. An hour after mid-day, the royal bride started in a superb coach for the Cathedral, accompanied by the Duchess Regent, [the Duchess Dowager] and the Princess Leonore.[2] [Maria's brother] the Duke, riding a generous steed, wore a suit of brocade, embroidered with pearls and gold, his hat-band and sword-hilt all diamonds. At his right rode the English ambassador, representing the Duke of York. Then came…their suites to the number of a hundred cavaliers, who by the richness of their dress, of their liveries and the pomp of their accoutrements raised wonder and delight in the beholders.

After winding their way through Modena, they arrived back at the ducal palace for Maria's wedding feast. Maria and the English ambassador sat at the head of the table. The table was decorated with sculptures made of sugar. They

---

2. Eleonore d'Este, Maria's paternal aunt, who was also mentioned as a possible bride for James. She entered a convent in May 1674.

included Poseidon in his seahorse-drawn chariot, Artemis with a leopard, and Atlas and his globe.

> The last course consisted of comfits and confectionary, but these were hardly touched by the guests, and as soon as removed, were speedily seized… by the *bassa gente* whom the inadvertence of the guards had allowed to enter, but which the generosity of the Duchess allowed….the guests for a little while went down into the Corso, still full of carriages, and cavaliers, and masqueraders, who, dressed in various guise according to their humor, gave and received no ordinary amusement. The night closed with a ball at the Ducal Palace, where the presence of the Princes, the jewels of the ladies and the splendour of the gentlemen made the night as resplendent as the day.

The people of Modena rejoiced for days. There were colorful masques, entertainments, and decorations everywhere.

With her marriage secure, Maria left for England and for her thirty-nine-year-old, pox-scarred husband. She needed to arrive before 23 October, when Parliament was set to open.

Maria's Journey to England

Maria took the scenic route from Modena, traveling overland. She left Modena on 5 October 1673, her fifteenth birthday, with her mother. Maria's brother Duke Francesco journeyed with her the first couple of days before it became prudent for him to return to the Ducal Palace. Maria cried at his departure. Like so many other noble or royal brides, Maria never saw her home again.

Maria arrived in Lyon on 22 October, making it impossible for her to arrive before Parliament opened in England. James scarcely received timely updates of Maria's journey toward England, likely due to the characteristically stormy weather of the English Channel. Parliament opened on schedule and within a week, pleas were being made to have James's marriage annulled. Charles II was forced to prorogue Parliament until after Maria's marriage with James was consummated.

She arrived at Louis XIV's Parisian court on 2 November, where she was given a gracious welcome. Louis was James's maternal cousin. As a Catholic, Louis was no doubt pleased that his Stuart cousin was married to a Catholic woman. This meant that both preeminent women in the Stuart monarchy were Catholics, hopefully increasing the chances that Scotland and England would return to the Catholic fold. Louis gave the new Duchess of York gifts, including an expensive broach.

On 3 November, Maria and her entourage were invited by Louis XIV to Versailles. Arriving in the morning, Louis took,

> the Royal bride by the hand [and] conducted her through that superb palace, so richly furnished and especially so rich in silver plate that there are some 3,000 pieces, without counting the cabinets full of jewels. They went through the gardens in a gilt chariot, the king himself acting as coachman, perhaps in order to give the second place to the Duchess of York, who thus sat beside the Queen [of France]. His Majesty showed them the fountains... and all the other rare and costly beauties of the place...After a delightful promenade they were led to an apartment where a splendid collation [of food] was spread... The supper[3] ended, they returned to Paris in the royal carriages arriving at 5 o'clock in the evening by torchlight.

Maria's good spirits were surely shattered when news of Parliament's vote to annul her marriage reached Paris. James swiftly dashed off a letter of reassurance to her. James wanted Maria to be in England as soon as possible.

Maria fell ill, making it dangerous to leave Paris as quickly as James would have preferred. It is thought that she was suffering from dysentery. She spent the next several weeks in Paris recovering.

Maria's Arrival in England

In late November, Maria was finally well enough to travel to Calais. The journey took her a week. Almost as soon as she arrived, Maria boarded a ship at seven o'clock in the morning named *Catherine* and set sail across the Channel with other accompanying ships. She arrived at Dover ten hours later.

England must have seemed a very depressing place for Maria when she first arrived. As seen, most of the men in Parliament were Protestant, and did not like the idea of welcoming yet another Catholic bride into the Stuart royal family. It was viewed as another papist plot. As a result, Maria barely had a welcome at all when she first stepped onto English soil at Dover.

Maria made an excellent impression on her new husband,

> The Duke, attended by only four gentlemen, awaited her, and greeted her (and then [her mother] the Duchess of Modena) and [Maria], with her beauty and manners so natural and appropriate, captivated the heart of the Duke...as she had captivated the French.

---

3. Remember, Dear Reader, that supper was earlier in the day than dinner, and in Louis XIV's court, at around 10 o'clock in the morning.

Maria was allegedly negatively overwhelmed by her husband's appearance and demeanor and cried.

The couple stayed at Dover for three days. They then journeyed to Canterbury and next to Rochester, resting a little at each spot. Charles II awaited them at Gravesend, from which they took a barge to Whitehall Palace. Charles led Maria inside the palace through a secret entrance, and her mother was escorted inside by James. It was now 6 December. Her mother stayed on into January 1674 before returning home to Modena.

Maria's Time as Duchess of York

Maria was only a few years older than James's daughters Mary and Anne. James introduced Maria to his surviving daughters as a playmate. Mary was happy enough to oblige, although Maria had to work a little to gain Anne's affection.

In Parliament, which sat again in early January 1674, all Catholic members were prevented from doing anything to interfere with Protestant attempts to annul Maria's marriage. The attempts at annulment were ultimately unsuccessful, but it must have been a harsh dose of reality for Maria to realize she was wholly unwelcome in her new country. Maria, however, through relying on her manners, bearing, and appearance, won herself friends at court.

Maria might have been pregnant already, as there were rumors that she had a stillborn child in March or May of 1674. This seems unlikely, between the timing of her first meeting with her husband and the birth of her child Catherine Laura on 10 January 1675. Either way, Maria was pregnant at least ten times over the span of ten years, having at least four little girls and a boy during her time as Duchess of York.

Little Catherine Laura was well received by her aunt and uncle, Catherine of Braganza and Charles II. She was baptized in the Anglican church, to Maria's dismay. That small bump in her baby girl's life could not hide Maria's delight in being a mother. She was getting along well with James, too, even if she did not feel a passion for him. In fact, when James was away from court with Charles II in early 1674, it was noted that, "the Duke's absence causes Her Royal Highness a little melancholy: she diverts herself, however, with the Princesses [Mary and Anne], whose conversation is much to her taste and satisfaction." At least her home life was going well.

Maria's maternal aunt Hortense Mancini, Duchess of Mazarin, caused a stir when she arrived for a visit to the Stuart court early in Maria's marriage. Her presence annoyed Maria and Catherine of Braganza. Hortense became a mistress to Charles II, to the chagrin and displeasure of the Duchess of York and the Queen.

Tragedy struck Maria and James on 3 October 1675. Catherine Laura, whom James recognized as his first child with Maria, died unexpectedly from convulsions. Maria withdrew from court for a time, claiming illness. Catherine Laura was buried in Mary, Queen of Scots's tomb. Maria was allegedly pregnant in October 1675, and either suffered a later-term miscarriage or stillbirth. That could be another explanation for her withdrawing from court. More evidence is needed.

Maria was pregnant again in the spring of 1676. At the same time, her husband declared that the couple and their family would no longer attend the Protestant church. This did not impress Charles II, although Maria may have felt that she was accomplishing the Pope's mission.

Maria's second, named child, Isabel, was born on 28 August 1676 at St. James's Palace. She was fourth in line to the throne for most of her life. Maria was slightly disappointed at having another girl, but James encouraged Maria, gladdening her heart. He also gifted her ten fruit dishes made of silver filagree, presented in an attractive casket.

Anti-Catholic sentiment at court and throughout England, and presumably Scotland, continued to rise during 1676. Maria, so confident in her faith and her royal position, threw a ball in December 1676. The dark hearts of the anti-Catholic faction were perhaps not unhappy to hear that, in January 1677, both Maria and her five-month-old daughter Isabel were terribly sick. It was thought that the infant would not survive. James complained of Maria being bled too often by the doctors.

Thankfully, both mother and daughter recovered, and Maria conceived again a couple of months later. Her first son, named Charles and recognized as Duke of Cambridge was born at St. James's Palace on 7 November 1677. His birth moved Isabel to being fifth in line to the throne; Isabel's elder half-sisters were in third and fourth place of the line of succession. Unfortunately, the baby was infected with smallpox and died on 12 December 1677. He was interred in Westminster Abbey the next day. Maria was depressed, Isabel was an only child again, and the former order of succession resumed.

Popish Plot

Titus Oates, a minister who could never quite sort which Protestant religion he preferred, managed to create mass hysteria in England between 1678 and 1681. A profligate liar, he never graduated from college but claimed he had. The hysteria he cooked up overtook common sense at court, impacting Maria and her family.

Oates and another co-conspirator wrote and published a tome about the Catholic plot to assassinate Charles II. Recalling that Charles's father had been killed and the ensuing inefficacy of the Protectorate, a threat of the island being violently dragged back to Catholicism was not outlandish. The publication implicated members of Maria of Modena's and Catherine of Braganza's Catholic-dominated courts. Things spun out of control from there.

Charles II's Privy Council repeatedly and inexplicably chose to believe every word that came out of Oates's mouth, so hungry were they to uncover a Catholic plot to cause chaos. After accusing Catherine of Braganza and her doctor of conspiring to poison Charles II, Charles ordered Oates arrested. Bafflingly, Oates was released by Parliament. He was awarded with apartments at Whitehall Palace and a healthy pension. Oates quickly sought to obtain a coat of arms, which was granted. He continued accusing innocent people of being involved in the Popish plot. Dozens were killed.

The tide turned against Oates in 1681. Finally, it was realized that he made up the entire plot. Oates was arrested, imprisoned, and fined.

Maria and her husband were hugely impacted by Oates's nonsense. From fear of their becoming the next Stuart monarchs because of Charles's lack of legitimate children, the Exclusionist movement began. The interested parties wanted to ban James from becoming king. Maria, Princess Anne, and toddler Isabel left for a visit to Holland in October 1678. Maria's stepdaughter Mary was the newest Princess of Orange, having married her paternal, Stuart first-cousin Willem Hendrik, or William of Orange, in 1677. James decided to join them.

Maria came back in early November 1678, finding the situation with Parliament not much improved. Writing to her brother on 3 November, she told him,

> Parliament met last Monday, and there are so many intrigues, supposed plots, and accusations that I could not describe the hundredth part of them...I shall say no more than that the Catholics here are in very ill case, and if God does not come to our aid I not know how it will end.

Later in the month, Maria provided an unencouraging update,

> Affairs here [in England] are getting rather worse than better, every day they invent new stories and new plots, which are too long and too confused to write, also all the couriers are stopped, and all letters opened, so that one can write nothing.

The rest of 1678 passed without much merriment. Maria may have had another child, a daughter named Elizabeth, who lived and died in 1678.

The plots intensified until, on 28 February 1679, King Charles II wrote a very affectionate letter to James, Duke of York, kicking him and Maria out of the country. They were not allowed to take fifteen-year-old Princess Anne or three-year-old Princess Isabel. Maria and her husband, escorted by Charles II, left from Greenwich on 4 March 1679, with a small retinue. They arrived in Brussels on 27 March. Maria became seasick and otherwise unwell on the journey.

Maria remained friendly to her stepdaughter Mary, going to Brussels on 16 April 1679 because the latter was suffering from body aches and a fever. She intended to stay with Mary until Mary was well again. Maria also supported the hope that her and James's exile would be only temporary, perhaps a month at most. As negative reports continued trickling into Brussels from England, Maria grew to understand that she would be out of England for some time.

Time in Brussels and Scotland

Maria's mother Laura, who was living in Rome, came to Brussels in July 1679 to visit. Maria hoped that her brother Francesco could come, but he never did make the journey. Laura was overjoyed with her healthy, intelligent, beautiful daughter. James was a respectful and kind son-in-law, thanking Laura for allowing him to wed Maria.

At around this time, Maria and James petitioned to have Princess Anne and Princess Isabel sent to them in Brussels. Their request was granted, and the young ladies duly conveyed. They arrived in early August. Laura was delighted to meet and dote upon her little granddaughter.

By the end of August, Charles II had reportedly taken quite ill. He requested that James come immediately to England. James did, which was viewed as utterly foolish. If Charles died and James was anywhere near his brother, James would be blamed. The government was wildly uncomfortable with James's presence in England, too. Weeks after his arrival, James was besought to leave England for Scotland. When he was brought to his brother, James was instead ordered to go first to Brussels. Once there, he was to collect his daughters and his wife, then go to The Hague, where Princess Mary Henrietta Stuart lived with her husband. The Yorks would then sail from The Hague to Scotland.

The crossing from Holland left Maria feeling poorly. She and her family were granted permission to travel overland through England on their way to Scotland. Maria was invited by Charles II to recover her health in London, but she preferred to stay with her husband and daughter. After spending time in the capital city, it was determined that Maria and James would go to Scotland without their young ladies. Princesses Anne and Isabel were left at St. James's Palace. Maria and James left for Edinburgh on 6 November 1679, with Princess Anne and several supportive nobles in their respective coaches following the couple for several miles.

Maria and James found the people outside of London to be ill-disposed toward them. They spent multiple nights in York and eventually arrived in Edinburgh on 4 December. They were fabulously welcomed to Edinburgh, the citizens of which were honored to have the Duke and Duchess of York live amongst them. Gun salvos were given, and every noble within a reasonable distance of Edinburgh was on hand to greet them. There were still those who conspired against Maria's family, but overall, things were calmer.

The couple stayed in Edinburgh for the winter of 1679 to 1680, before being unexpectedly invited back to London. They arrived there on 24 February 1680. The people of London were ready for them, celebrating with bonfires and bellringing well into the night. Maria's mother came for a visit in late March 1680.

Throughout this time, James's son-in-law Willem Hendrik, Prince of Orange, was gaining in popularity as a possible heir to the throne. James disregarded any rumors that displaced him as Charles II's heir. Another curious rumor spreading by the autumn of 1680 included that Maria was begging James to abandon Catholicism so he could secure his place in the line of succession. This was untrue.

Anxiety impinged upon Maria's life once more when her daughter Princess Isabel caught a fever in September 1680. It was made clear that, regardless of her little girl's health, Maria and James had to return to Scotland without their daughters.

Maria and James journeyed to Edinburgh, leaving London on Halloween 1680. They traveled by boat this time, and were in Edinburgh by 5 November 1680, with Maria recalling,

> We had only two days given us to prepare for such a journey: I had just risen from illness, and was weak to the last degree, but being free from fever I took courage and found strength for the voyage by sea, where I suffered much, but…we made land in six days; I recovered soon and am now perfectly well.

The couple petitioned Charles to allow them to return home after Parliament was dissolved in early 1681.

Tragedy struck on 2 March 1681 when Princess Isabel died of her ongoing illness, which caused her to develop convulsions. Her parents were still exiled in Edinburgh. Maria was childless again, having outlived at least four, if not up to six, children. The next month, Maria gave birth to a baby who did not live very long. Maria consoled herself,

> with the thought that I have more angels to pray for me, and I ought to esteem myself honoured that, while other women give their children to the world, I have given all mine to God, in whose mercy I still hope that He may someday comfort me by giving me a male child who shall live, and yet in the end gain Heaven.

Maria was pregnant by the very end of 1681, but likely did not know it.

Parliament, this time sitting at Oxford, continued their campaign against Maria's husband. That summer, Willem Hendrik of Orange decided to turn up in Windsor. He wanted reinforcements for his military exertions in Flanders but was denied and returned home empty-handed in August 1681.

Princess Anne's arrival at Edinburgh in July 1681 brought some mirth to the court. There was dancing and gaiety at the Palace of Holyroodhouse. Plays and masques were given. Maria's spirits appeared to revive after seeing Anne again. Maria had given herself over to praying fervently and daily to assuage her grief. After the arrival of Princess Anne, Maria found a new passion for horseback riding. James was delighted. The passion did not last long because Maria fell off her horse on 2 October and hurt her left side. Before giving up, though, Maria did try to resume her hobby, falling again and injuring herself more seriously. Maria stayed in Edinburgh recovering until the spring of 1682, although James had returned to London.

On 3 May 1682, James left England to retrieve Maria. This time, being aware of her penchant for seasickness, James sailed in a large frigate named *Gloucester*. It was hoped that the size of the vessel would minimize the pitching and rolling sensation so clearly felt on smaller ships. It did not go well, and the frigate was wrecked. James and his servants safely escaped the wreck, but many others were not so lucky.

He continued his journey to Edinburgh, successfully fetching Maria. They went back to London, meeting Charles II at Whitehall on 27 May 1682. Maria was roughly six months pregnant at this time, too. They again received a warm welcome from the people of London.

Also at around this time, Maria became very aware of her husband's long-term affair with Catherine Sedley. Catherine had been employed by Maria for the past several years. She was considered very plain, with her attractiveness stemming from her wit. The exposure of the long-term affair caused Maria a deep emotional wound.

Maria's grief and frustration over her husband's behavior was hopefully comforted by the birth of another daughter on 15 August 1682. She was named Charlotte Maria. She lived only two months, contracting a fever and dying of convulsions on 16 October 1682.[4] Maria had two more children while she was the Duchess of York, stillborn or late miscarriages. One arrived in October 1683 and the other in May 1684.

Maria's station in life changed dramatically the following year.

Queenship

Charles II died on 6 February 1685. Maria's husband was now king of England, Scotland, and Ireland as James VII & II. Maria was sad to lose her brother-in-law, but undoubtedly vindicated to now be queen. She never forgot her promise to the Pope.

Maria was installed at Somerset House, which had a certain Catholic flair to it thanks to her mother-in-law Henriette Marie of France. She also had apartments at Whitehall. After making herself comfortable, Maria went to visit Catherine of Braganza, now queen dowager, at St. James's Palace. Maria and James observed Holy Week in the Catholic fashion at St. James's Palace. James allowed his daughter Princess Anne to remain at Whitehall Palace and observe the Protestant service there.

The couple's coronation was held on 23 April 1685, St. George's Day. Celebrating their coronation on the saint's day for the patron saint of England sent a strong message to their kingdom. It was lavish to the degree of bordering absurdity. Maria and James were crowned and anointed privately before going to Westminster Abbey from Whitehall Palace by barge. Maria was still weak after the death of Isabel. She never quite recovered from the shock of the princess's death.

The royal couple entered the abbey through the west door, which is to say the main door. They walked on a blue carpet behind Herb Women, who strew herbs before the new king and queen to scent the air as the herbs were crushed underfoot. They were followed by the peers of the realm, who walked four abreast.

Maria was dressed in purple velvet for the occasion, with her train being seven yards long. The dress was heavily adorned with glittering diamonds. Maria's ladies-in-waiting carried her train. She wore a gold circlet decorated with diamonds on her way to the abbey. The Duke of Beaufort held Maria's crown. The earls of Rutland and Dorset carried her scepter and wand. A canopy of cloth of gold was borne over her head.

---

4. One should note that febrile seizures or convulsions are caused by very high fevers and can lead to death.

During the ceremony, an Imperial Crown was placed on Maria's head. Once the coronation service was over, Maria wore her third crown of the day. It was wholly encrusted with diamonds and pearls. All said, the ceremony lasted nine hours, from roughly 10 o'clock in the morning to 7 o'clock that evening.

After her part of the ceremony was over, Maria went to a closet where her stepdaughter Anne sat with husband George of Denmark. Anne had married George a few years before and had already suffered through her first stillbirth. She was heavily pregnant at her father's and stepmother's coronation.

Maria was instantly popular for her beauty and elegance. She was also benevolent and kind, personally paying the debts of all those imprisoned for debts of £5 or less. As a result, hundreds of people throughout the realm were released from debtor's prison.

Unfortunately, plots against Maria and James continued. In her personal life, Maria was growing increasingly irritated with James's behavior toward his favorite mistress, especially now that he was king. In December 1686, completed renovations at Whitehall Palace for the new royal couple included the addition of a Catholic chapel. Maria saw fit to remove to Whitehall from her usual residence of Somerset House, which Maria completed by February 1687.

Maria's mother passed away in summer 1687. In honor of her passing, the English court went into mourning for six months. Outside the palace walls, a general feeling of unrest and hatred toward the Catholic monarchs was growing, and Willem of Orange used the occasion of Maria's mother's death to send a spy to London, ostensibly to show the court in The Hague's sorrow over the death. In reality, the spy was gauging the country's mood toward the Protestant Willem coming across the sea to take the throne.

Maria, undoubtedly stressed by the low hum of hostility toward her and her husband's reign, wished to conceive again. She was only twenty-eight years old and hopeful of having a healthy pregnancy and providing an heir. To facilitate this, Maria went to the city of Bath in September 1687, whose famous waters could help a woman conceive. Her trip was successful, and Maria was pregnant in autumn 1687.

The baby boy was born 10 June 1688 at St. James's Palace. He was christened James Francis Edward, and hereinafter referred to as James Francis. James II wrote of the birth,

> For the past three or four days Her Majesty the Queen felt extremely well; last night she played at basset[5] and went tranquilly to bed, and this morning [10 June] was suddenly seized with pain, and at ten o'clock gave birth to a little prince, admirably formed, who promises to live.

---

5. A card game, an element of which is usually gambling.

The birth of Maria's son was a public affair. Catherine of Braganza was present, as were really any women who wished to be in Maria's chamber. The men were allowed to stay in the antechamber. Maria chose to nurse and raise James Francis herself, which was seen as terribly odd. Wet nurses were hired, just in case.

Despite the very public birth, horrendous rumors followed. First, there was the rumor that James Francis would not live. Second, there was the rumor that Maria had suffered a stillbirth, and the corpse of that infant was replaced with a living child. The second terrible rumor, and variations thereof, would dog the boy his entire life.

The birth of James Francis sped up the inevitable for Maria and James II. Maria, at first oblivious to any cruel rumors about her or her son, noticed that by mid-July her stepdaughter Mary, whom she nicknamed Lemon, failed to acknowledge little James Francis. Princess Mary was now displaced in the line of succession, and even worse, her replacement would likely be a Catholic.

At around the time of James Francis's birth, seven Protestant bishops in England were prosecuted for seditious libel. Uncleverly known to history as the Seven Bishops, they were prominent clergymen opposed to James's pro-Catholic proclamations made in Scotland in February of 1687 and in England in April 1687. Another version was issued in England in April 1688, and the Protestant clergy could not accept it. They were arrested without bail and thrown in the Tower. After a trial, the Seven Bishops were acquitted in June 1688.

In September 1688, Louis XIV of France declared war on the Dutch. Louis XIV was a maternal cousin of James II, and both monarchs were Catholics. Willem of Orange was afraid that, due to familial affinity and sharing a religion, James II and Maria of Modena would support the French king. Willem sailed to London with a force of 20,000 men and invaded the country.

Willem's invasion started on 5 November from Brixham, Devon, southwest of Exeter. He quickly moved toward London, and the Royal Army gave way during November and December. Maria slipped away from London with James Francis on 9 December 1688. She and her Modenese lady Victoria Davia-Montecuculi were dressed in disguise. They reached Calais safely, and there waited for Maria's husband.

Willem declared James deposed in England on 11 December. James was captured later in December in Kent, but Willem allowed him to flee to France. James left for Calais to join Maria on 23 December 1588. That spring, James was deposed in Scotland. There was no hope for them to return.

Final Exile and Death

Maria and her husband created a court-in-exile at Château de Saint-Germain-en-Laye, courtesy of Louis XIV's benevolence. The palace was Louis's birthplace, and a favorite location until he permanently began using Versailles as his main residence. For Maria's part, she spent most of her time at Versailles.

Maria's husband did try entering England in March 1689 in hopes of reclaiming the throne. James had strong support in Ireland, where he fought off his son-in-law's troops throughout early 1690 but was firmly defeated in July 1690 at the Battle of the Boyne. Strategically, James's army was still strong enough to attack Willem's again, but James gave up and returned to France.

Maria did her best to support James's efforts. She is said to have pawned her jewels and other expensive items to raise funds for his military campaign. She also did her best to convince Louis XIV to provide aid to James, which Louis willingly did.

Maria, as a queen, had to carefully navigate the strict etiquette of the French court. Maria Anna Christine Victoria of Bavaria was Louis XIV's daughter-in-law and was the highest-ranking lady at court after the death of Louis's wife in 1683. It is thought that Maria Anna avoided Maria of Modena so that there were no awkward etiquette issues. Maria Anna spent much of her time in her apartments with her German ladies. Added to that, Maria of Modena was regarded as very beautiful, whereas Maria Anna was considered unattractive at best. Maria Anna, who was frequently ill, died in April 1690, resolving the etiquette issues.

Maria struck up a friendship with nuns at the Convent of the Visitandines in Chaillot, particularly three women whose names all featured Angélique. This was the same convent founded by Maria's mother-in-law Henriette. Maria became involved with this large, important monastery as early as 1689. She had a small space there, where she would occasionally escape court and commune with the Angéliques. Friendship with the nuns at Chaillot would carry Maria through the increasingly difficult later years of her life.

Maria and her husband lived the rest of their lives in France. They did have one final child in June 1692, whom they named Louisa Maria Theresa Stuart. She was born at Saint-Germain-en-Laye, Maria's and James's official residence in France. James tried in vain to have his oldest daughter, now Queen Mary II, attend the birth. James was away from Maria when Louisa was born, suffering yet another failed attempt at, if not invading England, then at least crippling the Dutch navy. Possibly out of shame, James failed to return for weeks after Louisa's birth. Maria corresponded with the nuns at Chaillot, lamenting her husband's inexplicable absence during her lying-in.

None of the Protestant English women who were invited to witness Louisa's birth bothered coming.

Maria's daughter served as consolation and a companion during her lifetime. Maria and her husband were the Queen and King Over the Water, and Louisa became known as the Princess Over the Water.

Weeks after Louisa's birth, Maria's brother the Duke of Modena finally married. He tried negotiating for a French bride, but when that failed, he found an Italian noblewoman. The pair never had children. The Duke of Modena died in September 1694, leaving Maria in the lurch financially, among other issues with the administration of Modena.

Attempts at restoring James II and Maria of Modena continued in fits and spurts during the 1690s, never really gaining any ground. Ill health hit James in March 1701, leading to a regency for the Monarchs Over the Water. James suffered a stroke, impacting him heavily. He died six months later, on 16 September 1701. James suffered an intense seizure which, combined with his paralysis and after-effects of stroke from six months earlier, made the seizure deadly.

Maria, now regent for her son James Francis, once more leapt into action to assert her family's interests. James Francis was thirteen years old and was officially dubbed the "Jacobite pretender" in England. Maria had a pamphlet written and disseminated in Scotland and England, justifying James Francis's right to the throne and that he was, indeed, the king. No one paid Maria's attempts any mind in England. Interest was piqued in Scotland, but ultimately went nowhere.

Delegates from Scotland visited Maria in France, attempting to lay the groundwork for James Francis's return after his brother-in-law died, leaving the throne vacant. Maria, unwilling to be separated from her son when Willem died in 1702, would not allow James Francis to be taken to Scotland for purposes of setting him on the throne. That was the end of the Old Pretender's strong chance of gaining the reign.

Maria dressed in mourning clothes throughout her widowhood. Her visits to Chaillot increased, and she would bring her daughter Louisa with her. Maria's level of poverty slowly increased after James II's death, and her sorrows continued. Her daughter died of smallpox in 1712, not long before her twentieth birthday. This was crushing for Maria, who had hoped that Louisa could marry one of her Hanoverian cousins, thus restoring James II's heirs to the throne. By the time of Louisa's death, her elder sister Mary II and brother-in-law Willem were deceased. Louisa's sister Queen Anne had already lost seventeen children through miscarriage, stillbirth, or the tragedy of childhood illness, and so it seemed very unlikely that Anne would go on to have surviving children.

Maria died 26 April 1718/ 7 May 1718[6]. She was fifty-nine years old, a widow, had one child out of perhaps a dozen who outlived her and was impoverished. She was buried at the convent in Chaillot.

---

6. Using the Old and New Style of dating.

Chapter 14

Mary II & William III

Mary II's and William III's Early Years

Willem Hendrik van Oranje was born 4 November 1650 at Binnenhof Palace in Den Haag, or The Hague, in modern-day Netherlands. His mother was Mary Henrietta Stuart, Princess Royal, whose brothers Charles II and James II & VII became kings of England, Scotland, and Ireland. Willem's father William II, Prince of Orange, died of smallpox days before Willem was born. Mary Henrietta turned nineteen the same day that Willem was born, suffering the dual extremes of joy over the birth of her son and sorrow at losing her husband. What a way to turn nineteen.

Willem grew up amidst the power struggle between his mother and paternal grandmother. The first major issue was over Willem's name: the women sparred over whether he should be named Charles, a Stuart family name. The name Willem won out because apparently, it was known that that was the name his father preferred. How convenient for his paternal grandmother.

Willem's grandmother next decided to test her luck by petitioning the law court in April 1651. She wanted full custody of Willem, claiming that Princess Mary Henrietta was too immature and inexperienced. The law court instead appointed Princess Mary Henrietta and her mother-in-law as joint regents, and further appointed Willem's uncle Elector Frederick William of Brandenburg as joint regent with the women. Willem's paternal aunt was Elector Frederick William's wife.

Willem received a suitable education for his hoped-for status as Stadtholder of Orange. Willem's father and grandfather were appointed to the position, as it had not yet become hereditary. The young man received a lot of pushback, particularly during Oliver Cromwell's tenure as Lord Protector. The English had a tense relationship with the Dutch in the late 1650s to early 1660s. To smooth things, it was promised that Willem would not be elected to the position of Stadtholder. With the return of the monarchy, that agreement was dissolved. Willem became Stadtholder in due course.

Princess Mary Henrietta did not spend as much time with Willem as she could have. She was never embraced by the Dutch people, and so spent her time away from court. This does not mean that she did not care about her son, but rather that widowhood in a foreign country did not treat her well. Despite the public's distaste for Princess Mary Henrietta, she did manage to have appointed to Willem a few English and Scottish women for his nursery. This would have given him a meager exposure to his mother's culture, which would become extremely important in his adult life.

The future Mary II was born on 30 April 1662 at St. James's Palace. At the time of her birth, her uncle Charles II was safely on the throne. Charles II's bride Catherine of Braganza was en route to London. As seen, Mary's father James, Duke of York, would become James VII & II of England, Scotland, and Ireland. That was not known at the time of Mary's birth. James married Mary's mother Anne Hyde out of love, despite it being a source of disdain at court. Her parents' conversion to Catholicism in the late 1660s was another source of discomfort to Charles II, who determined that Mary and her siblings would be raised under Anglican teachings.

Mary was her parents' second child, although her elder brother died a year before Mary was born. Between Mary's birth and May 1667, she was one of four living legitimate children from James, Duke of York. Three more babies came and went, but by 6 December 1671, Mary and her younger sister Anne were the only children to survive.

Mary spent a lot of her time away from her parents. This does not mean that her mother and father did not care for her, but rather that raising the royal children and likely eventual heirs of Charles II required resources in which Mary's parents might not have wanted to invest. Mary learned French, music, and religion per Anglican theology, predominantly.

At some point, Mary encountered a young lady named Frances Apsley, who was nine years older than Mary. When Mary herself was roughly nine years old, she and Frances began a passionate correspondence, signing with code names. The letters were not sexual in nature but were emotional. Mary may have learned some of the writing style from reading romance novels, which she enjoyed. Frances eventually changed the tone of her letters, perhaps no longer wishing to indulge Mary as the princess grew into a teenager. Frances went on to serve Mary and Mary's sister when they were queens.

Mary and Willem Hendrik van Oranje Wed

Mary's marital negotiations were dominated by her uncle the king and by Parliament. Charles II initially wanted Mary to wed one of her French cousins, Louis the Grand Dauphin. He was five months older than Mary. The two were the great-grandchildren of Henri IV of France and Maria de' Medici. Louis's

Catholicism was intolerable to Parliament. Charles II received pushback over the marriage, so they sought a Stuart cousin.

Willem was almost twelve years older than Mary. To say she was displeased about marrying Willem would be an understatement. Regardless of her personal feelings, and daresay keeping in line with royal tradition, the wedding went ahead anyway.

At the time of their marriage, fifteen-year-old Mary had black hair, was close to six feet tall, had a clear complexion, and a lovely figure. She had excellent manners, enjoyed reading, and was well-versed in Protestantism. Willem was twenty-seven, five and a half feet tall, pox-scarred, slightly hunchbacked, and mostly interested in his military campaigns. He did see the value in wedding his attractive younger cousin, even though the couple was very mismatched physically.

Their unglamorous wedding took place on 4 November 1677 in Mary's apartments at St James's Palace. No one at the ceremony looked particularly pleased. Charles II tried to lighten the mood with jokes, for which no one was in the mood. The wedding took place at nine o'clock at night.

Despite the inauspicious beginning of the marriage, Mary and Willem grew to love each other. They traveled to the Netherlands in late November 1677. After surviving the brutal sea portion of the journey, the Prince and Princess Consort of Orange could not dock where they were originally supposed to because of ice. Instead, the couple and their entourage had to walk roughly 7 miles or 11 kilometers from their landing place of Ter Heijde to Den Haag or The Hague. Once safely arrived and recovered, they enjoyed their joyous entry, a tradition in the Netherlands, Belgium, and occasionally Scotland for when a ruler or new spouse arrived.

The couple's marriage was viewed favorably in Britain. Mary, second in line to the throne after her father, was married to Willem, who was fourth in line. Mary herself was popular at the Dutch court. Unfortunately, the couple never successfully conceived a child, causing Mary's younger sister Anne to eventually become the heir apparent.

Even though it was a foregone conclusion that Mary's father James would become the next reigning monarch of England, Scotland, and Ireland, Mary must have still been surprised when the day came. As the story goes, Mary was playing a card game when Willem came to tell her of her father James II's accession in February 1685. With the news, she would have realized that her uncle was dead, her father was king, and she was first in line to the throne.

The Glorious Revolution

The tide turned against Mary's father and stepmother soon enough. James and his wife Maria of Modena being Catholics was unbearable to Parliament, which made Protestant Willem and Anglican Mary the best candidates for the throne. Aside from that, Maria of Modena's children up to the couple's ascension had not lived to adulthood. Maria did give birth to a baby boy in June 1688, upon whose legitimacy or even existence the Protestant-leaning persons at court did their best to cast in doubt.

Princess Mary had no interest in her new baby half-brother, James Francis. After receiving several letters from her stepmother Maria bemoaning Mary's lack of concern for the infant, Mary coolly brushed it off by writing, "all the King's children shall ever find as much affection and kindness from me as can be expected from children of the same father."

Willem was more overt in not recognizing his new brother-in-law. When the English ambassador at The Hague invited members of the court to a celebration of the prince's birth, no one loyal to Willem attended the event. In a petty move, Willem refused to allow his trumpeters and court musicians to participate in the party. It was upheld at the Dutch court that James Francis was of dubious birth. This was to make Willem and Mary's own ascension to the thrones of England and Scotland as smooth as possible.

That autumn, eleven years after Mary and Willem had married at St. James's Palace, Willem led a force to England. It was a rash move on his part to effectively invade, but he landed successfully at Brixham in Devon on 5 November 1688. Willem bade Mary come to London in February 1689. By April, Willem and Mary Henrietta were recognized as the co-monarchs William III and Mary II of England and Ireland. In June, they were recognized in Scotland. Of the year 1689, Mary reflected,

> When I look back on what I was last year and what I now am, it amazes me to see how well I ended the last and how ill I begin this year.
>
> I was then in good temper of mind. The melancholy prospect for me, to see my husband and father so far engaged against each other took all of the satisfaction I could have in this world, and made me find by experience it was not the place of rest or content. The sad example of my father showed sufficiently it was not greatness could secure me; which example touch me so much the more by the nearness of the concern I had every way in it.
>
> On the other side I saw my husband in a prosperous way and blessed God for it, and was sorry I could not so much rejoice as his wife ought; neither was I so sad as became the daughter of a distressed king. I bless my

God decided between the daughter and the wife, and showed me, when Religion was at a stake I should know no man after the flesh, but wait the Lord's leisure and trust his goodne[ss] for the event.

The new king and queen held their joint coronation at Westminster Abbey on 11 April 1689.

Coronation of the Monarchs and Mary II's Reign

A new chair was required for the coronation. It was the first and only time in Scottish, or greater British, history that a joint coronation was held for co-monarchs. An immediate issue that needed solving was that there was only one coronation chair. Given the ceremonial importance, it was deemed that a second chair would be made for Mary, and William would use the traditional coronation chair.

To prepare herself for the coronation, Mary drafted a prayer. She wrote of the time leading up to the coronation,

> The coronation came on [the 11 April 1689]; that was to be all vanity, yet the Bishop of London spoke seriously of it and showed me it ought to be an act of devotion and accordingly they made some very good alterations [for a Protestant ceremony] in the Office. Easter came, the king [William] and I received the sacrament together at Hampton Court. I bless my God I then began to make more serious reflections, and upon Good Friday writ down a confession and prayer fit for the time, and though the coronation took up too much of my thoughts, yet blessed be God, I made a prayer which I used constantly before [the coronation] to prepare myself for it. I also composed some ejaculations[1] which I used at the time of the coronation. One thing was to be done which I was much against, it was receiving the sacrament; this all I could say they would have it, because it had been left out by my father, and wordly consideration prevailing it was done; but I confess myself much to blame in the matter, and never had anything so much troubled me as that did; for there was so much pomp and vanity in all the ceremony that left little time for devotion, and my thought there was so much...and so little true devotion in the matter, that I must reproach it myself as long as I live.

It does not seem that Mary enjoyed herself.

---

1. Meaning, "an abrupt, exclamatory utterance", per Merriam-Webster.

The co-monarchs swore to uphold the Protestant religion. Each was presented with the orb and scepter, girded with the sword of state, and crowned. In addition, they took the important step of agreeing to uphold a constitutional monarchy.

Mary was pious and dutiful to William. As reflected in her memoirs, Mary seemed very concerned over how she was received by the public. All this combined to create her thoughts and beliefs,

> And my opinion having ever been that women should not meddle in government, I have never given myself to be inquisitive into those kind of matters. I have ever used myself not to trouble the king about his business, since I was married to him; for I saw him so full of it that I thought, and he has told me so himself, that when he could get from it, he was glad to come to me and have his thoughts diverted by other discourse; and I found this so reasonable, and seeing it pleased him, I who desired nothing else, have continued still to live so with him; which has made me very ignorant in all kind of business, and I have this notion fully fixt in my mind that, all wisdom being the gift of God, he does impart it where he sees necessary, and since it has pleased Him to take all of my hands by giving me such a husband, I think I ought only to make it my business to serve God, and do all the good I can in the world.

She did her best to adhere to these thoughts throughout her reign with William. William, who was busy fighting wars to keep his positions in Scotland, England, Ireland, and the Netherlands secure, was frequently away from court during the summer months. This meant that Mary did have to administer the government, despite her desires. She had the help of a council, which must have eased her troubles. Mary, in her memoirs, comes across as very anxious to avoid looking foolish. The real Mary was quite competent, impressing her husband.

During her time as queen, Mary oversaw the navy when William was away. This was not a particularly exciting prospect. Mary did just fine with the management of it when necessary. This surely eased William's mind, particularly when he was fighting her father at the Battle of the Boyne in the summer of 1690.

Mary was unafraid of taking decisive action when necessary. She was unwilling to bend the law, even if she felt uncomfortable with the outcome. Examples of these attributes include how she dealt with her maternal uncle Henry Hyde, 2d Earl of Clarendon. She oversaw executions during her reign, but only if that was the only way to satisfy the demands of the law. Otherwise, Mary was perfectly willing to show mercy and leniency.

Her maternal uncle Clarendon chose to support James VII & II during Mary's and William's early reign. He spoke against James's ouster in Parliament.

Adding insult to injury, he refused to sign the necessary oaths of allegiance to Mary and her husband. This earned him a stay in the Tower of London during the summer of 1690. He was released. Later, on New Year's Eve 1690, one of Clarendon's co-conspirators was arrested. He happened to be carrying a letter from Clarendon to James VII & II, earning Clarendon another trip to the Tower in January 1691. One co-conspirator wound up executed, another was set free after some torture and exposing the identities of other miscreants, and Clarendon was allowed to retire to the countryside, never to be seen in London again. Mary preferred that the realms not suffer executions under her watch, but the law was the law.

Mary proved to be a capable, trustworthy leader. She awaited her husband's direction when necessary, even halting departure of the post so she had time to respond to his most recent letter. Mary wrote to William directly three or four times per week, and each had a secretary of state with them who also conveyed messages between the monarchs. Mary and William were able to accomplish a level of synchronicity during William's time away that was nothing short of impressive.

Mary was designated William's vicegerent when he was away. Different from the viceregent, a person who is appointed by the monarch to temporarily act in the monarch's stead, the vicegerent is typically a position occupied by a spiritual authority. For example, the Pope can be considered God's vicegerent on earth. Another example from the Tudor period would be Henry VIII of England appointing Thomas Cromwell as vicegerent. William's appointment of Mary as vicegerent makes sense because she was already a monarch in her own right, and thus could not be made a viceregent. As vicegerent, Mary was William's spiritual representative when he was overseas. She acted on both their behalf, in spirit.

Mary did not have long to rule. She fell ill in December 1694, failing to write her usual reflection for the year. She was afflicted with smallpox. Despite having robust health when compared with her husband William and sister Anne, Mary's body simply could not fend off the smallpox infection and any other secondary infections that went along with it. The chilly, damp English winter did not help matters, either. Mary passed away on 28 December 1694. Her husband William was with her at Kensington Palace until hours before her death, when she sent him away for being too distraught. She passed away around midnight. The winter of 1694 into 1695 was particularly cold. Mary's body was left to lie in state at the Banqueting House, which is still standing, of Whitehall Palace. She was finally buried on 5 March 1695 in Westminster Abbey.

William was devastated. It was rumored that the physically frail king would soon follow Mary, especially since she was the healthier of the two.

William III's Reign

William's frequent campaigns gave him convenient excuses for his health and his diversions. He suffered from asthma, and the classic English weather simply did not agree with him. William had it in his head that by the end of 1689, he would return to the Netherlands permanently and manage his affairs there. Surely Mary would be just fine ruling England, Scotland, and Ireland with the support of a council. Mary did not agree and was vehemently opposed to William's idea. He capitulated to his wife's wishes, but instead busied himself each summer with his ongoing war against Mary's cousin Louis XIV of France.

William had an illicit relationship with Elizabeth Villiers between 1680 and 1695. Elizabeth and her sisters accompanied Mary II to the Netherlands when Mary officially began her life there as Princess of Orange. Elizabeth's mother had served as governess for both Mary II and Queen Anne. William almost certainly indulged in this relationship when he was away from the British Isles. Mary may have seen a small degree of comfort in William having only one mistress his whole life, unlike her raucous uncle Charles II.

William diligently corresponded with Mary. He appreciated her desire to accept his will, and her stance that the husband was the head of the family and the king, the head of the realm. This allowed him to maintain a sense of control over his island realms, even if his heart was in the Netherlands and its wars.

To say that William was involved in the Nine Years' War is an understatement. Also called the War of the League of Augsburg or the War of the Grand Alliance, the war saw William's old nemesis Louis XIV of France attempt to make claims on territory belonging to the Holy Roman Empire. Not caring that Louis XIV was a cousin to his wife, William dutifully participated in the war from its inception in 1688, just before William invaded England.

William and Louis XIV had a history of warring against each other, having fought the Franco-Dutch War from 1672 to 1678 when the French invaded and took over a large portion of the Dutch Republic in early 1672. The French were later repulsed. Louis XIV desired to expand French territory. During the war, each side and its allies took and then lost land. The war ended in September 1678 with the Peace of Nijmegen. France walked away having regained Hainault, Franch Comté, and Artois. William regained the areas originally lost to the French during their invasion of 1672.

William busied himself with the Nine Years' War each summer until the war ended in 1697. Sometimes, William simply marched his troops around Europe, never really engaging in battle. The most serious fighting took place in the summers of 1692 and 1693, with William's efforts being overall successful. Even after burying his wife in March 1695, William was back in the Netherlands, fighting the French. William hosted peace talks at one of his palaces in the Netherlands in the spring of 1697. This resulted in the Treaty of Ryswick, which was concluded between September and October of 1697.

In other unpopular developments, inflation became rife under William's watch in England and Scotland. This left no one happy. William was tone-deaf to the needs of his people, seemingly pursuing glory and indulging in his indiscretions by awarding his mistress some of Mary's former property.

By the turn of the century, it was obvious that neither William nor his sister-in-law Anne would have any surviving, legitimate children. There is no record of William fathering any children. Anne birthed her last child, a stillborn son, in January 1700. Her longest-surviving child died that July. William, in the Netherlands, had to act quickly to secure the succession.

In 1701, William met with his cousin Sophia of Hannover. She was a granddaughter of James VI & I through his daughter Elizabeth Stuart, the Winter Queen of Bohemia. In 1700, Protestant Sophia had five living children, four of whom were male. It was decided through the 1701 Act of Settlement that, should William and his successor Anne die without issue, the thrones of England, Scotland, and Ireland would pass to Sophia and her line. It was around this time that Maria of Modena hoped her daughter Louisa might marry her cousin Georg Ludwig, a Hanoverian cousin through Sophia, or one of his brothers.

William fell off his horse in February 1702, breaking his collarbone. This wound healed. The Jacobites enjoyed the idea that William's horse tripped on a molehill, causing William's fall. They also said it was this fall that killed him. While the riding accident certainly did not help, he easily survived his injuries.

That winter, William struggled with his respiratory health. He allegedly fell asleep near an open window not long after his riding accident, causing him to catch a cold. He suffered from asthma his entire life, which provided another convenient excuse to go abroad in the summers. Due to his age, temporary immobility from the riding injury, and asthma, the cold developed into pneumonia. William died on the morning of 8 March 1702. He was buried in Westminster Abbey next to his wife after a simple ceremony. Their tomb in Henry VII's Lady Chapel is not marked with a monument.

Chapter 15

George of Denmark

Birth and Early Years

On 2 April 1653, King Frederick III of Denmark and his wife, Sophia Amelie of Brunswick-Lüneberg, welcomed their third son. Born in Copenhagen, they named the little boy Jørgen von Oldenburg. Jørgen's birth must have been a welcome joy that spring. Their second son, named Frederick, died fourteen months earlier, in March 1652.

Jørgen was raised at court in Copenhagen. He had at least two tutors, the first being the German Baron Otto Grote zu Schauen. He was seventeen years older than Jørgen. The baron was appointed Jørgen's tutor in 1661 but showed a talent for statecraft. In 1665, the baron became a privy counselor and served in this capacity until his death in 1693.

Jørgen's second tutor was Christen Jensen Lodberg. Lodberg proved to be better suited to the task of instructing Jørgen. From a farming family, Lodberg began his education in around 1636, when he was eleven. He pursued a course in theology, and by 1652, began an interesting round of travel. He traveled through Italy, coming into the employ of the Spanish Guard at Naples to make ends meet. After five years abroad, Lodberg returned to Denmark and pursued a master's degree. He also wrote books and lectured, at Sorø Academy, between 1663 and 1665. He was at Sorø Academy when he was asked to tutor Jørgen. Tales of this adventurous background were inspiring to Jørgen.

In 1668, when Jørgen was roughly fifteen, he went on a Grand Tour. He ventured through Germany, Italy, France, and England. He was back in Denmark by 1670. His father died that year, and his brother became King Christian V of Denmark.

Jørgen had an interesting path forward in his youth. After his Grand Tour and the death of his father, Jørgen was considered a candidate for the king of Poland. He was interested in obtaining the position, but not interested enough to abandon Lutheranism for Catholicism. He remained a prince in Denmark.

Jørgen began his military career during the Scanian War of the 1670s. A simplified version of events follows. The Danes were friendly with the Dutch, creating the Grand Alliance. Sweden, Denmark's neighbor, allied with France. Denmark invaded the Swedish territory of Scania in 1675 to distract the Swedes and the French from attacking the Dutch. The Scanian War was a side-bit to the wider Franco-Dutch war, mentioned in the previous chapter. The Danes succeeded in taking land from the Swedes, given back through the Treaties of Nijmegen in 1679. Jørgen participated in the war during 1677, which saw land and sea campaigns against the Swedes. He was recognized for his service to his brother the king.

Jørgen Starts Life in England

James VII & II sought a Danish marriage for his younger daughter Anne. James's daughter Mary wedded the Dutch William of Orange in 1677. The Netherlands had a strong position on the North Sea, and James wished to balance the Netherlands' naval power with that of Scotland and England. Strengthening ties to Denmark would do just that. As such, Jørgen, who became known as George, was engaged to Princess Anne.

Charles II, who wanted Anne and her sister to be raised as Protestants, was happy with the devoutly Lutheran George. Charles met George in 1669 during the latter's Grand Tour when George was a roughly sixteen-year-old teenager. Four-year-old Anne was not around when George visited England, but it's doubtful she would have formed much of an opinion of George had she met him.

William of Orange would not have approved of George's marriage to Anne, had William known of it. The entire proceedings were kept a secret. Louis XIV of France liked the idea of weakening the Dutch position. Charles II, Louis's cousin, preferred to keep his fellow monarch happy over his niece Mary's husband William.

George and Anne married on 28 July 1683. The wedding was attended by Catherine of Braganza, Maria of Modena, Charles II, and the future James II. The intimate ceremony took place in the Chapel Royal at St. James's Palace. As part of the marriage treaty, George was designated a prince of the Blood Royal. This put him on the same dynastic level as his new bride Anne, in the sense that George had the same status as a legitimate blood-son of James VII & II.

The new couple were granted living space at Whitehall Palace. This allowed George and Anne to develop their separate, Protestant court alongside the Catholic court of the then-Duke of York. Later that summer, it was apparent that three separate courts existed in London, namely that of Charles II and Catherine of Braganza, that of James, Duke of York and Maria of Modena, and that of Prince George of Denmark and Princess Anne of Denmark.[1]

---

1. Anne was recognized as Princess of Denmark after her marriage to George.

George and Anne became a focus of Protestants in London immediately after their marriage. The couple did outwardly support Anne's father, James, even if things were to change quickly. The marriage further signified that the Church of England would remain alive and well, calming Protestant fears over the succession.

George and his wife expected a baby not long after their wedding. Their first baby, a daughter, was not alive when she was born on 12 May 1684. This was the first in a string of familial tragedies. Their next four pregnancies saw mixed results. A daughter Mary, born 2 June 1685. Anne Sophia came on 12 May 1686. Both died in February 1687, a couple of weeks after their mother miscarried. A stillborn son, likely also premature, arrived on 22 October 1687. Another miscarriage in April 1688 followed.

Even with this never-ending string of child deaths and false starts, George was well-liked by his father-in-law. The month of February 1685 was emotionally tumultuous for George. Charles II died on 6 February, leaving George's father-in-law as the new king of England, Scotland, and Ireland. George's mother Sophia Amalia died on 20 February 1685, at the age of fifty-four. George lost two important people in his life within a couple of weeks.

When James VII & II became king in 1685, George was appointed to the Privy Council. He was frequently invited to join his father-in-law for events, including a royal progress in 1686. James granted to George, who was a trained soldier, a military regiment. Leaders of the military were frequent visitors to George's and Anne's court, and all were Protestants. George remained true to his Lutheran roots throughout his life but viewed all forms of Protestantism as relevant. He had no concerns with supporting the Church of England.

The politics of James VII & II's and his French cousin Louis XIV's worried George and Anne. James increasingly tried to persuade his daughters to convert to Catholicism. Anne felt the brunt of her father's pressing because Mary was in the Netherlands with William. Louis's persecution of French Protestants increased. James tried to maintain a separate political agenda from Louis, but James's favoring of Catholics at his court did not ease George's or Anne's minds. There was also the threat of James and Maria of Modena successfully raising a Catholic heir to adulthood.

George went to Denmark with members of his and Anne's court in the summer of 1687. He left to visit his homeland on 17 June 1687. Anne stayed in England because she was pregnant, and was likely despairing over the recent deaths of her daughters. George picked an excellent time to visit Denmark, whether he knew it or not. Maria Sophia of Neuburg, the niece of George's sister-in-law, was set to wed the Portuguese king in July 1687[2]. Maria Sophia was living at her aunt's court in Denmark. In honor of Maria Sophia's impending nuptials, festivities were held, with Protestant leaders throughout the Scandinavian peninsula and the Holy Roman Empire present. This gave George a chance to catch up on the French situation in Europe and strengthen ties with friends and allies.

The Glorious Revolution

George, like Anne, Mary, and William, was displeased when Maria of Modena produced a healthy son in June 1688. This all but ensured a Catholic succession if the boy survived his father. George's sister-in-law Mary had not successfully conceived a child since the early 1670s. This meant that George and Anne, who continued at least conceiving, still stood a chance at their Protestant line continuing. Thus, George remained invested in the Stuart succession.

The French invaded the German Rhineland in September 1688. This was upsetting to George, who wished to see the preservation of Protestant territories within the Holy Roman Empire. The following month, several German leaders, including some of George's relatives, formed the Magdeburg Concert in opposition to the French, part of which included support for William of Orange. His brother-in-law William, fed up with French ambitions and fearing a Catholic Anglo-French alliance, decided it was time to act. As mentioned in prior chapters, William took a huge gamble and invaded England.

George supported James VII & II during the early months of the Glorious Revolution in 1688. Whether he truly did wish to support James, or if it was simply a ruse as he awaited William's invasion, is up for interpretation. With news of William's impending arrival, George defected from supporting James in November 1688. James tried to play it off that he was not terribly upset by George's actions, but this was a serious event. George was, after all, a member of the Stuart Blood Royal. George showed whose rule he preferred by joining with William at the end of November for the latter's progress. Later explaining his behavior to his brother Christian V of Denmark, George wrote that he was pleased with "the king" no longer being in league with the French, as it meant safety for the Protestants. George did not state which king he meant, although one could assume that he was referring to the change in monarchs from James VII & II to William III and Mary II.

When Anne defected from her father's court, she left a letter for her stepmother Maria of Modena. In the letter, Anne explained that she had no choice but to join

---

2. This is the same wedding of Maria Sophia of Neuburg and King Pedro of Portugal discussed in Chapter 12; Pedro was Catherine of Braganza's brother.

her husband George. To do otherwise would be unnatural. It was a convenient excuse. Thankfully, the couple chose the correct side of history.

Reign of Mary II and William III

William, and presumably Mary, were grateful for George's help during the Glorious Revolution. Right before their April coronation, George was made a denizen of England. He was no longer a foreigner, and as a member of the Blood Royal, this paved the way for George and Anne to be William's and Mary's heirs as co-monarchs. George was created Duke of Cumberland, possibly as a nod to his Germanic heritage. The previous holder of the title, Prince Rupert of the Rhine, was a nephew of Charles I through his sister Elizabeth. Rupert passed away in 1682, leaving another creation of the dukedom a possibility. Adding to the joyous time for George and Anne was Anne's seventh pregnancy.

On 24 July 1689, George and Anne welcomed a little boy at Hampton Court Palace. They named him William after his uncle, the king. William had health concerns from the start. He reportedly suffered from convulsions very early on, but he survived infancy. That was more than any of George's and Anne's other children would do.

George did not enjoy the English court's penchant for moving frequently or the never-ending goings-out for tea. George was a military man and approaching later life for someone in the 17th century. He was thirty-seven by the time of Mary and William's coronation. Regardless of earlier support, George also proved to be a less-than-ideal relative to Mary and William.

George remained a member of Parliament in the early 1690s. Because of his nearness in blood to William, the two were seated next to each other whenever they were present in the House of Lords. The men needed to project a united front not only at home but also in their respective homelands. Regardless of outward appearance, George was not a good political ally for William once the latter was king. William worked hard to undo his predecessors' actions in expanding royal authority. William wanted to re-establish a parliamentary monarchy. While George may have agreed with this in theory, that did not mean he signed off on every law or policy William wanted implemented. George's bristling against William caused a strain between the two couples, leaving them largely estranged.

One thing upon which George and William could agree was Protestantism. William allowed George to establish a Lutheran chapel at St. James's Palace, in George's apartments. It was 1699, George's son Prince William still lived, and Protestantism was the religion of the land.

George's and Anne's obstetric history remained tragic throughout the 1690s. Another baby girl, whom they named Mary, was born on 14 October 1690 at St. James's Palace. She died a couple of hours after her birth, having arrived prematurely. A baby boy, George, arrived on 17 April 1692. He took a few breaths, was baptized, and died. A stillborn daughter arrived eleven months later, on 23 March 1693. Another miscarriage followed in January 1694, and then another, in February 1696. Another miscarriage came seven months later, in September 1696; it is debated whether Anne miscarried twins. They conceived quickly enough after this tragedy, but Anne miscarried in March 1697. Another miscarriage happened in December of that year. Anne quickly fell pregnant once more and delivered a stillborn son on 15 September 1698 at Windsor Castle. George and Anne were expecting again in 1699. Their final child, a boy, arrived on 24 January 1700 at St. James's Palace. He was dead.

The Last Years of William III's Rule

Even greater tragedy hit George and Anne in the summer of 1700. Prince William, who suffered from hydrocephalus possibly from an infection leading to meningitis in his infancy, frequently had fevers and other maladies. His head was drained of excess fluid throughout his life, which could not have been a pleasant experience for the boy. Prince William saw his eleventh birthday on 24 July 1689. After dancing at his birthday party, he complained of feeling rather tired. It was assumed that his tiredness was from the frail lad overdoing things at his party. His condition worsened over the next few days, and the physicians decided to bleed him. His condition continued to deteriorate. He died on 30 July 1700, of an unspecified disease.

To give the reader a visualization of George's and Anne's eighteen lost souls, behold this line of letters, showing whether the child was stillborn (S), miscarried (D), or the child's first initial (A, G, M, W):

S·M·A·D·S·D·W·M·G·S·D·D·D·DD·D·S·S

Think about that for a moment and be glad for modern medicine.

Prince Consort

After William's death on 8 March 1702, George's wife Anne became queen regnant of England, Scotland, and Ireland. George, who had a slight claim for the position of king regnant, chose to live quietly as Anne's prince consort.

He was supportive of his wife behind the scenes and avoided the appearance of meddling.

Anne's coronation took place on 23 April 1702, St. George's Day. Anne, wearing crimson velvet, entered Westminster Abbey through the west door to the sound of song. She walked through the church and through the choir. She walked past the throne so that she could pray at the altar. She then returned to a sitting chair, as she was quite obese and suffered multiple maladies by this point. The sitting chair was below the throne. Anne stood for homage to be given to her. She walked again to the altar and kneeled for part of the coronation ceremony. A litany followed, for which Anne returned to her chair and kneeled on a footstool placed before it. She next sat for the appropriate declaration and coronation oath. She rose from her chair and went to the altar again to swear to God that she would keep her oath.

Anne went back to her chair, knelt on her footstool, and was anointed. That done, she stood to be girded with the Sword of State, then sat down. Anne continued to stand up and sit down for the rest of the ceremony. She received purple Robes of State, and the orb. She was given the Queen's Ring, which is a solid gold ring adorned with a ruby. The ruby has the cross of St. George engraved into it. Anne next received the Scepter Royal and the Rod of Equity and Mercy. St. Edward's Crown, made for the coronation of Anne's uncle Charles II, was placed on her head. Anne was finally queen. She sat on the Coronation Chair. She was then presented with the Holy Bible. More singing and ceremony followed, but at the end, Anne was the queen and George remained a prince.

Anne gave George several military titles upon her accession. The War of the Spanish Succession loomed in the Netherlands. It began in 1700 but was not a serious threat to England's and Scotland's allies until 1702. George was made Lord High Admiral and appointed the Lord Warden of the Cinque Ports, too. He never did engage in open war during Anne's reign.

George's struggle with asthma, much like that of William, bothered him throughout his life. The royal couple visited Bath when they could, hoping to take in better air. George became ill in the spring of 1706. He largely remained away from public engagements after that, most notably the thanksgiving service in May 1707 celebrating the Acts of Union.

The Acts of Union were a century in the making. England, Scotland, and Ireland received their first joint monarch in 1603 with the accession of James VI & I. Finally, James's great-granddaughter made the union official. First, the Treaty of Union was agreed to by the governments of Scotland and England in July 1706. England passed its Union with Scotland Act in 1706,[3] which was followed by the Scottish ratification of the Treaty of the Union in January 1707.[4] The Scottish ratification was called the Union with England Act 1707. This done, the kingdoms of Scotland and England, having shared the same monarch since 1603, became Great Britain. This made Anne the first monarch of Great Britain.

George's health continued to decline. He was horribly sick by the autumn of 1708 and died at Kensington Palace in the afternoon of 28 October 1708. Anne was utterly beside herself with grief and did not want to leave her husband's body. She repeatedly kissed him as he lay dying, such was her love for George. The shy but strong couple felt a genuine love for each other. Anne mourned and missed George for the rest of her life.

George was laid to rest in Westminster Abbey in the Stuart vault. Along with him are Charles II, Mary II and William III, and several of George's and Anne's deceased children. Anne was buried in the same vault when she passed away in 1714. George's coffin plate bears an inscription, translated into English as,

> The remains of the most illustrious and exalted Prince George, Hereditary Prince of Denmark and Norway and of the Goths and Vandals, Duke of Schleswig-Holstein, Storman, Dithmarschen, and Cumberland; Earl of Oldenburgh, Delmenhorst, and Kendal; and Baron Wokingham; the only brother of the most serene and puissant Christian, the fifth of that name, lately King of Denmark and Norway etc.; most beloved husband of the most serene and excellent prince[5] Anne, by the grace of God Queen of Great Britain, France and Ireland, Defender of the Faith etc.; Supreme Prefect of all the armies of the Queen both by land and sea, Lord High Admiral of Great Britain and Ireland, Governor of the royal castle of Dover, Warden of the Cinque Ports, Privy Councillor of the Queen's Majesty, Knight of the Most Royal Order of the Garter. Born at Copenhagen, capital of Denmark, on 2nd of April 1653, he died at Kensington on 28th October 1708 aged 56.

George's death saw the end of centuries of royal Stuart Spouses.

---

3. This was passed in the early part of 1707 because the administrative new year still began on 25 March, not 1 January.
4. January 1708 to the modern person; see footnote 2 in A Selection of Poems.
5. Yes, prince.

Epilogue
The Introduction of the Hanoverians

After the death of Queen Anne of Great Britain, the succession fell to the descendants of James VI & I's German granddaughter Sophia of Hannover. Per the 1701 Act of Succession, Sophia and her descendants were to inherit the thrones of England, Scotland, and Ireland to maintain Protestantism within the realms. The Act of Succession omitted dozens of closer-related Catholic cousins to the Stuarts, including Maria of Modena's still-living son James Francis Edward Stuart.

Eighty-three-year-old Sophia collapsed and died at Herrenhausen Palace in Hannover, Lower Saxony, in June 1714, a couple of months before Queen Anne died in England. Next in line to the British throne was Sophia's eldest son Duke Georg Ludwig von Braunschweig-Lüneburg. Braunschweig-Lüneburg is usually called Hanover by English speakers, after the territory's capital city of Hannover.[1] Georg Ludwig was born in late spring 1660. Georg Ludwig married his cousin Sophia Dorothea in 1682 but divorced in 1694. Thankfully, the couple conceived a healthy son who lived to adulthood. Georg Ludwig became Elector of Hannover in 1698, amongst other titles within the Holy Roman Empire.

Georg Ludwig was duly declared king of Great Britain as George I in 1714 very quickly after Queen Anne's death. He arrived in his new kingdom in mid-September and celebrated his coronation the following month. He was not fully embraced by the people of England and faced plenty of opposition during his thirteen-year reign, but not enough to cast the Hanovers off the throne. George I's line still exists today in the persons of Charles III, Prince William of Wales, and William's children George, Charlotte, and Louis.

---

1. The German name for the city is spelt with two Ns, whereas the English spelling has one N.

Appendix
A Selection of Poems

Dear Reader, below are a few poems relevant to our Stuart spouses. I did my best to transcribe poems into modern English for those that still needed to be done. My transcriptions are imperfect; the meaning of some words in the original poem might be lost to the sands of time, and so on. Ultimately, I hope my transcriptions facilitate the modern enjoyment of these works.

The Thistle and the Rose

by William Dunbar, on the occasion of Princess Margaret of England's marriage to James IV of Scotland

Modern English

I.
When March was with variant winds passed,
And April had, with her silver showers,
Took dearly to Nature with one orient blast;
And lusty May, that mother of flowers,
Had made the birds begin their hours
Among the tender odors red and white,
Whose harmony to hear it was delight;

II.
In bed at morrow, sleeping as I lay,
I thought Aurora,[1] with her crystal eyes,
In at the window looked by day
And turned her neck to me, with visage pale and green;
On whose hand a lark sang from the spleen;
Awake, lovers, out of your slumbering,
See how the lusty morrow does upspring.

---

1. In Greek mythology, Aurora is Lady of the Dawn. Her siblings are the sun and moon.

III.
I thought fresh May before my bed up stood,
In weeds painted of many diverse hue,
In bright attire of flowers forged new,
Heavenly color, white, red, brown and blue,
'Balmed in dew, and gilt with Phoebus'[2] beams,
While all the houses illuminate her brightly.

IV.
'Sluggish,' she said, 'Awake now, for shame,
And in my honor something thou go write,
The lark he's done the merry day proclaim,
To raise up lovers with comfort and delight,
Yet naught increases thy courage to indict,
Whose heart sometime has glad and blissful been,
Sung to make under heavy green.'

V.
'Whereto,' quoth I, 'shall I uprise at morrow,
For in this May few birds heard I sing?
They have more cause to weep and 'plain their sorrow,
Thy air it is not wholesome or benign,
Lord Aeolus[3] does in thy season ring;
So blusterous are the blasts of his home,
Among thy boughs to walk I have forborne.'

VI.
With that this lady soberly did smile,
And said, 'Uprise and do thy observance,
Thou did promise, May's lust while,
For to describe the Rose of most pleasance.
Go see the birds how they sing and dance,
Illuminated hour with orient skies bright,
Animated richly with new azure light.'

---

2. Phoebus is part of Phoebus Apollo's name in Greek mythology, like how Athena's name is Pallas Athena. Phoebus Apollo is the God of the Sun.
3. Son of Hippotes, a mortal king; Aelous is the Keeper of the Winds in Greek mythology.

VII.
When this was said, departed she, this queen,
And entered in a lusty guarding gent;
And then, me thought, full hastily be seen,
In sark and mantle [after her] I went into this garth,[4] most dulce and redolent
Of herb and flower, and tender plants sweet,
And green leaves doing of dew down fleet.

VIII.
The purple sun, with tender beams red,
In orient bright as angel did appear,
Through golden skies putting up his head,
Whose gilt tresses shown so wonderously clear,
That all the world took comfort, far and near,
To look upon his fresh and blissful face,
Doing all sable from the heavens chase.

IX.
And as the blissful sun of cherarchy
The fouls' song through comfort of the light;
The birds did with open voices cry,
O lovers' foe, away thou dully night,
And welcome day that comforts every wight;
Hail May, hail Flora, hail Aurora sheen,
Hail princess Nature, hail Venus love's queen !

X.
Dame Nature gave an inhibition there
To fierce Neptune, and Eolus the bald,
Not to perturb the water nor the air,
And that no showers [sharp,] nor blasts cold,
Affray should flowers nor fouls on the fold,
Show bad eek Juno, goddess of the sky.
That show the heaven should keep amene and dry.

XI.
She ordained eek that every bird and beast
Before her highness should anon compare,

---

4. another word for garden

And every flower of virtue, most and least,
And every herb by field far or near,
As they had wont in May, from year to year,
To her there maker to make obedient,
Full law inclined with all due reverence.

XII.
With that anon she send the swift Ro
To bring in beasts of all condition;
The restless swallow commanded she also
To fetch all foul of small and great renown,
And to gar flowers compare of all fashion,
Full craftily conjured she the Yarrow,
Which did forth surge al swift as any arrow.

XIII.
All present were in twinkling of an eye,
Both beast, and bird and flower, before the queen,
And first the lion, greatest of degree,
Was called there, and he most fair to be seen,
With a full hardy countenance and keen,
Before Dame Nature come, and did incline,
With visage bald, and courage leonine.

XIV.
This awful beast full terrible was of cheer,
Piercing of look, and stout of countenance,
Right strong of corpse, of fashion fair, but fear,
Lusty of shape, light of deliverance,
Red of his color, as is the ruby glance;
On field of gold he stood full mightily,
With flower delicious circled lustily.

XV.
This lady lifted up his claws clear,
And let him listlessly lean upon her knee,
And crowned him with diadem full dear,
Of radiant stones, most royal for to see;
Saying, 'The King of Beasts make I thee,
And the chief protector in the woods and shaws;
Onto thy legs go forth, and keep the laws.

XVI.
Exert justice with mercy and conscience,
And let no small beast suffer scathe, nor scorns
Of great beasts that been of more puissance;
Do law elect to apes and unicorns,
And let no bugle, with his busteous horns,
The meek plow ox oppress, for all his pride,
But in the yoke go peaceable him beside.'

XVII.
When this was said, with noise and sound of joy,
All kind of beasts unto their degree,
At once cried loud, '*Vive le roi!*'
And to his feet fell with humility,
And all they made him homage and fealty;
And he did them resave with princely laits,
Whose noble ire is *parcere prostratis*.

XVII.
Since crowned she the eagle King of Fowls,
And as the steel darts sharpened she his pens,
And bade him be just to aps and owls,
As unto peacocks, parrots, or cranes,
And make a law for wight fowls and for wrens;
And let no fowl of raven do affray,
Nor devour birds but his own prey.

XIX.
Then called she all flowers that grew on field,
Discerning all their fashions and affairs;
Upon the awful Thistle she beheld,
And saw him kept with a bush of spears;
Considering him so able for the wears,
A radius crown of rubies she him gave,
And said, 'In field go forth, fend the laith:

XX.
'And, since thou art a king, thou be discreet;
Herb without virtue though had not of such price
As herb of virtue and of odor sweet;

And let no nettle vile, and full of vice,
Her fallow to goodly flower delice;
Nor let no wild weed, full of churlishness,
Compare her to the lily's nobleness.

XXI.
'Nor hold none other flower in such dainty
As the fresh Rose, of color red and white;
For give thou does, hurt is thine honesty,
Considering that no flower is so perfect,
So full of virtue, pleasance and delight,
So full of blissful angelic beauty,
Imperial birth, honor, and dignity.'

XII.
Then to the rose she turned her visage,
And said, 'O lusty daughter most benign,
Above the lily, illustrious of lineage,
From the stock royal rising fresh and eying,
But any spot or macule doing spring;
Come bloom of joy with gems to be crowned,
For our the love of thy beauty is renowned.'

XXIII.
A costly crown, with clarified stones bright,
This comely queen did on her head enclose,
Which all the land illumined of the light;
Wherefore me thought all flowers did rejoice,
Crying at once, 'Hail be, though richest Rose!
Hail, herbs' empress, hail, freshest queen of flowers,
To thee be glory and honor at all hours.'

XXIV.
Then all the birds' song with voice on high,
Whose mirthful sound was marvelous to hear;
The mave's song, 'Hail, rose most rich and right,
That does up flourish under Phoebus' sphere;
Hail, plant of youth, hail, prince's daughter dear,
Hail, blossom breaking out of the blood royal,
Whose precious virtue is imperial.'

XXV.

The merle she sang, 'Hail, rose of most delight,
Hail, of all flowers queen and sovereign;'
The lark she sand, 'Hail, rose, both red and white,
Most pleasant flower, of mighty colors between;'
The nightingale sang, 'Hail, nature's suffragan,
In beauty, nurture and every nobleness,
In riche array, renown, and gentleness.'

XXVI.

The common voice uprise of birds small,
Upon the wise, 'O blessed be the hour
That thou was chosen to be our principal;
Welcome to be our princess of honor,
Our pearl, our pleasance and our paramour,
Our peace, our play, our plain felicity,
Christ thee conserve from all adversity!'

XXVII.

Then all the birds sang with such a shout,
That I anon awoke where I lay,
And with a braid I turned me about
To see this court; but all were went away:
Then up I leaned, halflings in affray,
And thus I write, as ye have hard to-forrow,
Of lust May upon the nynt morrow.

The Thrissill and the Rois

16th-century Scots

I.

Quhen Merch ewes with variand windis past,
And Appryll had, with her siluer schouris
Tane leif at nature with ane orient blast;
And lusty May, that mvddir is of flouris,
Had maid the birdis to begyn their houris
Amang the tendir odouris reid and quhyt,
Quhois armony to heir it wes delyt;

II.

In bed at morrow, sleeping as I lay,
Me thocht Aurora, with her cristall ene,
In at the window lukit by day
And halsit me, with visage hei and grene;
On quhois hand a lark sang fro the splene;
Awalk, luvaris, out of your slomering,
Se how the lusty morrow dois vp spring.

III.

Me thocht fresche May befoir my bed upstude,
In weid depaynt of mony diuerss hew,
Sobir, benyng, and full of mansuetude,
In brycht atteir of flouris forgit new,
Hevinly of color, quhyt, reid, broun and blew,
Balmit in dew, and gilt with Phebus bemys,
Quhill all the houss illumynit hir lemys.

IV.

'Slugitf,' scho said, 'Awalk annone, for schame,
And in my honour sum thing thow go wryt,
The lark hes done the mirry day proclame,
To raiss vp luvaris with confort and delyt,
Yit nocht incressis thy curage to indyt,
Quhois hairt sum tyme hes glaid and blissful bene,
Sangid to mak vndir evis grene.'

V.

'Quhairto,' quod I, 'sall I vpryss at morrow,
For in this May few birdis herd I sing?
Thai haif moir causs to weip and plane their sorrow,
Thy air it is nocht holsum nor benyng;
Lord Eolus dois in thy sessone ring;
So busteous ar the blastis of his home,
Amang thy bewis to walk I haif forborne.'

VI.

With that this lady soberly did smyll,
And said, 'Vpryss and do thy observance;
Thow did promyt, Mayis lusty quhyle,

For to discryve the Roiss of most pleasance.
Go se the birdis how thay sing and dance,
Illumynit our with orient skyis brycht,
Annamyllit richely with new asur lycht.'

VII.
Quhen this wes said, depairtit scho, this quene,
And enterit in a lusty gairding gent;
And than, me thocht, full hestely besene,
In serk and mantill [eftir hir] I went
Into this garth, most dulce and redolent
Off herb and flour, and tendir plantis sueit,
And grene levis doing of dew doun fleit.

VIII.
The purpour sone, with tendir bemys reid,
In orient bricht as angell did appeir,
Throw goldin skyis putting vp his heid,
Quhois gilt tressis schone so wondir cleir,
That all the world tuke confort, fer and neir,
To luke vpone his fresche and blisfull face,
Doing all sable fro the hevynnis chace.

IX.
And as the blisfull soune of cherarchy
The fowlis song throw confort of the licht;
The birdis did with oppin vocis cry,
O luvaris fo, away thow dully nycht,
And welcum day that confortis every wicht;
Haill May, haill Flora, haill Aurora schene,
Haill princes Natur, haill Venus luvis quene!

X.
Dame Nature gaif ane inhibitioun thair
To ferss Neptunus, and Eolus the bawld,
Nocht to perturb the wattir nor the air,
And that no schouris [scharp,] nor blastis cawld,
Effray suld flouris nor fowlis on the fold;
Scho bad cik Juno, goddess of the sky,
That scho the hevin suld keip amene and dry.

XI.
Scho ordand eik that every bird and beist
Befoir hir hienes suld annone compeer,
And every flour of vertew, most and leist,
And every herb be I fer and neir,
As thay had wont in May, fro yeir to yeir,
To hir thair makar to mak obediens,
Full law inclynnand with all dew reuerens.

XII.
With that annone scho send the swyft[e] Ro
To bring in beistis of all conditioun;
The restles Suallow commandit scho also
To feche all fowll of small and greit renown;
And to gar flouris compeir of all fassoun,
Full craftely conjurit scho the Yarrow,
Quhilk did furth swirk als swift as ony arrow.

XIII.
All present wer in twynkling of ane e,
Baith beist, and bird and flour, befoir the quene,
And first the lyone, gretast of degre,
Was called thair, and he, most fair to sene,
With a full hardy contenance and kene,
Befoir Dame Natur come, and did incline,
With visage bawld, and curage leonine.

XIV.
This awfull beist full terrible wes of cheir,
Persing of luke, and stout of countenance,
Rycht strong of corpis, of fassoun fair, but feir,
Lusty of schaip, lycht of deliuerance,
Reid of his cullour, as is the ruby glance;
On I of gold he stude full mychtely,
With flour delycis sirculit lustily.

XV.
This lady liftit vp his cluvis cleir,
And leit him listly lene vpone hir kne,
And crownit him with dyademe full deir,

Of radyous stonis, most ryall for to se;
Saying, 'The king of beistis mak I thee,
And the chief protector in the woddis and schawis;
Onto thi leigis go furth, and keip the lawis.

XVI.
'Exerce justice with mercy and conscience,
And lat no small beist suffir skaith, na skornis
Of greit beistis that bene of moir piscence;
Do law elyk to aipis and vnicornis,
And lat no bowgle, with his busteous hornis,
The meik pluch ox oppress, for all his pryd,
Bot in the yok go peciable him besyd.'

XVII.
Quhen this was said, with noyis and soun of joy,
All kynd of beistis into their degre,
At onis cryit lawd, '*Viue le roy!*'
And till his feit fell with humilite,
And all thay maid him homege and fewte;
And he did thame ressaif with princely laitis,
Quhois noble yre is *parcere prostratis*.

XVIII.
Syne crownit scho the Egle King of Fowlis,
And as steill dertis scherpit scho his pennis,
And bawd him be als just to awppis and owlis,
As vnto pacokkis, papingais, or crennis,
And mak a law for wycht fowlis and for wrennis;
And lat no fowl of ravyne do efferay,
Nor devoir birdis bot his awin pray.

XIX.
Than callit scho all flouris that grew on I,
Discirnyng all thair fassionis and effeiris;
Vpone the awfull Thrissill scho beheld,
And saw him kepit with a busche of speiris;
Concedring him so able for the weiris,
A radius croun of rubeis scho him gaif,
And said, 'In I go furth, and fend the laif;

XX.
'And, sen art a king, thow be discreit;
Herb without vertew thow hald nocht of sic pryce
As herb of vertew and of odor sueit;
And lat no nettill vyle, and full of vyce,
Hir fallow to the gudly flour delyce;
Nor latt no wyld weid, full of churlichenes,
I hir till the lilleis nobilnes.

XXI.
'Nor hald non vdir flour in sic denty
As the fresche Roiss, of cullour reid and quhyt;
For gife thow dois, hurt is thyne honesty,
Conciddering that no flour is so perfyt,
So full of vertew, plesans and delyt,
So full of blisfull angelik bewty,
Imperiall birth, honour, and dignite.'

XXII.
Than to the Roiss scho turnyt hir visage,
And said, 'O lusty dochtir most benyng,
Aboif the lilly, illustare of lynnage,
Fro the stok ryell rysing fresche and ying,
But ony spot or macull doing spring;
Cum blowme of joy with jemis to be cround,
For our the laif thy bewty is renownd.'

XXIII.
A coistly croun, with clarefeid stonis brycht,
This cumly quene did on hir heid inclois,
Quhill all the land illumynit of the licht;
Quhairfoir me thocht all flouris did reioiss,
Crying attonis, 'Haill be, thow richest Roiss!
Haill, hairbis empryce, haill, freschest quene of flouris,
To the be glory and honour at all houris.'

XXIV.
Thane all the birdis song with voce on hicht,
Quhois mirthfull soun wes mervelus to heir;
The mavyss song, 'Haill, Roiss most riche and richt,

That dois vp flureiss vndir Phebus speir;
Haill, plant of yowth, haill, princes dochtir deir,
Haill, blosome breking out of the blud royall,
Quhois pretius vertew is imperiall.'

XXV.
The merle scho sang, 'Haill, Roiss of most delyt,
Haill, of all flouris quene and soverane;'
The lark scho song, 'Haill, Rois, both reid and quhyt,
Most plesand flour, of michty cullouris twane;'
The nychtingaill song, 'Haill, naturis suffragene,
In bewty, nurtour and every nobilness,
In riche array, renown, and gentilness.'

XXVI.
The ffray voce vprais of birdis small,
Apone this wyss, 'O blissit be the hour
That thow wes chosin to be our principall;
Welcome to be our princes of honour,
Our perle, our plesans and our paramour,
Our peax, our play, our plane felicite,
Chryst thee conserfe frome all aduersite!'

XXVII.
Than all the birdis song with sic a schout,
That I annone awoilk quhair that I lay,
And with a braid I turnyt me about
To se this court; bot all wer went away:
Than vp I lenyt, halflingis in affrey,
And thuss I wret, as ye haif hard to-forrow,
Off lusty May vpone the nynt morrow.

The Deploration of the Death of Queen Madeleine

by David Lindsay, written after the early death of Madeleine de Valois, the Summer Queen of Scots.

Modern English

I.
O cruel Death! too great is thy puissance,
Devourer of all earthly living things:
Adam, we may thee wit of this mischance,
In thy default, this cruel tyrant rings,
And spares neither emperor, nor kings:
And now, alas! he's 'reft forth of this land,
The Flower of France, and comfort of Scotland.

II.
Father Adam, alas! that thou abused
Thy free will, being not obedient
Thou chased death, and listing life refused:
Thy succession, alas! that may repent,
That though he's made mankind so impotent;
That it may make to Death no resistance,
Example of our queen, the Flower of France.

III.
O dreadful dragon! With thy doleful dart,
Which did naught spare of the feminine the flower;
But, cruelly, did pierce her through the heart,
And would not give her respite for an hour,
To remain with her prince, and paramour,
That she at leisure, might have taken license:
Scotland on thee, may cry aloud vengeance.

IV.
Though light Methuselah leave nine hundred year,
Three score and nine, but in thy furious rage
Thou did devour this young princess, but per,
Or she was complete seventeen year of age.
Greedy gourmand! Why did thou not assuage

Thy furious rage, contrary to that lusty queen,
Till we some fruit had of her body seen.

V.
O dame Nature! thou did no diligence,
Contrarywise this thief, which all the world confounds;
Had thou with natural targets made defense,
That briber had not committed within her bounds,
And had been saved, from such mortal stounds,
This many a year, but where was thy discretion
That let her pass, till we had seen succession.

VI.
O Venus! with thy blind son, Cupido,
Fie on you both! That made no resistance;
Into your court, ye never had such two,
So loyal lovers, without dissemblance,
As James the Fifth and Madeleine of France,
Descending both of blood imperial,
To whom in love, I find no parallel.

VII.
For, as Leander swam out through the flood,
To his fair lady Hero, many nights,
So did this prince, through burbling streams would,
With earls, barons, squires, and with knights,
Contrary Neptune, and Aeolus,[5] and their mights,
And left his realm, in great disseverance,
To seek his love, the first Daughter of France.

VIII.
And she, like prudent Queen Penelope,
Full constantly would change him for none other,
And for his pleasure left her own country,
Without regard to father, or to mother,
Taking no cure of sister, nor of brother;
But shortly took her life, and left them all,
For love of him to whom love made her thrall.

---

5. Here, likely the son of Neptune/Poseidon.

IX.
O dame Fortune! Where was thy great comfort
To her, to whom thou was so favorable?
Thy sliding gifts made her no support,
Her high lineage, nor riches untellable,
I see thy puissance been but variable;
When her father, the most Christian king,
To his dear child, might make no supporting.

X.
The potent prince, her lusty love, and knight,
With his most hardy nobles of Scotland,
Contrary that baleful briber had no might,
Though all the men had been at his command
Of France, Flanders, Italy, and England
With fifty thousand million of treasure,
Might not prolong that lady's life an hour.

XI.
O Paris! of all cities principal,
Which did receive our prince, with laud, and glory
Solemnly through arches triumphal
For as Pompey, after his victory,
Was into Rome received, with great joy,
So thou received our right redoubted roy.[6]

XII.
But, at his marriage, made upon the morn,
Such solace, and solemnization,
Was never seen afore, since Christ was born,
Nor to Scotland such consolation;
There sealed was the confirmation
Of the well-kept ancient alliance,
Made betwixt Scotland and the realm of France.

XIII.
I never did see one day more glorious,
So many, in rich habiliments,

---

6. The old French spelling of the word "*roi*," or king, is "roy."

Of silk, and gold, with stones precious,
Such banqueting, such sound of instruments,
With song, and dance, and martial tournaments:
But like a storm, after a pleasant morrow,
Soon was our solace changed into sorrow.

XIV.
O traitor Death! Whom none may countermand,
Thou might have seen the preparation
Made by the Three Estates of Scotland,
With great comfort and consolation
In every city, castle, tower, and town,
And how such noble set his hail intent,
To be excellent in habiliment.

XV.
Thief! saw thou not the great preparedness
Of Edinburgh, the noble famous town;
Thou saw the people, laboring for their lives,
To make triumph, with trump, and clarion;
Such pleasure was never, into this region,
As should have been the day of her entrance;
With great propinesm[7] given to her Grace.

XVI.
Thou saw mankind right costly scaffolding,
Painted well, with gold, and azure fine,
Ready-prepared for the upsetting,
With fountains, flowing water clear, and wine,
Disguised folks, like creatures divine,
On the scaffold, to play in sundry stories,
But, all in greeting turned thou that glory.

XVII.
Thou saw many a lust fresh gallant,
Well-ordered for resaving their Queen,
Such craftsman, with bent bow, in his hand,

---

7. a gift of money

Full regalia[8] in short clothing of green:
The honest burghs, clad thou should have seen,
Some in scarlet, some in cloth of green,
For to have met their Lady Sovereign.

XVIII.
Provost, baileys, and lords of the town,
The senators, in order consequent,
Clad into silk of purple, black, and brown;
Syne[9] the great lords of the Parliament,
With many knightly barons, and baronets,
In silk, and gold, in colors conformable;
But thou, alas! all turned into sable.

XIX.
Syne all the lords of religion,
And princes of the priests venerable,
Full pleasantly in their procession,
With all the cunning clerks honorable;
But, thiftwisly,[10] thou tyrant treasonable,
All great solace, and solemnities,
Thou turned into doleful dirges.

XX.
Syne next, in order, passing through the town,
Thou should have heard the din of instruments,
Of tabor, trumpet, shawm,[11] and clarion,[12]
With roar resounded, through the elements,
The heralds, with their awful[13] vestments,
With maces upon either of their hands,
To rule the press, with burnished silver wands.

---

8. I was unable to translate this word but felt that "regalia" fit the context.
9. next
10. by way of theft
11. a medieval instrument like an oboe
12. a type of trumpet
13. "awful" and "awesome" used to have similar meanings, with "awful" here meaning "full of awe" or "awe-inducing."

XXI.
Syne, last of all, in order triumphal,
That most illustrious Princess honorable,
With her lusty ladies of Scotland,
Which should have been a sight most delectable;
Her raiment to rehearse, I am not able,
Of gold, and pearl, and precious stones bright,
Twinkling like stars, in a frosty night.

XXII.
Under a pall of gold, she should have past,
By burgesses born, clothed in silks fine,
The great master of household, all their last,
With him, in order, all the king's tryne,[14]
Whose ordinance was lengthy to define;
On this manner, such passing through the town
Should have resaved many benisoun.[15]

XXIII.
Of virgins, lusty burgesses' wives,
Which should have been a sight celestial;
Vive la Reine! crying for their lives,
With a harmonious sound angelical;
In every corner, mirth musical;
But thou tyrant, in whom is found no grace,
Our Alleluia has turned into Alas!

XXIV.
Thou should have heard the ornate orators,
Making Her Highness salutation,
Both of the clergy, town, and counselors,
With many notable narration;
Thou should have seen her coronation,
In the fair Abbey of the Holy Rood,
In presence of a mirthful multitude.

---

14. Retinue. I kept the original word to preserve the rhyme scheme.
15. Blessings. Again, I kept the original word to preserve the rhyme scheme.

XXV.
Such banqueting, such awful tournaments,
On horse, and foot, that time which should have been;
Such chapel royal, with such instruments,
And crafty music, singing from the spleen,
In this country, never heard, nor seen;
But, all this great solemnity, and gam,
Turned thou hence, *In Requiem aeternam*.

XXVI.
Inconstant world! Thy friendship, I defy;
Since strength, nor wisdom, riches, nor honor,
Virtue, nor beauty, none may certify,
Within thy bounds, for to remain an hour;
What vail to be king, or emperor,
Since princely puissance may not be exempt
From death, whose dolor cannot be expressed!

XXVII.
Since man in earth has no place permanent,
But all men pass by that horrible port;
Let us pray to the Lord Omnipotent,
That doleful day to be our great comfort,
That in His realm, we may with Him resort,
Which from Hell, with His blood ransomed been,
With Magdalene, while of Scotland, queen.

XXVIII.
O Death! that thou the body may devour
Of every man, yet, have thou no puissance,
Of their virtue, for to consume the glory,
As shall be seen of Magdalene of France,
While our queen, whom poets shall advance,
And put her in perpetual memory,
So shall her fame of thee of have victory.

XXIX.
Though thou have slain the heavenly Flower of France,
Which imputed was to the Thistle brave,
Wherein all Scotland saw their hail pleasance,

And made the Lion rejoice from the spleen;
Though rude be pulled from lives green,
The smell of it shall, in despite of thee,
Keep always to realms in peace, and amity.

16th-century Scots

I.
O Crewell Deith! too greit is thy puissance,
Devorar of all erthlie levyng thingis:
Adam, we may thee wyit of this mischance,
In thy default, this cruell tyrane ringis;
And sparis nother Empryour, nor Kingis:
And now, allace! hes reft furth of this land,
The flour of France, and confort of Scotland.

II.
Father Adam, allace! that thow abusit
Thy fre wyll, being inobedient
Thow chesit deith, and lestyng lyfe refusit:
Thy successioun, allace! that may repent,
That thow hes maid mankind so impotent;
That it may mak to deith no resistance,
Exemple of our Quene, the flour of France.

III.
O dreidfull dragoun! With thy dulefull dart,
Quhilk did noght spair of the feminine the flour;
Bot, crewellie, did perse hir throuch the hart,
And wald nocht give hir respite for ane hour,
To remane with hir Prynce, and paramour,
That scho at laiser, mycht have tane licence:
Scotland on thee, may cry ane loud vengeance.

IV.
Thow leit Methusalem leif nine houndreth yeir,
Thre score and nyne, bot in thy furious rage
Thow did devore this young Princess, but per,
Or scho was compleit sevintene yeir of age.
Gredie gorman! quhy did thow nocht assuage

Thy furious rage, contrair that lustine Quene,
Till we sum fruct had of hir bodye sene.

V.
O dame Nature! thow did na diligence,
Contrair this theif, quhilk all the warld counfoundis;
Had thow with natural targis maid defence,
That brybour had nocht commit within hir boundis,
And had been savit, frome sic mortall stoundis,
This mony ane yeir, bot quhare was thy discretioun
That leit hir pas, till we had sene successioun.

VI.
O Venus! with thy blind sone, Cupido,
Fy on yow baith! that maid na resistance;
In to your court, ye never had sic two,
So leill luffaris, without dissimulance,
As James the Fyft and Magdalene of France,
Discendyng baith of blude Imperiall,
To quhome in lufe, I find na paregall.

VII.
For, as Leander swame outthrow the flude,
To his fair Lady Hero, mony nichtis,
So did this Prynce, throw bulryng stremis wode,
With erlis, baronis, squyaris, and with knychtis,
Contrair Neptune, and Eoll, and their mychtis,
And left his Realme, in greit disesperance,
To seik his lufe, the first Dochter of France.

VIII.
And scho, like prudent Quene Penelope,
Full constantlie wald change hym for none uther,
And for his plesour left hir awin countre,
Without regard to Fader, or to Mother,
Taking no cure of sister, nor of brother;
Bot schortlie tuke her leif, and left thame all,
For lufe of him to quhom lufe maid her thrall.

IX.
O dame Fortune! quhare was thy greit confort
Till hir, to quhome thow was so favorabill?
Thy sliding giftis maid hir na support,
Hir hie linage, nor riches intellebill,
I se thy puissance bene bot variabill;
Quhen hir Father, the maist hie Cristin King,
Till his deir child, micht mak no supporting.

X.
The potent Prince, hir lustye lufe, and kniht,
With his maist hardie Noblis of Scotland,
Contrair that bailfull bribour had no micht,
Thocht all the men had bene at his command
Of France, Flanderis, Italie, and Ingland,
With fiftie thousand million of tresour,
Might nocht prolong that Ladyis lyfe an hour.

XI.
O Paris! of all citeis principall,
Quhilk did resave our Prince, with laud, and glorie
Solempnitlie throw arkis triumphall,
Quhilk day bene digne, to put in memorie;
For as Pompey, efter his victorie,
Was into Rome resavit, with greit joy,
So thow resavit our richt redoutit Roy.

XII.
Bot, at his marriage, maid upon the morne,
Sic solace, and solempnizatioun,
Was never sene afore, sen Christ was borne,
Nor to Scotland sic consolatioun;
Thare selit was the confirmatioun
Of the weill keipit ancient Alliance,
Maid betuix Scotland and the realme of France.

XIII.
I never did se one day mair glorious,
So mony, in so riche abilzementis
Of silk, and gold, with stonis precious,

Sic bankettyng, sic sound of instrumentis,
With sang, and dance, and martiall tornamentis:
Botm lyke ane storme, efter ane pleasand morrow,
Sone was our solace changit in to sorrow.

XIV.
O traytour Deith! quhome none may contramand,
Thow mycht have sene the preparatioun
Maid be the Thre Estaitis of Scotland,
With greit confort and consolatioun
IN everlik cietie, castell, toure, and town,
And how ilk Nobill set his haill intent,
To be excellent in abilzement.

XV.
Theif! saw thow nocht the greit preparatyvis
Of Edinburgh, the nobill famous toun;
Thow saw the peple, labouring for their lyvis,
To make triumphe, with trump, and clarioun;
Sic plesour was never, in to this region,
As suld have bene the day of hir entrace;
With greit propynis, gevin till her Grace.

XVI.
Thow saw mankind rycht costlie scaffolding,
Depayntit weill, with gold, and asure fine,
Reddie preparit for the upsetting,
With fontanis, flowing watter cleir, and wyne,
Disagysit folkis, lyke creaturis divine,
On ilk scaffold, to play ane syndrie storie,
Bot, all in greeting turnit thow that glorie.

XVII.
Thow saw mony ane lustie fresche galland,
Weill ordourit for resaving of their Quene:
Ilk craftisman, with bent bow, in his hand,
Full galzeartlie in schort clothing of grene:
The honest Burges, cled thow suld have sene,
Sum in scarlot, and sum in claith of grane,
For till have met their Lady Soverane.

XVIII.
Provest, Baillies, and Lordies of the toun,
The Senatouris, in ordour consequent,
Cled into silk of purpure, blak, and brown;
Syne the greit Lordis of the Parliament,
With mony knychtlie Barroun, and Banrent,
In silk, and gold, in coulouris confortable;
Bot, thow, allace! all turnit in to sable.

XIX.
Syne all the Lordis of Religioun,
And Princes of the preists venerable,
Full plesandlie in their processioun,
With all the cunning Clerkis honorable;
Bot, thiftuouslie, thow tyrane treasonable,
All greit solace, and solempniteis,
Thow turnit in till dulefull Diregeis.

XX.
Syne nixt, in ordour, passing thow the toun,
Thow suld have hard the din of instrumentis,
Of tabrone, trumpet, schalme, and clarioun,
With reird redounand, throw the elemtis:
The Herauldis, with their awful vestimentis,
With Maseris, upon ather of their handis,
To rewle the preis, with burneist silver wandis.

XXI.
Syne, last of all, in ordour triumphall,
That most illuster Princess honorable,
With hir lustie ladyis of Scotland,
Quhilk suld have bene ane sicht most delectable;
Hir rayment to rehers, I am nocht able,
Of gold, and perle, and precious stonis brycht,
Twinklyng lyke sterris, in ane frostie nycht.

XXII.
Under ane pall of gold, scho sulde have past,
Be burgessis borne, clothit in silkis fine,
The greit maister of householde, all thare laste,

With hym, in ordour, all the Kingis tryne,
Quhais ordinance war langsum to deftne;
On this maner, scho passing throw the toun
Suld have resavit mony benisoun,

XXIII.
Of virginis, and of lustie burges wyiffis;
Quhilk suld have bene ane sicht celestiall;
Vive la Royne! cryand for their lyiffis,
With ane harmonious sound angelicall;
In everilk corner, myrthis musicall:
Bot thow tyrane, in quhome is found no grace,
Our Alleluya hes turnit in Allace!

XXIV.
Thow sulde have hard the ornate Oratouris,
Makand hir Hienes salutatioun,
Baith of the Clergy, Toun, and Counsalouris,
With mony notable narratioun:
Thow suld have sene hir Coronatioun,
In the fair Abbay of the Haly Rude,
In presence of ane myrthfull multitude.

XXV.
Sic banketting, sic awfull tornamentis,
On hors, and fute, that time quhilk suld haife bene;
Sic Chapell Royall, with sic instrumentis,
And craftie musick, singing from the splene,
In this countre, never hard, nor sene:
Bot, all this greit solempnitie, and gam,
Turnit thow hes, *In Requiem aeternam.*

XXVI.
Inconstant warld! Thy freindschip, I defy;
Sen strength, nor wisdom, riches, nor honour,
Vertew, nor bewtie, none may certify,
Within thy boundis, for to remane ane hour;
Quhat vailith to be Kyng, or Empryour,
Sen princely puissance may nocht be exemit
From deith, quhais dolour can nocht be expremit!

XXVII.
Sen man in erth hes na place permanent,
Bótall mon passe be that horrible port;
Lat us pray to the Lord Omnipotent,
That dulefull day to be our greit confort,
That in His realme, we may with Him resort,
Quhilkis from the hell, with His blude ransomit bene,
With Magdalene, umquhyle of Scotland Quene.

XXVIII.
O Deith! thocht thow the bodie may devore
Of every man, yit hes thow na puissance,
Of their vertew, for to consume the glore,
As salbe sene of Magdalene of France,
Umquhyle our Quene, quhome Poetis shall avance,
And put hir in perpetuall memorie,
So sall hir fame of thee haif victorie.

XXIX.
Thocht thow hes slane the hevinly Flour of France,
Quhilk impit was in to the Thrissill kene,
Quhairin all Scotland saw their haill pleasance,
And maid the Lyoun rejoysit frome the splene:
Thocht rute be pullit from the levis grene,
The smell of it sall, in despite of thee,
Keip ay twa Realmes in peace, and amitie.

Laing, David, LL.D. (ed). "The Deploratioun of the Deith of Quene Magdalene."
The Poetical Works of Sir David Lyndsay of the Mount. Vol. I. Edinburgh: William
Paterson (1879) pp. 117–124.

Epithalamium for Mary Stuart and the Dauphin of France

by George Buchanan (edited and abridged)

Whence the sudden stir that roars through my vitals? Why is my breast, unused to the experience of Apollo's inspiration, by breathless excitement agitated, and amid Parnassus' long silent shade do the mob raise anew...? But lately, I remember, the laurels were untended, drooping, dumb the tortoise-shell, glum Apollo, and the lyre's inventor an Arcadian.... You [Francis II], do you without backwardness, no belier of your royal progenitors, and like a true-born Frenchman, wholeheartedly take as your wedded wife [Mary, Queen of Scots] this woman whom law has made spouse to you, nurture sister, sex servant of your command, courtesy mistress of your life, whom as life-partner to you have united her parents, and pedigree and goodness and beauty and eligible age and promise to obey and what, fastening these many chains together, makes tighter and faster the fastenings on all these individual chains—namely her love.

If unto you the Goddesses with unanimous consent to suit you with a wife made offer...and allowed you to join the nuptial torches according to your free choice, what, however ambitious are your desires, could you ask for that would be better? Is the charm of exceptional beauty your delight? See the great nobility of her brow, what charm through her winsome cheeks is suffused, how ripe a flame from eyes how lovely flashes its lightnings, in what friendly alliance harmonises with fresh youth mature seriousness, and soft, easy gracefulness with queenly dignity! No whit behind her body is her brain, being well trained in the employments of Pallas, and, as it has received the culture of the Muses' arts, so tranquillises her moods as to render them gentle and obedient to wisdom's rule.

If unbroken family-tree and long pedigree are looked for, this royal house from its one stock a hundred descendants, who all successively bore the sceptret...his is the only house that covers in its historical records twice ten centuries...whatever antiquity is claimed for the other nations by traditions, tales or the boldness of myth, or is credited to them by our generation on the strengtrh of old records...is mere modernity. If splendour of dowry is what stirs you, take as your dowry these war-brave hearts, the Scots.... But the real boast of the quivered Scots is this:...fighting to defend their native land, and to hold life cheap when their good name has to be maintained unimpaired; once a promise has been made, to keep faith; to revere the holy spirit of friendship; and to love not magnificence but character. It was due to these qualities that...one solitary nation in its old home still bade on, and still enjoyed its traditional freedom. Here the fury of the Angles halted, here stuck fast the deadly onset of the Saxons, here the Danes stuck after defeating the Saxons, and when the fierce Danes were subjugated, the Normans too....Rome built a long wall as defence against the battle axes of the Scots. Here all hopes of advancing further were abandoned, and by the Solway water the boundary stone marks the limit of the Roman Empire. And think not that, so accustomed as they are to cruel Mars' pursuits, their hearts have attained not to the refinement of the cultural arts. Scotland too, when barbarian invasions shook the Roman world, almost alone among nations gave hospitality to the banished muses. From here the teachings of Greek culture and Latin culture, and teachers and shapers of unlearned youth, Charlemagne brought across to the Gauls;...to the French joined by treaty the Scots; a treaty which neither the War-God with iron, nor unruly sedition can undo, nor mad lust for power, nor the succession of years, nor any other force, but a holier treaty, binding with closer bonds. Tell over the list of your nation's triumphs since that age and of the conspiracies of the world in all its airs for the destruction of the French name—without the help of Scottish soldiers never victory shone upon the French camp...[Scotland] has shared the brunt of all the vicissitudes of French fortune, has this one nation; and the swords that threatened the French it has often diverted against itself. The bellicose English know this, the wild Netherlanders know this.... This is the dowry your wife offers you, a nation for so many centuries faithful to your subjects and conjoined with them by a treaty of alliance...a people unsubjugated by arms throughout so many dangerous crises.... Rejoice! Now she is yours to kiss, and more than kiss. But check your haste. Give us a share of the happiness today; you will monopolise all the joys tonight—and yet you won't monopolise all the joys today!...Let there be untroubled bright sunshine, and smiling is the countryside, placidly rippling the sea, bland, untempestuous the air.... Thus to your people as a whole the contentment wedlock brings you assures corresponding contentment....Nature, too, is throughout agog with eagerness to honour this wedding: see how the sun comes northward and daily lengthens his stay in the sky as if to behold the honeymoon couple! How the earth puts forth buds and greenery as if to promise happiness and fruitfulness to the union! Lucky couple! I pray that no quarrels will shake your concord and that your wedlock will endure steadfastly and long, like the alliance that joins your respective nations.

Bride, your beauty and ability will doubtless so impress your husband that he will offer to let you control his life and guide his kingdom. Be you true to the nature of your sex and refuse to exercise rule. Land, where it presents a rough craggy front, has to suffer Sea's buffets and fierce waves, but where it makes no stand but lies open, sand-strewn with a fine beach, then Sea puts away its violent moods and woos Land with gentle kisses. Ivy by clinging and obeying climbs as high as the tree to which it is wedded. So too in marriage, submission is the woman's role. Do not be too dismayed by your absence from your native land. In France you have many noble kinsmen (the Guises), there too you will everywhere find the allies of your own race...and there besides you have a husband who will soon mean more to you than either kinsmen or native land, and soon too you will have children to delight you with their baby ways.... Grant me, Fates, this length of days—until Scotland and France, joined through so many centuries by mutual kindnesses, and by poets and by the fetters of laws, are now ruled by the sceptres of brothers and are growing one in spirit; and those whom sea with waves, and sky and earth by huge distances sunder, unity of purpose unites into one people, unity of purpose destined to endure as long as the everlasting fires of the stars.

Gife Langour

by Henry Stewart, Lord Darnley, about or to Mary, Queen of Scots

Modern English

Give languor makes men light,
Or dolor them I,
In earth there is not which
May me compare in ...
Give careful thoughts restore
My heavy heart from sorrow,
I am forevermore
In joy both evening and morrow.

Give pleasure be to pance,[16]
I plaint me not oppressed;
Or absence might advance,
My heart is hail possessed.
Give want of quiet rest
From cares might me convey,
My mind is not molested,
But evermore in joy.

Thou that I pance in pain
In passing to and fro,
I labor all in vain,
For so have many mo'
That have not served so
In suiting of their suit,
The near the fire I go,
The greater is my heat.

The torture for her make
More dule may not endure
Nor I do for her sake,
Even her who has in cure
My heart, which shall be sure

---

16. The act of thinking about something.

In service to the deed
Unto that lady pure,
The well of womanhood.

So schedule to that suite,
My part so permanent,
That no mirth while we meet
Shall cause me be content;
But still my heart lament
In sorrowful sighing sore
Until time she be present,
Farewell, I say no more.

16th-century Scots

Gife heir makis men licht,
Or dolour thame decoir,
In erth heir is no wicht
May me I in gloir.
Gif cairfull thochtis restoir
My havy hairt frome sorrow,
I am for evirmoir
In joy both evin and morrow.

Gif plesour be to pance,
I playnt me nocht opprest;
Or absence micht avance,
My hairt is haill possest.
Gif want of quiet rest
From cairis micht me convoy,
My mind is nocht heir,
Bot evirmoir in joy.

Thocht that I pance in pane
In passing to and fro,
I laubor all in vane;
For so hes mony mo
That hes nocht servit so
In suting of heir sueit.
The nar the fyre I go,
The grittar is my heit.

The turtour for hir maik
Mair dule may nocht indure
Nor I do for hir saik,
Evin hir quha hes in cure
My hart, quhilk sal be sure
In service to the deid
Unto that lady pure,
The well of womanheid.

Schaw schedull to that sueit,
My pairt so permanent,
That no mirth quhill we meit
Sall cause me be content;
Bot still my hairt lament
In sorrowful siching soir
Till tyme scho be present.
Fairweill. I say no moir.

To the Queen

by Henry Stewart, Lord Darnley, to Mary, Queen of Scots

Modern English

Be governor both good and gracious,
Be loyal and loving to thy lieges all,
Be large of freedom and no thing desirous;
Be just to [the] pure for anything may fall;
Be firm of faith and constant as a wall;
Be ready ever to staunch evil and discord;
Be charitable and surely thou shall
Be obedient always to know thy God and Lord.

Be not too proud of worldly goods here;
Be well bethought that will remain at no time;
Be assured also that though men die by war;
Beware therewith the time will no man bide;
Be virtuous and set all vice aside;
Be patient, humble, and misericord;
Be ruled so wherever thou go or bide;
Be obedient always to know thy God and Lord.

Be well-advised of whom thou counsel takes;
Be sure of them that they be loyal and true;
Bethink thee also whether they be friends, or foes.
Be to thy soul, their solace or thou pursue;
Be never over hasty to work and syne to rue;
Be not their friend that makes the false record;
Be ready ever all good works to renew;
Be obedient always to know thy God and Lord.

Be true and conquer thy own heritage
Be enemies of old now occupying
Be strong and force thou sober the man assuage
Be law of God—there may no man deny it;
Be not as lantern in murkiness unespied;
Be thou in right these lands should be restored,
Be worship so thy name be magnified;
Be obedient always to know thy God and Lord.

Be to rebels strong as lion also;
Be fierce to follow them wherever they may be found;
Be to thy liegemen both soft and meek;
Be their succor and help them hail and sound;
Be busy ever that justice be not smothered;
Be blithe in heart; their words oft expound;
Be obedient always to know thy God and Lord.

16th-century Scots

Be governour baith guid and gratious;
Be leill and luifand to thy liegis all;
Be large of fredome and no thing heirth;
Be just to pure for ony thing may fall;
Be ferme of faith and constant as ane wall;
Be reddye evir to stanche evill and discord;
Be cheretabill, and sickerlye thou sall
Be bowsum ay to knaw thy God and Lord.

Be nocht to proud of wardlie guidis heir;
Be weill bethocht thai will remane na tyde;
Be sicker als that thou man die but weir;

Be war thairwith the tyme will no man byde;
Be vertewus and set all vyce on syde;
Be patient, lawlie and misericord;
Be rewlit so quhairevir thou go or byde;
Be bowsum ay to knaw thy God and Lord.

Be weill avysit of quhome thow counsale tais;
Be sewer of thame that thai be leill and trew;
Bethink the als quhidder thai be friendis, or fais.
Be to thy saull, heir sawis or thou persew:
Be nevir our hastye to wirk and syne to rew;
Be nocht heir I that makis the fals record;
Be reddye evir all guid workis to renew;
Be bowsum ay to knaw thy God and Lord.

Be traist and conquese thy awin heirth
Be ennemyes of auld now occupyit;
Be heirth and force thou sobir thai man swage
Be law of God—heir may no man deny it;
Be nocht as lantern in mirknes unspyit;
Be thou in rycht thi landis suld be restored,
Be wirschop so thy name beis magnefeit;
Be bowsum ay to knaw thy God and Lord.

Be to rebellis strong as Iyoun eik;
Be ferce to follow thame quhairevir thai found;
Be to thy liegemen bayth soft and meik;
Be heir succour and help thame haill and sound;
Be knaw thy cure and caus quhy thow was cround;
Be besye evir that justice be nocht smord;
Be blyith in hart; thir wordis oft expound;
Be bowsum ay to knaw thy God and Lord.

To the Queen

By James VI & I, for Anna of Denmark
Add MS 24195, f.5r

As on the wings of your enchanting fame
I was transported ov'r the stormy seas
Who could not quench that restless burning flame
Which only ye by sympathy died mease
So can I troubled be with no disease
But ye my only medicine remains
And easily whenever that ye please
May salve my sores and mitigate my pains
Your smiling is an antidote agains[t]
The melancholy that oppresseth me
And when a raging wrath into me reigns
Your loving looks may me me calm to be
How oft you see me have an heavy heart
Remember then sweet doctor on your art.

To the Queen

Anonymous
By James VI & I, for Anna of Denmark
Add MS 24195, f.5v

That blessed hour when first was brought to light
Our earthly Juno, and our gracious Queen
Three goddesses how soon they had her seen
Contended who protect her should by right
But being as goddesses of equal might
And as of female sex like stiff in will
It was agreed by sacred Phoebus' skill
To join their powers to bless that blessed wight.
Then happy monarch sprung of Fergus' race
That talks with wise Minerva when pleaseth thee
And when thou list some princely sport to see
Thy chaste Diana rides with thee in chase
Then when to bed thou gladly does repair
Clasps in thine arms thy Cytherea [Aphrodite] fair.

Prologue to the Duchess, on Her Return from Scotland

written by John Dryden in c. 1682 about Maria of Modena, then Duchess of York

When factious rage to cruel exile drove
The Queen of beauty and the Court of love,
The Muses droop'd, with their forsaken arts,
And the sad Cupids broke their useless darts.

Love was no more, when loyalty was gone,
The great supporter of his awful throne,
Love could no longer go after beauty stay,
But wandered northward to the verge of day,
As if the sun and he had lost their way.

Pleasing, yet cold, like Cynthia's silver beam,
The people's wonder, and the poet's theme –
Distemper'd Zeal, Sedition, canker'd Hate
No more shall vex the Church, and tear the State;
No more shall Faction civil discords move,
Or only discords of too tender love;

Discord, that only this dispute shall bring,
Who best shall love the Duke, and serve the King.

Funeral Sentences

written by Henry Purcell for the occasion of Mary II's funeral.
The text, from the 1662 *Book of Common Prayer*, was set to music.

1. Man that is born of a woman
hath but a short time to live,
and is full of misery.
He cometh up, and is cut down like a flower;
he fleeth as it were a shadow,
and ne'er continueth in one stay.

2. In the midst of life we are in death:
of whom may we seek for succour,
but of thee, O Lord,
who for our sins art justly displeased?

Yet, O Lord, O Lord most mighty,
O holy and most merciful Saviour,
deliver us not into the bitter pains
of eternal death.

3. Thou knowest, Lord, the secrets of our hearts;
shut not thy merciful ears unto our pray'rs;
but spare us, Lord most holy, O God most mighty.

O holy and most merciful Saviour,
thou most worthy Judge eternal,
suffer us not, at our last hour,
for any pains of death, to fall from thee. Amen.

Bibliography

Primary Sources

Amours, F. J., ed. *Scottish Alliterative Poems in Riming Stanzas*. Edinburgh & London: William Blackwood & Sons (1897).

Baillon, Charles, Comte de. *Lettres Inedites de Henriette-Marie, Reine d'Angleterre*. Paris : Emile Perrin (1884).

BL Harl. MS. 1581, sigs. 39–40; reprinted in Cabala, pp. 278–279.

Bannatyne Miscellany. Vol. I. Edinburgh (1827).

Bower, Walter; edited by Der Watt. *A History Book for Scots: Selections from the Scotichronicon*. Edinburgh: John Donald Publishing (2012).

Brown, K. M. et al., eds. *The Records of the Parliaments of Scotland to 1707*. A1371/1. St. Andrews (2007–2022). 20 June 2023.

Brown, K. M. et al., eds. *The Records of the Parliaments of Scotland to 1707*. 1425/3/19. St. Andrews (2007–2022). Accessed: 26 June 2022.

Brown, K. M. et al., eds. *The Records of the Parliaments of Scotland to 1707*. 1426/15. St. Andrews (2007–2022). Accessed: 26 June 2022.

Brown, K. M. et al., eds. *The Records of the Parliaments of Scotland to 1707*. 1428/7/2. St. Andrews (2007–2022). Accessed: 26 June 2022.

Brown, K. M. et al., eds. *The Records of the Parliaments of Scotland to 1707*. 1428/7/3. St. Andrews (2007–2022). Accessed: 28 June 2022.

Brown, K. M. et al., eds. *The Records of the Parliaments of Scotland to 1707*. 1435/4. St. Andrews 2007–2022). Accessed: 7 July 2022.

Brown, K. M. et al., eds. *The Records of the Parliaments of Scotland to 1707*. 1439/9/1. St. Andrews (2007–2022). Accessed: 7 July 2022.

Brown, K. M. et al., eds. *The Records of the Parliaments of Scotland to 1707*. 1451/6/3. St. Andrews (2007–2022). Accessed: 10 July 2022.

Brown, K. M. et al., eds. *The Records of the Parliaments of Scotland to 1707*. A1454/4. St. Andrews (2007–2022). Accessed: 25 July 2022.

Brown, K. M. et al., eds. *The Records of the Parliaments of Scotland to 1707*. A1504/3/147. St. Andrews (2007–2022). Accessed: 5 December 2022.

Brown, K. M. et al., eds. *The Records of the Parliaments of Scotland to 1707*. A1513/1. St. Andrews (2007–2022). Accessed: 5 December 2022.

Brown, K. M. et al., eds. *The Records of the Parliaments of Scotland to 1707*. A1516/11/5. St. Andrews (2007–2022). Accessed: 5 December 2022.

Brown, K. M. et al., eds. *The Records of the Parliaments of Scotland to 1707*. A1524/11/1. St. Andrews (2007–2022). Accessed: 5 December 2022.

Brown, K. M. et al., eds. *The Records of the Parliaments of Scotland to 1707*. 1528/9/15. St. Andrews (2007–2022). Accessed: 5 December 2022.

Brown, K. M. et al., eds. *The Records of the Parliaments of Scotland to 1707*. 1540/12/56. St. Andrews (2007–2023). Accessed: 23 May 2023.

Brown, K. M. et al., eds. *The Records of the Parliaments of Scotland to 1707*. A1547/9/1. St. Andrews (2007–2023), Accessed: 8 June 2023.

Brown, K. M. et al., eds. *The Records of the Parliaments of Scotland to 1707.* A1548/7/1. St. Andrews (2007–2023). Accessed: 2 June 2023.
Brown, K. M. et al., eds. *The Records of the Parliaments of Scotland to 1707.* A1554/4/1. St. Andrews (2007–2023). Accessed: 2 June 2023.
Brown, K. M. et al., eds. *The Records of the Parliaments of Scotland to 1707.* A1554/4/3. St. Andrews (2007–2023). Accessed: 4 June 2023.
Brown, K. M. et al., eds. *The Records of the Parliaments of Scotland to 1707.* A1555/6/40. St. Andrews (2007–2023). Accessed: 4 June 2023.
Brown, K. M. et al., eds. *The Records of the Parliaments of Scotland to 1707.* A1557/12/3. St. Andrews (2007–2023). Accessed: 9 June 2023.
Buchanan, George. *Rerum Scoticarum Historia.* Edinburgh (1582).
Clifford, Arthur, ed. *The State Papers and Letters of Sir Ralph Sadler, Knight-Banneret.* Vol. I. Edinburgh: Archibald Constable & Co. (1809).
Doebner, Richard. *Memoirs of Mary, Queen of England, (1689–1693) Together with Her Letters and those of Kings James II and William III to the Electress, Sophia of Hanover.* London: D. Nutt, 270 Strand (1886).
Holinshed, Raphael. *The Scottish Chronicle, Or A Complete History and Description of Scotland Being an Accurate Narration of the Beginning, Increase, Proceedings, Wars, Acts, and Government of the Scottish Nation, from the Original Thereof Unto the Year 1585.* Vol. I. Arbroath: J. Finlay (1805).
Holinshead, Raphael. *The Scottish Chronicle, Or A Complete History and Decsription of Scotland Being an Accurate Narration of the Beginning, Increase, Proceedings, Wars, Acts, and Government of the Scottish Nation, from the Original Thereof Unto the Year 1585.* Vol. II. Arbroath: J. Finlay (1805).
MacKean, William, ed. "James I of Scotland," *Kingis Quair.* London: Alexander Gardner (1886).
Keith, Robert. *The History of the Affairs of Church and State in Scotland: From the Beginning of the Reformation in the Reign of King James V. to the Retreat of Queen Mary Into England.* Vol. I. Edinburgh: Thomas & Walter Ruddiman (1734).
Knox, John, W., W. Croft Dickinson, ed. *History of the Reformation in Scotland.* Edinburgh: Thomas Nelson & Sons (1949).
Labanoff, Alexandre. *Lettres, instructions, et mémoires de Maria Stuart, publiées sur les originaux et les manuscrits du State Paper Office de Londres et des principales archivest bibliothèques de l'Europe, par le Prince Alexandre Labanaoff.* London & Paris (1844).
Lindesay, Robert of Pitscottie, J. G. McKay, ed. *The Historie and Cronicles of Scotland from the Slauchter of King James the First to the Ane Thousande Fyve Hundreith Thrie Scoir Fyftein Zeir.* Vol. I. Edinburgh & London: William Blackwood & Sons (1899).
Moir, James, ed. "Blind Harry/Harry the Minstrel." *The Actis and Deidis of the Illustre and Vailzeand Campioun Schir William Wallace knicht of Ellerslie.* Edinburgh & London: William Blackwood & Sons (1889).
National Records of Scotland. *Ratification by King Henry VII of Indenture of Treaty of Perpetual Peace Between England and Scotland. At Westminster. Signed by the King.* SP6/31. 31 October 1502.
Patten, William, J. G. Dalyell, ed. "The Expedicion into Scotlande (1548)." *Fragments of Scottish History.* Edinburgh (1798).
Pepys, Samuel, Henry B. Wheatley, ed. *The Diary of Samuel Pepys.* Vol. II. Boston: Francis A. Niccolls & Co. (1893).
Pepys, Samuel, Henry B. Wheatley, ed. *The Diary of Samuel Pepys.* Vol. IV. London & Cambridge: George Bell & Sons, York St., Covent Garden, and Deighton, Bell & Co. (1893).

The Diary of Samuel Pepys: Daily Entries from the 17th Century London Diary. www.pepysdiary.com/diary/ Accessed numerous times.

Resen, Peter Hansen. *Kong Frederichs den Andens Krönicke*. Copenhagen: Mathias Jörgens Encke (1680).

Robert III: Translation, 1391, 7 March, Scone, Parliament. Parliamentary Records, March 1391. Charter: to Queen Anabella Drummond, of 2,500 merks. www.rps.ac.uk/trans/A1371/1.

Stewart, William, William B. Turnbull, ed. *The Buik of the Cronicles of Scotland*. Vol. III. Published by the Authority of the Lords Commissioners of Her Majesty's Treasury, Under the Direction of the Master of the Rolls. London: Longman, Brown, Green, Longmans, & Roberts (1858).

Teulet, A. *Papiers d'État à l'Histoire de l'Écosse au XVIe Siècle*. Vol. I. Paris : Typographie Plon Frères, Rue de Vaugirard (1851).

Thoms, William J. *The Book of the Court: Exhibiting the History, Duties, and Privilefes of the Several Ranks of the English Nobility and Gentry*. 2d edition. London: Henry G. Bohn, York Street, Covent Garden (1844).

Thomson, Thomas. *The Auchinleck Chronicle: Ane Schort Memoriale of the Scottis Corniklis for Addicioun*. Edinburgh: Printed for Private Circulation (1819).

Volume of King James I & VI's Poems and Sonnets. Add. MS 24195 www.bl.uk/manuscripts/Viewer.aspx?ref=add_ms_24195_f001r Accessed 18 May 2023.

Wood, Marguerite, ed. *Foreign Correspondence with Marie de Lorraine, Queen of Scotland, from the Originals in the Balcarres Papers*. Edinburgh: Scottish Historical Society (1922–1925).

Secondary Sources

Ashley, Mike, *The Mammoth Book of British Kings and Queens*. London: Robinson Publishers (1999).

Barrow, Geoffrey W. S. *Robert Bruce and the Community of the Realm of Scotland*. Edinburgh: Edinburgh University Press (1988).

Beddard, R. A. "Six Unpublished Letters of Queen Henrietta Maria." *The British Library Journal* 25, no. 2 (1999): pp. 129–143. www.jstor.org/stable/42554519.

Bonner, Elizabeth. "Scotland's 'Auld Alliance' with France, 1295–1560." *History*. Vol. 84, No. 273, pp. 5–30. Wiley (January 1999).

Bradbury, Jim. *Stephen and Matilda: The Civil War of 1139–53*. Stroud: The History Press (2009).

Breem, Charles. "'I am Her Majesty's Subject:' Prince George of Denmark and the Transformation of the English Male Consort," *Canadian Journal of History*, p. 39 (2004).

Britannica, editors of Encyclopaedia. "Anne, duke de Montmorency." *Encyclopedia Britannica*, 11 March 2023, www.britannica.com/biography/Anne-duc-de-Montmorency. Accessed: 9 June 2023.

Britannica, editors of Encyclopaedia. "Mary Of Lorraine." *Encyclopedia Britannica*, 7 June 2023. www.britannica.com/biography/Mary-of-Lorraine.

Broomhall, Susan. "In the Orbit of the King: Women, Power, and Authority at the French Court, 1483–1563." In *Women and Power at the French Court, 1483–1563*, edited by Susan Broomhall, pp. 9–40. Amsterdam University Press, 2018. https://doi.org/10.2307/j.ctv8pzd9w.3.

Bryce, Moir. "Mary Stuart's Voyage to France in 1548." *The English Historical Review*, Vol. 22, No. 85, pp. 43–50. Oxford: Oxford University Press (1907).

Buchanan, Patricia H. *Margaret Tudor Queen of Scots*. Edinburgh: Scottish Academic Press (1985).

Colvin, H. M. & Brown, R. A. "The Royal Castles 1066–1485." The History of the King's Works, Volume II: The Middle Ages. London: Her Majesty's Stationery Office (1963).
Creighton, Charles. *A History of Epidemics in Britain from A.D. 664 to the Extinction of the Plague.* Cambridge: Cambridge University Press (1891).
de Bourdeïlle, Pierre, translated by Katherine Prescott Wormeley. *The Book of the Ladies (Illustrious Dames).* Hardy, Pratt & Company (1899).
de Lisle, Leanda. *Henrietta Maria: The Warrior Queen Who Divided a Nation.* New York & London: Pegasus Books (2002).
Dunn, Jane. *Elizabeth and Mary: Cousins, Rivals, Queens.* London: Harper Collins Publishers (2003).
Edinburgh Evening Chronicle (21 September 1847).
Ewan, Elizabeth, Sue Innes, and Sian Reynolds: *The Biographical Dictionary of Scottish Women.* Edinburgh: Edinburgh University Press (2007).
Farguson, Julie. "Dynastic Politics, International Protestantism and Royal Rebellion: Prince George of Denmark and the Glorious Revolution." *The English Historical Review* 131, no. 550 (2016): pp 540–569. www.jstor.org/stable/43896662.
Field, J. F. "Battle of Lund." *Encyclopedia Britannica*, 27 November 2022. www.britannica.com/event/Battle-of-Lund.
Firth, C. H. "Cromwell, Oliver (1599–1658*)" in* Stephen, Leslie *(ed.). Dictionary of National Biography. Vol. 13: pp. 155–180.* London: Smith, Elder & Co. (1888).
Fraser, Antonia. King Charles II. London: Orion Publishing Co. (2002 reprint).
Glenne, Michael. *King Harry's Sister: Margaret Tudor, Queen of Scotland.* Long (1952).
Gough, Melinda J. "A Newly Discovered Performance by Henrietta Maria." *Huntington Library Quarterly* 65, no. 3/4 (2002): pp. 435–447. www.jstor.org/stable/3817983.
Green, David. *Queen Anne.* London: Charles Scribner's Sons (1970).
Green, Mary, Anne Everett, ed. *Letters of Henrietta Maria including Her Private Correspondence with Charles First.* London: Forgotten Books (orig. 1857, again in 2018).
Gregg, William H. *Controversial Issues in Scottish History: A Contrast of the Early Chronicles with the Works of Modern Historians.* New York & London: The Knickerbocker Press (1910).
Grose, Clyde L. "The Anglo-Portuguese Marriage of 1662." *The Hispanic American Historical Review* 10, no. 3 (1930): pp. 313–352. https://doi.org/10.2307/2506378.
Haile, Martin. *Queen Mary of Modena: Her Life and Letters.* London: J. M. Dent & Co. (1905).
Henderson, Thomas Finlayson. "Mary (d. 1463)." *Dictionary of National Biography.* Vol. 36. (1885–1900).
Heron, Robert. *A New General History of Scotland from the Earliest Times, to the Æra of the Abolition of the Hereditary Jurisdictions of Subjects in Scotland, in the Year 1748.* Vol. I. Perth: R. Morison Junior (1794).
Heron, Robert. *A New General History of Scotland from the Earliest Times, to the Æra of the Abolition of the Hereditary Jurisdictions of Subjects in Scotland, in the Year 1748.* Vol. V, Part I. Perth: R. Morison Junior (1799).
Jensen, De Lamar. "French Diplomacy and the Wars of Religion." *The Sixteenth Century Journal* 5, no. 2 (1974): pp. 23–46. https://doi.org/10.2307/2539820.
Laing, David. *Remarks on the Character of Mary of Guelders, Consort of King James the Second of Scotland; In Connexion with an Attempt to Determine the Place of her Interment in Trinity College Church, Edinburgh.* Society of Antiquaries (18 December 1848).
Lang, Andrew. *A Short History of Scotland.* New York: Dodd, Mead & Company (1912).
Lenz, Harvey Nancy. *The Rose and the Thorn: The Lives of Mary and Margaret Tudor.* Macmillan (1975).

Lesley, John, Bishop of Ross. *The History of Scotland, from the Death of King James I. in the Year M.CCCC.XXXVI to the Year M.D.LXI*. Edinburgh (1830).

Mackean, William, ed., and James I of Scotland. *Kingis Quair*. London: Alexander Gardner at Paternoster Row (1886). Stanzas 30–50.

Marshall, Rosalind. *Scottish Queens, 1034–1714*. East Linton: Tuckwell Press (2003).

Mather, Increase & John Sherman. *Kometographia: Or a Discourse Concerning Comets*. London: Samuel Green for Samuel Sewell (1680).

Maurer, Helen E. *Margaret of Anjou: Queenship and Power in Late Medieval England*. Woodbridge: Boydell (2004).

McGowan, Margaret M. "Form and Themes in Henri II's Entry into Rouen." *Renaissance Drama* 1 (1968): pp. 199–251. www.jstor.org/stable/41917415.

Melo, João Vicente. "Catherine of Braganza (1638–1705)." In *Lives in Transit in Early Modern England: Identity and Belonging*, edited by Nandini Das, Amsterdam University Press (2022) pp. 61–68. https://doi.org/10.2307/j.ctv2fzkpnj.12.

Noble, Mark. *Memoirs of the Protectoral-House of Cromwell*. Vol. I, 3rd edition. London: G. G. J. & J. Robinson, Paternoster Row (1787).

Norrie, Aidan, Carolyn Harris, J.L. Laynesmith, Danna R. Messer, Elena Woodacre, eds. *Tudor and Stuart Consorts: Power, Influence, and Dynasty*. London: Palgrave Macmillan (2022).

Ogg, David. *England in the Reigns of James II and William III*, 2nd edition. Oxford: Clarendon Press (1957).

Porter, Linda. *Royal Renegades: The Children of Charles I and the English Civil Wars*. Pan, Main Market Edition (2017).

Price, Richard. "An Incomparable Lady: Queen Mary II's Share in the Government of England, 1689–94." *Huntington Library Quarterly* 75, no. 3 (2012): pp. 307–26. https://doi.org/10.1525/hlq.2012.75.3.307.

Reid, W. Stanford. "The Scottish Counter-Reformation before 1560." *Church History* 14, no. 2 (1945): pp. 104–125. https://doi.org/10.2307/3160932.

Robertson, William. *The History of Scotland During the Reigns of Queen Mary and of King James VI*. Vol. I. Dublin: James Williams (1778).

Robertson, William. *The History of Scotland During the Reigns of Queen Mary and of King James VI*. Vol. II. London: Cadell & Davies, et al. (1817).

Robertson, William. *Scotland Under Her Early Kings: A History of the Kingdom to the Close of the Thirteenth Century*. Vol. II. Edinburgh: Edmonston & Douglas (1862).

Schiern, Frederik, translated by Rev. David Berry. *Life of James Hepburn, Earl of Bothwell*. Edinburgh: David Douglas (1880).

Scott, Walter. *Tales of a Grandfather: Being the History of Scotland from the Earliest Period to the Close of the Reign of James the Fifth*. Boston: Ginn & Company, Publishers (1891).

Theobald, Mary Miley. "A Love Story: King William and Queen Mary." *William & Mary Magazine*. 14 February 2023. https://magazine.wm.edu/online-exclusives/love-story-king-william-and-queen-mary.php. Accessed: 22 July 2023.

Van der Kiste, Johns. *James II and the first modern revolution*. Barnsley: Pen & Sword (2021).

Vaughan, Richard. "Philip III." *Encyclopedia Britannica*, 27 July 2022. www.britannica.com/biography/Philip-III-duke-of-Burgundy. Accessed: 7 May 2023.

Weir, Alison. *Britain's Royal Families, the Complete Genealogy*. London: Vintage Books (2008).

Weir, Alison. *The Wars of the Roses*. New York: Ballantine Books (1995).

"Windsor Castle Gardens." www.rct.uk/collection/themes/Trails/royal-gardens/windsor-castle-gardens Accessed: 29 March 2023.

Index

Aberdeen
　William Elphinstone, Bishop of, 39
　Burgh of, 19, 39
Aberdeenshire, 117
Acts of Union, xii, 190
Ainslie Tavern Bond, 115
Afonso of Portugal, 153
Albany, Duke of
　Alexander Stewart (1454–1485),
　　second creation, son of James II of
　　Scotland, 20
　Robert Stewart (c. 1340–1420),
　　third son of Robert II of Scotland,
　　xxii–xxvi, 8
　John Stewart (1482–1536), Duke of
　　Albany and Count of Auvergne and
　　Lauraguais, xvii, 48–50, 58
　Robert Stewart (1541) *see* Stewart,
　　Robert, son of James V of Scotland
　Henry Stewart (1545–1567) *see* Stewart,
　　Henry, Lord Darnley
Albrecht VI of Austria, 17
d'Albret, Jeanne, 86, 90
Aldpark, 18
Alexander III of Scotland, xv
Alexander of Islay, 8
Alfonso IV d'Este, Duke of Modena and
　Reggio, 87, 159
Alnwick Castle, 23
Alvarotto, Julio, 85
Amboise, 89, 90
Ancrum Moor, 1545 Battle of *see*
　Rough Wooing
Angéliques, 173
Angoulême, Château, 133
Angoulême, Marguerite de, Queen
　Consort of Navarre, 56, 58
Angus, 24
Anjou, Louis II of, 17
Anjou, Margaret of, 21, 22, 32, 36

Anjou, René of, 22
Anne of Austria, 134, 136
Anne, Duchess of Brittany, 34, 55, 56, 85
Anne, Queen of Great Britain and Ireland,
　xi–xiv, xix, 164, 166–171, 174, 176, 177,
　181–183, 185–192
Antipope
　Benedict XIII, 24
　Clement VII, xxiv
Antoine of Navarre, 86, 89, 90
Antonio, Cardinal Trivulzio, 86
Aragon, Ferdinand of, 41
Aragon, Katharine of, 42, 48, 56, 66, 67,
　80, 128
Arran, Earl of
　Thomas Boyd (??–c. 1473), 30
　James Hamilton, 2d Earl (1519–1575),
　　70, 71, 73, 75, 76, 81, 93, 106–109
Artois, 33, 182
Atholl, Earl of *see* Stewart, Walter, son of
　Euphemia de Ross
Auld Alliance, xiii, xv–xvii, 6, 7, 17, 34, 36,
　47, 49, 58, 62, 65, 69, 70, 72, 85, 152
d'Aumale, Claude, 86
Austria, Claudia Felicitas of, 159
Ayala
　Pedro, 41
　1498 Treaty of, 41
Aylesbury, Frances, 156
Ayliffe, Anne, 156
Ayrshire, 19

Balcomie Castle, 67
Balliol, John *see* John I of Scotland
Basilica of St. Denis, 91, 149
Bass Rock, xxvi
Bath, 171, 190
Bavaria, Maria Anna Christine
　Victoria, 173
Beaufort, Henry, 5

Beaufort, Joan, ix, xiii, 1, 3, 4, 6–14, 104
  wedding, ix, 4, 5
  coronation, 5
  death, ix, 15
Beaufort, John, 1, 4
Beaufort, Margaret, 15, 38, 43
Beaujeu, Anne de, 32
Belasyse, Thomas, 1st Earl of Fauconberg, 143
Bemposta Palace, 153, 155
Bening, Alexander, 32
Bening, Simon, 32
Bergenhus Fortress, 118
Berkeley, Euphemia de, xx
Berwick, 21, 43, 117
Berwick-upon-Tweed, 102
Bidaossa River, 57
Biggar, Sir Walter de, 21
Birrell, Robert, 116
Black Knight of Lorne, 12
Blackness Castle, 19
Blairlogie, 18
Blargib, 18
Blois, 76, 133
Blois, Stephen of, 18
Boglio, Madame de, 87
Boleyn, Anne, 66, 92
Bombay *see* Mumbai
Bonnytoun, 19
Bordeaux, 23, 57, 90
Borders, Scottish, 21, 70, 111
Bothwell, Earl of
  James Hepburn, 4th Earl *see* Hepburn, James, Earl of Bothwell
  Patrick Hepburn, 3d Earl *see* Hepburn, Patrick, 3d Earl of Bothwell
Boulogne, 1550 Treaty of, 75
Bourbon, Antoine of *see* Antoine of Navarre
Bourbon, Antoinette of, 63, 65, 69, 86
Bourbon, Charles of, 56, 86
Bourbon, Christine of, French princess and daughter of Henri IV of France, 133, 135
Bourbon, Gaston of, French prince son of Henri IV of France, 133
Bourbon, Henriette Marie de *see* Henriette Marie of France
Bourbon, Louis of, 63, 89, 90
Bourbon, Mary of, 59, 62, 63, 66
Bourchier, Elizabeth, xiii, 142–145
Bourchier, James, 142
Bourdeille, Pierre de, 56
Bourg, Anne de, 89
Bower, Walter, xxiv, xxvi, xxvii, 8, 10
Boyd, Thomas *see* Arran, Earl of
Boyne, 1690 Battle of the, 173
Brabant,
Bragança, Catarina Henriqueta de *see* Braganza, Catherine of
Braganza, Catherine of, xi, 148–155
  wedding, xi, 150, 151
  death, xi, 154, 155
Braganza, Joanna of, 149
Brahe, Tycho, 119, 124
Brandenburg, Frederick William of, 175
Brandenburg-Kulmbach, Dorothea of, 28, 29
Brantôme *see* Bourdeille, Pierre de
Branxton, 1509 Battle of *see also* Flodden, 1509 Battle of, 48
Brechin, 18, 24, 95
  Cathedral, 24
Breda
  city of, 156
  1658 Declaration of, 148
Brest, 140
Brixham, 172, 178
Brotherhood of Misericordia, 155
Broughty Castle, 75
Bruce, Marjorie, xviii, 70
Bruce, Matilda, xx
Bruce, Maud *see* Bruce, Matilda
Bruce, Robert the, xvi, xviii–xx
Bruce, Robert (Presbyterian minister), 125
Bruges, 16, 31, 33
Brunswick-Lüneburg, Sophia Amalia of, 184, 186
Brussels, 16, 167
Buchanan, George, 41, 219
Burgundy, 17, 24, 32, 33, 35, 40
Burgundy, Charles, Duke of *see* Charles I of Burgundy, Duke
Burgundy, Isabella of *see* Portugal, Isabella of

Index   237

Burgundy, Philip III of *see* Philip III
  of Burgundy

Caithness, Earl of
  Walter Stewart *see* Stewart, Walter, son
    of Euphemia de Ross
  George Crichton *see* Crichton, George,
    Earl of Caithness
Calais, 22, 61, 163, 172
Callendar, 126
Cambrai, 1529 Treaty of, 56
Cambuskenneth Abbey, 37
Canterbury, 136, 164
Capiteux Abbey, 57
Capua Castle, 22
Carberry Hill, 1567 Battle of, 116, 117
Carlisle, 69
Carrick, Earl of *see* Robert III of Scotland
Carrick, Sir John de *see* Robert III
  of Scotland
Casa de Rainhas, 154
Casa do Infantado, 154
Casket Letters, 113
Castille, Juana of, 56
Castille and Leon, Isabella of, 41
Cateau-Cambrésis, 1559 Treaty of, 78, 81
Chaillot, Convent of the Visitandines, 149,
  150, 173, 174
Chalon, René of, Prince of Orange, 66
Chapman, Walter, 39
Charlemagne, xv, 220
Charles, Duke of Vendôme, 58
Charles the Bold of Burgundy *see* Charles
  I of Burgundy, Duke
Charles I of Burgundy, Duke, 31–34, 40
Charles I of England, Scotland and
  Ireland, xi, 126, 127, 131, 134–142, 145,
  148, 156, 162, 164–166, 188
Charles II of England, Scotland and
  Ireland, xi, 140, 142, 144, 145, 148–153,
  156, 157, 159, 166–170, 175–177, 182,
  185, 186, 190, 191
Charles II of Spain, 160
Charles III, Duke of Lorraine
Charles III of the United Kingdom,
  16, 192
Charles IV of France, xvi
Charles IV of Maine, 17

Charles V of France, xvi, 85
Charles VI of France, xvi
Charles VII of France, 6, 7, 9, 17
Charles VIII of France, xvi, 29
Charles IX of France, 88
Chase-About Raid of 1565, 95–97, 109
Chartres, 76
Château de Saint-Germain-en-Laye,
  172, 173
Châteaudun
  Castle, 76
  Sainte Chappelle, 66
Chrestien, Marguerite, 106
Christian I of Denmark and Norway, 28,
  29, 35
Christian II of Denmark and Sweden, 119
Christian IV of Denmark and Norway,
  120, 121, 128, 139
Christian V of Denmark and Norway, 184,
  187, 191
Christopher III of Denmark, 29
Clackmannan, 18
Clarence, George, Duke of, 33
Claude, Duke of Longueville, 64
Claude, Queen of France, 54–56, 85
Claypole, John, 146
Clerkington, 75
Cleves, Anna of, 16, 66, 87, 132
Cleves, Catherine of, 16
Cleves, Duchy of, 16, 17
Cleves Duke John I of, 16
Cleves, Francis of, 87
Cleves, Maria of, 17
Cleves, Sybylla of, 16
Cleves, William V of, 66
Cockburn, Alexander, 107
Cockburn, John, Laird of Ormiston,
  106, 107
Cockburnspath, 45
Cognac, 54
Col du Pin-Bouchain, 58
Collyweston, 43
Conflans, 1465 Treaty of, 32
Copenhagen, 28, 118, 184, 191
Corbeil, xvi
Cragorth, 19
Craigmillar Castle, 102, 112, 117
Cranbourne Lodge, 156

Crichton Castle, 106, 111
Crichton, George, Earl of Caithness, 19
Crichton, James, son of George
    Crichton, 19
Crichton, Margaret, daughter of William
    Crichton, 3d Lord Crichton, 20
Crichton, William, Chancellor of
    Scotland, 17
Crichton, William, 3d Lord Crichton, 20
Cromwell, Anna, 146, 147
Cromwell, Bettie *see* Cromwell, Elizabeth
Cromwell, Bridget, 143
Cromwell, Dorothy, 146, 147
Cromwell, Elizabeth, 143
Cromwell, Elizabeth, daughter of Richard
    Cromwell, 146
Cromwell, Frances, 144
Cromwell, Henry, 143
Cromwell, Joan *see* Bourchier, Elizabeth
Cromwell, Katherine, 143
Cromwell, Mary, 144
Cromwell, Oliver, Lord Protector of
    England, xiii, 142, 143, 145, 148, 175
Cromwell, Oliver, son of Oliver Cromwell,
    Lord Protector of England, 143
Cromwell, Oliver, son of Richard, Lord
    Protector or England, 146, 147
Cromwell, Richard, Lord Protector of
    England, xiv, 142, 143, 146, 147
Cromwell, Robert, 143
Cromwell, Thomas, 142, 181
Croÿ, Charles II de, Duke of Chimay, 66
Cumbria, 69
Cupar, 18

Dalkeith, 6, 72, 126
Danés, Pierre, 83
Darcy, Lord Thomas, 92
Davia-Montecuculi, Victoria, 172
David I of Scotland, 18
David II of Scotland, xvi, xviii–xx,
Den Haag *see* The Hague
Denmark, Anna of, x, xi, 29, 82,
    119–131, 227
    wedding, x, 122, 124
    death, xi, 131
Denmark, Christina of, Duchess of Milan,
    58, 65

Denmark, George of, xi, xii, xiv, 29,
    171, 184–191
    Wedding, xi, 185
    death, xii, 191
Denmark, Margaret of, ix, 28–32, 35
    –37, 39
    wedding, ix, 30
    coronation, 30
    death, x, 37
Dissolution of the Monasteries, 143
Douglas, Archibald, husband of Margaret
    Tudor *see* Douglas, Earl of, Archibald,
    6th Earl
Douglas, Catherine *see* Kate Barlass
Douglas, Elizabeth *see* Kate Barlass
Douglas, James de, xxi
Douglas, Earl of
    Archibald, 4th Earl, xxv
    Archibald, 5th Earl, 12
    Archibald, 6th Earl, xvi, 49–52, 92
    William Douglas, 1st Earl, xxi
Douglas, Gavin, 39
Douglas, Margaret, 92, 93, 97
Douglas, Marjory, xxiv
Doune
    Castle, 18, 46
    Lordship, 46
Dover, 163, 164, 191
Dragsholm Castle, 118
Drumcors, 19
Drummond, Anabella, ix, xxii, xxiii
Drury, William, 117
Dryden, John, 228
Dumbarton, 73, 75
Dunbar
    Castle, 15, 45, 100, 111–113
    Lordship, 45
    town, 45, 115, 116
Dunbar, Elizabeth de, xxiv
Dunbar, William, 39, 44, 193
Dunfermline
    Abbey, xxiv, 124
    Palace, xv, xxiii, 36, 124
Durham, 1424 Treaty of, 5
Dunstanburgh Castle, 23

Edinburgh, xvii, 8, 17–19, 21, 25, 28, 31,
    39, 44, 46, 47, 50, 67–69, 71, 73, 75, 84,

94, 96, 100–103, 105 –108, 110, 111, 113–117, 122, 124, 126, 127, 168, 169, 209, 216
  1544 burning of *see also* Rough Wooing, 70
  Canongate, 110, 114
  Castle, xxi, xxiv, 8, 11, 21, 36, 39, 47, 68, 76, 78, 79, 97, 114
  Park, 72
  Royal Mile, 8, 97
  1560 Treaty of, xvii
Edinburghshire, 114
Edward I of England, xv
Edward III of England, xvi, 4
Edward IV of England, 22–24, 32, 33, 35–38, 40
Edward V of England, 40
Edward VI of England, 65, 70, 73, 76, 83, 84, 128
Edward of Lancaster *see* Edward of Westminster
Edward of Westminster, 21, 22
Eglinton, Hugh of, xxi
Egmond, Arnold von, 16, 17, 34
Elizabeth I of England, x, xi, xiii, 66, 76–78, 82, 89, 93, 94, 96, 97, 102, 108, 115, 124, 126, 128, 153
Elizabeth II of the United Kingdom, 16, 70
Elphinstone, 73
Elphinstone, James, 122
Elphinstone, William *see* Aberdeen, Bishop of
Ely, 143, 144
English Civil War *see* Wars of the Three Kingdoms
Erasmus, Desiderius, 47, 64, 80
Ercole II, Duke of Ferrara, 85
Erskine, Sir Robert de, xxi
d'Este, Alfonso, 87
d'Este, Alfonso IV *see* Alfonso IV d'Este, Duke of Modena and Reggio
d'Este, Anne, 86
d'Este, Eleonore, 161
d'Este, Francesco, elder brother of Maria of Modena, 159
d'Este, Francesco, younger brother of Maria of Modena, 159

d'Este, Maria Beatrice Eleonora Anna Margherita *see* Modena, Maria of
Ettrick Forest, 45
Exeter, 140, 172
Eyck, Jan van, 16
Eyemouth, 109

Falkland
  Palace, xxv, 18, 39, 67, 69, 108, 121
  Park, 18
Falmouth, 140
Fåreveile Church, 118
Fa'side Castle, 116, 117
Falside, 71
Felstead Church, 143
Fethelcroft, 19
Fife, xv, 18, 67, 93
Fleetwood, Charles, 143
Fontainebleau, 55, 83
Forth
  Firth of, xxvi, 17, 67, 73
  River, 17
Fitzalan, Walter, xviii
Fitzroy, Henry, 51, 66
Fitzwalter, Alan, xviii
Flamborough Head, xxvi
Flanders, 9, 33, 169, 218
Flodden, 1509 Battle of, 16, 48, 49, 57, 69, 104
Foix, Françoise de, 55
Fontainebleau
  Chapel of the Trinity, 83
  Palace, 55, 83
  School, 55
Forfar, 18
Fossachy, 18
France, Madeleine of *see* Valois, Madeleine de
Franch Comté, 33, 182
Francis I of Brittany, 34
Francis II of Brittany, 34
Francis I of France, xvii, 54–61, 63–66, 72, 76
Francis II of France, x, xvii, 73, 74, 82–86, 89, 90, 105, 106, 113, 219
  wedding, x, 85–88
  coronation, x, 89
  death, x, 91

Francis I, Duke of Lorraine, 66, 86
Franco-Dutch War *see* Nine Years' War
Frederick I of Denmark and Norway, 28
Frederick II of Denmark and Norway, 118–121
Frederick III, Holy Roman Emperor *see* Holy Roman Emperor
Frederick V, Count Palatine of the Rhine, 131
Frederick III of Denmark and Norway, 184
Frederick Henry, Prince of Orange, 139
French Wars of Religion, 80, 89
Friesland, 33

Galbraith, Robert, 51
Gaunt, John of, 1, 4
Ghent, 4, 31
Glasgow, 75 102
Goes, Hugo van der, 31, 32, 35
Golden Rose, 37
Gordon, Catherine, 40, 41
Gordon, George, 4th Earl of Huntly, 109
Gordon, George, 5th Earl of Huntly, 110–112
Gordon, Jean, 96, 97, 109–111, 113, 117
Grafton, Richard, 43
Graham, Margaret de, xx
Gravesend, 164
Greenwich, 22, 167
    Palace, 64, 128–131
    Queen's House, 130
    1543 Treaty of, 70, 84
Guelders, 20, 24, 33–35
Guelders, Arnold of *see* Egmond, Arnold von
Guelders, Margaret of, 17
Guelders, Mary of, ix, 16–27, 35, 36, 67
    wedding, ix, 18
    coronation, 18
    death, ix, 24, 25
Guelders, Philippa of, 63
Guise, Renée de, Abbess of St. Pierre, Reims, 63
Guise, Louise de, 66
Guise, Marie de, x, 63–70, 72–79, 81, 82, 84–86, 90, 93, 95, 104, 105, 112, 130
    wedding, x, 66, 67
    coronation, 67, 68
    death, x, 78, 79
Guzman, Luisa de *see* Luisa of Portugal

Habsburg, Charles von *see* Holy Roman Emperor, Charles V
Habsburg, Frederick von *see* Holy Roman Emperor, Frederick III
Habsburg, Eleonore von, 56, 57
Habsburg, Philip von, 56
Hachberg-Sausenberg, Johanna of, 64
Hadden Rig, 1542 Battle of, 69
Haddington, 73, 75, 84
    Abbey, 74
    1548 Treaty of, 73
Hainault, 33, 182
Halidon Hill, 1332 Battle of, xvi
Hamilton, Elizabeth, Countess of Lennox, 92
Hamilton, Lord James, 30
Hamilton, Patrick, Scottish martyr, 80, 81
Hampton Court Palace, 138, 143, 144, 146, 179, 188
Hanover, Georg Ludwig of, 183, 192
Hanover, Sophia of, 183, 192
Hebrides, 29
d'Heilly, Anne de Pisseleu, 57
Hermitage Castle, 112
Henri II of France, 54, 59, 72–78, 83–90
Henri III of France, 88
Henri IV of France, 55, 132, 176
Henriette Marie of France, xi, 132–142, 148, 149, 151, 152, 157, 158, 170, 173
    wedding, xi, 136
    death, xi, 149
Henry I of England, xviii
Henry II of England, xviii
Henry IV of England, xvi, xxiii, xxiv, xxvi, 1
Henry IV of France, 80
Henry V of England, 1, 4
Henry VI of England, 7, 20–22
Henry VII of England, 15, 35, 37, 38, 41–45, 47, 93, 131, 146, 183
Henry VIII of England, xvii, 38, 39, 41, 42, 47, 49–52, 58, 65–67, 69, 70, 76, 80, 83, 87, 92, 93, 104, 132, 137, 142, 181
Hepburn, James, 4th Earl of Bothwell, x, 78, 82, 86, 96, 97, 99, 100, 104–119

Hepburn, Janet or Jean, 104
Hepburn, Patrick, 3d Earl of Bothwell, 43, 104
Hepburn, William, 107
Hermitage Castle, 112
Herrenhausen Palace, 202
Hesdin, 16
Holland, 33, 166, 167
Holland, Margaret, 1, 4
Holy Roman Emperor
 Frederick III, 17
 Charles V, 17, 56–58, 64
 Leopold I, 160
Holy Island, 108
Holy Trinity, Edinburgh, 31
Holyrood
 Abbey, 8, 11, 18, 21, 25, 27, 30, 45, 61, 62, 68, 70, 126, 211
 Monastery, 94
 Palace, 18, 44, 45, 61, 68, 94, 97, 102, 103, 109–111, 113–115, 124, 126, 127, 169
Holyroodhouse *see* Holyrood
Hornshole, 69
Howard, Charles, 93
Howard, Katheryn, 93
Howard, Lord Thomas, 92
Høyevarde, 118
Huguenots *see* French Wars of Religion
Hundred Years' War, xvi
Huntingdon, 142, 143
Huntly Castle, 117
Huntly, George Gordon, 4th Earl of *see* Gordon, George, 4th Earl of Huntly
Huntly, George Gordon, 5th Earl of *see* Gordon, George, 5th Earl of Huntly
Hursley Park and Lodge, 147
Hyde, Anne, xi, 156–158, 176
Hyde, Edward, 156
Hyde, Henry, 2d Earl of Clarendon, 180

Inchmahome Priory, 72
Inverallen, 18
Inverlochy, 1431 Battle of, 10
Inverness, 8, 30
Ireton, Henry, 143
Irish Confederate Wars *see* Wars of the Three Kingdoms

Isle of May, 17, 18, 67, 68

James I of Scotland, ix, xvi, xxi, xxiii, xxv, xxvi, 1–7, 9–12, 15, 104
James II of Scotland, ix, 7, 8, 11–14, 17–21, 23, 24, 27, 48, 80, 92, 104
James III of Scotland, ix, x, xvi, 20, 21, 24, 28–32, 34–38
James IV of Scotland, x, xvi, 32, 35–48, 193
James V of Scotland, x, xvi, xvii, 47–52, 57–63, 65–67, 69, 70, 75, 81, 93, 103, 122, 131, 134, 136, 207, 214
James VI of Scotland and I of England, x, xi, xiii, 53, 82, 101, 102, 111, 112, 117, 120–123, 183, 185, 190, 192, 227
James VII of Scotland and II of England, xi, 137, 140, 150, 153, 156–178, 180, 181, 185–187
James Hepburn, 4th Earl of Bothwell *see* Hepburn, James, 4th Earl of Bothwell
James of Ross, 36
Jedburgh, 101, 102, 112
Jermyn, Henry, 157
John of Brittany, 34
John of Denmark and Norway, 28
John I of Scotland, xv, xvi, 28
John II of France, xvi
John IV of Portugal, 148, 149
Joux, 58
Jülich-Berg, 17
Jülich-Berg, Maria of, 16
Jülich-Cleves-Berg, Johann Wilhelm of, 132

Kalmar Union, 29, 119, 120
Kate Barlass, 11
Kelso, 21, 69, 70
Kensington Palace, 181, 201
Kincavil, 19
King Over the Water *see* James VII & II of England, Scotland, and Ireland
Kinghorn, xv
Kingsfield, 19
Kinclaven, 18, 19, 21
Kirk o' Fields Parsonage, 102, 103, 107, 113, 114
Knox, John, 106, 107, 112

La Rochelle, 9
Ladies' Peace *see* Cambrai, 1529 Treaty of
Lambton Kirk, 43
Lauder, Robert, xxvi
Leeds, 92
Leith, 18, 61, 72, 122, 124
Les Pull, 18
Lethbertschel, 18
Leuven, 80
Lille, 16
Limburg, 33
Lindesay, Robert, of Pitscottie, 59, 61
Lindores, xxv
Lindsay, David, xxi, 39, 216
Linlithgow, 19, 46–49, 69, 115, 121, 126
Linlithgowshire, 46
Lisbon, 148, 150, 153, 154
Litil Salchy, 18
Little Sauchie *see* Litil Salchy
Livingston, Alexander, 12
Lochmaben Castle, 69
Lodberg, Chrisen Jensen, 184
Logie, 18
Lollards, 80
London, 1, 4, 22, 42, 49, 76, 97, 126, 127, 129, 130, 138–142, 147–149, 151, 167–169, 171, 172, 176, 178, 179, 181, 185, 186
Longueville, 64
Lords of the Congregation, 77, 78
Lorraine, Grand Cardinal of
   Antoine Sanguin de Medum, 86
   Charles of Lorraine, 86, 88
   Louis of Guise, 86
   Robert de Lenoncourt, 86
Lorraine, Anne of, 66
Lorraine, Claude of, 63, 86
Lorraine, Francis of *see* Francis I, Duke of Lorraine
Lorraine, Francis of, 2d Duke of Guise, 86–90
Lorraine, Isabella of, 22
Lorraine, Marie of *see* Guise, Marie de
Lorraine, René II of, Marquis d'Elbeuf, 106
Lossyntrule, 18
Lotharingia, 33

Louis I de Bourbon, Prince of Condé *see* Bourbon, Louis of
Louis II of Anjou, 17
Louis IX of France, Saint, 89
Louis XI of France, xvi, 7, 9, 22, 32–34, 36
Louis XII of France, xvi, xvii, 55, 56, 64, 85
Louis XIII of France, 132–134, 137
Louis XIV of France, 162, 163, 172, 173, 182, 185, 186
Louis the Grand Dauphin, 176, 177
Louvre Palace, 64, 132, 133, 140
Lubnach, 18
Luisa of Portugal, 148–150
Luther, Martin, 47, 80, 81
Lutheranism, 81, 125, 184–186, 188
Luxembourg, 33
Lyon, 58, 91, 162
Lyon, John, xi

Madrid
   city of, 134
   1526 Treaty of, 57
Maijor, Dorothy, xiv, 146, 147
Malcolm IV of Scotland, xviii, 129
Malines, 33
Malmö Castle, 118
Mancini, Hortense, Duchess of Mazarin, 164
Mar, John, Earl of, son of James III of Scotland, 36
Marches, 24
Maria Anna of Spain, 134, 136
Marignano, 1515 Battle of, 54, 63
Martinozzi, Laura, 163, 164
Mary of Orange *see* Stuart, Mary, daughter of Charles I of England, Scotland and Ireland
Mary, Queen of Scots, x, xiii, xvii, xxii, 69, 70, 72–78, 80–87, 89, 90, 93–119, 122, 128, 158, 165, 219, 220, 222, 224, 228
Mary I, Queen of England, 50, 65, 66, 76–78
Mary II, Queen of England, Scotland, and Ireland, xi, xiv, 153, 158, 164, 166, 167, 172–174, 176–178, 180, 182, 185–189, 191
   wedding, xi, 176

coronation, xi, 179
death, xi
Matilda of England, Holy Roman Empress Consort, 18
Maxwell, Robert, 5th Lord Maxwell, 66
May, Isle of *see* Isle of May
Mazarin, Jules, Cardinal, 159
Mecklenburg-Guestrow, Sophia of, 119–121, 124
Medici, Catherine de', 83, 86, 87, 89, 132
Medici, Marie de', 132, 133, 135–137, 176
Medum Antoine Sanguin de, 86
Melrose Abbey, xviii
Melville, Robert, Lord Seton, 122
Menteith
  Lake, 72
  Earldom/Lordship of, 18, 46
Mercat Cross, 94
Methven
  Lordship, 18, 46
  Castle, 18, 46, 52, 69
Milan, 56
Minette *see* Stuart, Henrietta
Mitte, 139
Modena
  Duchy of, 160–162, 164
  Ducal Palace, 159
Modena, Maria of, xi, 153, 156, 159–174, 178, 183, 185–187
  wedding, xi, 161, 162
  death, xii
Modena, Mary of *see* Modena, Maria of
Mont-de-Marsan, 57
Montalembert, André de, 74
Montglat, Françoise de, 1, 133
Montglat, Jeanne de, 132, 133
Montmorency, Anne de, 85
Moray, John Randolph, 3d Earl of, xx
Mumbai, 150
Mure, Elizabeth, ix, xix, xx, xxii
Murray, Elizabeth, Countess of Dysart, 145
Musselburgh, 116
Myllar, Andrew, 39, 47

Namur, 33
Naples, 22, 194
  Egg of, 86

Navarre, 56
Navarre, Isabella of, 58
Neuburg, Maria Sophia of, 186, 187
Neuchâtel, 64
Neville's Cross, 1346 Battle of, xvi
Neville, Richard, Earl of Warwick, 33
Newark, 45
Nieul Priory, 9
Nijmegen, 1678 Peace of, 182
Nine Years' War, 182, 183
North Berwick, 108
North Sea, 107, 108, 121, 123, 195
Northern Seven Years' War, 119
Northamptonshire, 146
Northumberland, 22, 44, 48, 108
Notre Dame Cathedral, Paris, 55, 60, 85, 87, 136
Norway, Margaret of, xv, xvi
Nydie, xxv

Oates, Titus, 165, 166
Oatlands Palace, 131
Old Pretender *see* Stuart, James Francis Edward
Oldenburg, Jørgen von *see* George of Denmark
Oldenburg, Anna von *see* Denmark, Anna of
Oldenburg, Christina von *see* Denmark, Christina of, Duchess of Milan
Oldenburg, Dietrich von, 29
Oldenburg, Elisabeth von, 120, 121, 124
Oldenburg, Frederick von, 28
Oldenburg, Knut von, 28
Oldenburg, Olav von, 28
Oldpark *see* Aldpark
Oranje, Willem Henrik of *see* William III of England, Scotland and Ireland
Order of the Garter, 16, 128, 191
Order of the Golden Fleece, 16
Order of St. Michael, 96
Oresund, 118
Orléans, 91
d'Orléans, Anne Marie, 149
d'Orléans, Claude, Duke of Longueville, 64
d'Orléans, Francis III, Duke of Longueville, 65, 66, 75, 76

244 Stuart Spouses

d'Orléans, Louis II, Duke of Longueville, 64–66
d'Orléans, Louis, post-humous son of Louis II, Duke of Longueville, 65
Orkney, xv, xvi, 29, 30, 35, 117, 120
Oslo, 124
Oxford, 80, 139, 140, 169

Pantheon of the House of Braganza *see* St. Vincente de Fora, Convent of
Paré, Ambroise, 91
Paris
   city of, xv, xvi, 55, 56, 60, 64, 66, 83, 85, 98, 105, 134, 136, 140, 163, 208
   Eustache du Bellay, Bishop of, 86
Parr, Catherine, 76
Patten, William, 71
Pavia, 1525 Battle of, 56
Pedro II of Portugal, 153, 154, 187
Pesaro, Bartolomeo da, 88
Perth, xxii, 7, 11, 18, 19, 46
   Monastery, Blackfriars, 10, 11, 15
   1266 Treaty of, 29
Perthshire, 21
Peter, Constable of Portugal, 32, 33
Peter II of Brittany, 34
Philip II of Spain, 78
Philip III of Burgundy, 16, 17, 22, 33
Philip IV of France, xv
Philip IV of Spain, 134
Philip VI of France, xvi
Philip the Good *see* Philip III of Burgundy
Picardy, 58, 89
Pilgrimage of Grace, 1537, 92
Pinkie Cleuch, 1547 Battle of *see* Rough Wooing
Pitscottie, Robert Lindesay of *see* Lindesay, Robert, of Pitscottie
Place de Grève, 90
Poitiers, Diane de, 83, 86
Pole, Anne de la, 37
Pont-à-Mousson, 22, 63
Ponthieu, 32
Pope
   Boniface IX, xxiv
   Clement VI, xx
   Clement X, 160
   Innocent VIII, 37

Leo X, 47
Paul III, 57
Pious II, 23
Portsmouth, 76, 150
Portugal, Isabella of, 16, 33
Portugal, Maria of, 65
Princess Over the Water *see* Stuart, Louisa Maria Theresa
Procession of the Golden Tree, 31, 33
Purcell, Henry, 228

Queen's Haugh *see* Quenishalch
Queen Over the Water *see* Modena, Maria of
Quenishalch, 18

Ramsay, James, 1st Lord of Bothwell, 37
Randolph, John, 3d Earl of Moray *see* Moray, John Randolph, 3d Earl of
Ravaillac, François, 132
Ravenscraig Castle, 23, 24
Redgorton, 19
Reims
   Cathedral, 89
   Saint-Pierre-Les-Dames, 63, 79
René, Duke of Anjou, 22
Rhône River, 22
Riccio, David, 96, 98, 99, 110
Richard II of England, xxiii, 4
Richard III of England, 33, 37, 40
Richard, Duke of York, 22
Richmond
   Earl of, 42
   Palace,
Rich, Robert, 2d Earl of Warwick, 144
River Clyde, 75
River Tyne, 75
Robert II of Scotland, ix, xvi, xviii–xxii, 9, 10, 70
Robert III of Scotland, ix, x, xxi–xxvii
Rochester, 164
Rohan, Jacqueline de, Marchioness de Rotbelin, 86
Roplauch, 18
Rosenkrantz, Erik, 118
Ross, Earldom of, 8
Ross, Euphemia de, Queen Consort of Scotland, ix, xx, xxi, 9

Ross, Hugh, Earl of, xx
Ross, James of, 36
Rothesay Castle, xxvi
Rouen
   1517 Treaty of, 58
   city of, 75
Rough Wooing, 93
   Battle of Ancrum Moor, 70
   Battle of Pinkie Cleuch, 70, 71, 73
Rovere, Guidobaldo della, 88
Rowallan Castle, xix
Roxburgh Castle, 9, 21
Royal Mile *see* Edinburgh
Rump Parliament of 1649, 142
Rupert of the Rhine, 188
Russell, John, 122, 144
Ruthven, Patrick, 97–100, 110
Ryswick, 1697 Treaty of, 183

Saint Adrian
   Chapel of, 17, 67
   history of, 17, 18
Saint Andrews
   Beaton, James, Archbishop of, 81
   Bishop of
      Kennedy, James, 21
      Landels, William de, xx, xxi
      Wardlaw, Henry, 5
   Castle, xxiv, 68, 108
   Cathedral, 67
   Saint Salvator's Chapel, 81
Saint Anthony Convent, 18
Saint Giles Church, Edinburgh, 94, 95, 127
Saint Giles-without-Cripplegate, London, 142
Saint Margaret's Chapel at Edinburgh Castle, 79
Saint Ninian, 36
Saint-Pierre-Les-Dames *see* Reims
Salinas, Maria de *see* Willoughby, Maria
Salins, 33
Salle, Antoine de la, 22
Sandleth, 18
Sargentland *see* Sergandlande
Scanian War, 194, 195
Schauen, Otto Grote zu, 184
Scone

Abbey, xx, 5, 11, 148
Hill, xx
Palace, xxii, xxiii, xxiv
Scotland Yard, 49
Scots Makars, 39
Scottish Bishop's War *see* Wars of the Three Kingdoms
Scottish Council of Twelve, xv
Scottish Marches, 24
Sedley, Catherine, 169
Selkirk, 45
Sergandlande, 18
Seton, George, 97
Settlement, 1701 Act of, 183, 192
Seven Bishops, 172
Seymour, Edward, Duke of Somerset and Lord Protector of England, 70, 71
Seymour, Jane, Queen Consort of England, 65, 66
Shetland, 29, 30, 35, 117, 118, 120
ships
   Catherine, of England, 163
   Gloucester, of England, 169
   Little Unicorn, of Scotland, 67
   Mary Willoughby, originally of England, but stolen by Scotland, 67
   Salamander, of France, 60
   Unicorn, of Scotland, 67
Shrewsbury, Richard of, 40, 41
Shropshire, xviii
Sinclair, Agnes, 104
Sinclair, John, Dean of Restarlig and Bishop of Brechin, 95
Skeoch *see* Skeok
Skeok, 18
Sluis, 17
smallpox, 24, 102, 128, 143, 149, 156–158, 165, 174, 175, 181
Solway Moss, 1542 Battle of, 69, 70
Somerset House, 131, 170, 171
Southwark Cathedral, 4
Soutra Aisle, 23
St. Adrian *see* Saint Adrian
St. Andrews *see* Saint Andrews
St. Anthony *see* *Saint Anthony*
St. Catherine of Alexandria, 151
St. Denis, Basilica of, 91, 149
St. Edward's Crown, 190

St. Ethernan *see* Saint Adrian
St. Germain, 84, 172, 173
St. Giles *see* Saint Giles Church, Edinburgh
St. Giles-without-Cripplegate, 142
St. Ives, 143
St. James's Palace, 141, 146, 158, 165, 168, 170, 171, 176–178, 185, 188, 189
St. John's Town *see* Perth
St. Margaret of Scotland, 79, 129, 130
St. Mary's Church, Ely, 143, 144
St. Mary Overy *see* Southwark Cathedral
St. Ninian *see* Saint Ninian
St. Vincent de Fora, Convent of, 155
Stewart, Alan, son of Walter Stewart, Earl of Atholl and Strathearn, 9
Stewart, Alexander, 4th High Steward of Scotland, 12
Stewart, Alexander, son of James I of Scotland and twin brother of James II, 7
Stewart, Alexander, son of James II *see* Duke of Albany
Stewart, Alexander, son of James IV of Scotland, 47, 49
Stewart, Alexander, posthumous son of James IV of Scotland, 49
Stewart, Annabella, daughter of James I of Scotland, 7
Stewart, Arthur, son of James IV of Scotland, 46
Stewart, Charles, son of Margaret Douglas and Matthew Stewart, 92, 97
Stewart, David, xx
Stewart, David, son of Walter Stewart, Earl of Atholl and Strathearn, 9
Stewart, David, son of Euphemia de Ross and Robert II, xx, xxi, xxiii
Stewart, David, son of Robert III of Scotland, xxii–xxv, 8
Stewart, David, son of James II of Scotland, 20, 24
Stewart, Dorothea, daughter of Henry Stewart, Lord Methven, 52
Stewart, Egidia, daughter of Robert III of Scotland, xxii
Stewart, Eleanor, daughter of James I of Scotland, 7
Stewart, Elizabeth, daughter of Euphemia de Ross, xxi
Stewart, Elizabeth, daughter of Robert III of Scotland, xxii
Stewart, Euphemia, xxi
Stewart, Francis, 5th Earl of Bothwell, 122
Stewart, Henry, Lord Darnley, x, xiii, 81, 82, 92–103, 109–115, 118, 222, 224
  wedding, x, 94
  death, x, 102, 103, 113, 114
Stewart, Henry, Lord Methven,
Stewart, Isabella, daughter of James I of Scotland, 34
Stewart, James, son of Robert III *see* James I of Scotland
Stewart, James, son of James I of Scotland *see* James II of Scotland
Stewart, James, Black Knight of Lorne *see* Black Knight of Lorne
Stewart, James, first son of James III of Scotland *see* James IV of Scotland
Stewart, James, second son of James III of Scotland *see* Ross, James of
Stewart, James, first son of James IV of Scotland *see* James V of Scotland
Stewart, James, son of James V of Scotland, 68
Stewart, James, 1st Earl of Moray, 76, 95, 96, 108, 109
Stewart, James Mor, 8
Stewart, Joan, daughter of James I of Scotland, 6
Stewart, John, later Robert III *see* Robert III of Scotland
Stewart, John, 2d Duke of Albany *see* Albany, John Stewart, 2d Duke of
Stewart, John, Duke of Albany and Count of Auvergne and Lauraguais *see* Albany, Duke of
Stewart, John, son of James II of Scotland, 20, 24
Stewart, John, son of James III of Scotland *see* Mar, Earl of, John
Stewart, John, 4th Earl of Atholl, 95, 110
Stewart, Margaret, daughter of Robert III of Scotland, xxii
Stewart, Margaret, daughter of James I of Scotland, 5, 7–9,

Stewart, Margaret, daughter of James II of Scotland, 20, 21, 34, 36
Stewart, Mary, daughter of Robert III of Scotland, xxii
Stewart, Mary, daughter of James I of Scotland, 7
Stewart, Mary, daughter of James II of Scotland, 20, 30
Stewart, Matthew, 4th Earl of Lennox, 92, 93, 95, 115
Stewart, Robert *see* Robert II of Scotland
Stewart, Robert, third son of Robert II of Scotland, Duke of Albany *see* Albany, Duke of
Stewart, Robert, son of Robert III of Scotland, xxii
Stewart, Robert, grandson of Walter Stewart, Earl of Atholl and Strathearn, 10, 11
Stewart, Robert, son of James V of Scotland, 68
Stewart, Walter, xviii
Stewart, Walter, son of Euphemia de Ross, xxi, 9, 10, 12, 18
Stewart, Walter, Earl of Atholl, Earl of Strathearn and relative of Euphemia de Ross, xxi, 9, 10, 18
Stirling, xvi, 18, 46, 102
   Castle, 12–14, 18, 35, 37, 39, 46–50, 52, 68, 102, 125–127
Stirlingshire, 46
Strait of Gibraltar, 150
Straiton, Walter, 10
Strath Gartney, 18
Strathearn, Earl of
   David Stewart *see* Stewart, David
   Walter Stewart *see* Stewart, Walter, son of Euphemia de Ross
Strathtyrum, xxv
Stuart, Anne, daughter of Charles I of England, Scotland, and Ireland, 137
Stuart, Anne Sophia, daughter of Queen Anne, 186
Stuart, Catherine, daughter of Charles I of England, Scotland, and Ireland, 137
Stuart, Catherine, daughter of James VII & II of England, Scotland and Ireland, 158
Stuart, Catherine Laura, 164, 165
Stuart, Charles, son of James VI & I of Scotland *see* Charles I of England, Scotland, and Ireland
Stuart, Charles, son of Charles I of England, Scotland, and Ireland *see* Charles II of England, Scotland, and Ireland
Stuart, Charles, Duke of Cambridge, son of James VII & II of England, Scotland and Ireland and Anne Hyde 157
Stuart, Charles, Duke of Cambridge, son of James VII & II of England, Scotland and Ireland and Maria of Modena, 165
Stuart, Charles, Duke of Kendal, son of James VII & II of England, Scotland and Ireland, 158
Stuart, Charles James, son of Charles I of England, Scotland, and Ireland, 137
Stuart, Charlotte Maria, 170
Stuart, Edgar, Duke of Cambridge, 158
Stuart, Elizabeth, Queen of Bohemia, daughter of James I & VI of England, Scotland and Ireland, 125–127, 131, 183, 188
Stuart, Elizabeth, daughter of Charles I of England, Scotland and Ireland, 137, 140, 141
Stuart, Elizabeth, daughter of James II & VII of England, Scotland and Ireland, 167
Stuart, George, son of Queen Anne, 189
Stuart, Henrietta, daughter of Charles I of England, Scotland and Ireland, 137, 140
Stuart, Henrietta, daughter of James VII & II of England, Scotland and Ireland, 158
Stuart, Henry, son of Charles I of England, Scotland, and Ireland, 137, 140, 141, 149
Stuart, Henry Frederick, son of James VI & I of England, Scotland and Ireland, 125–128, 131
Stuart, Isabel, 165
Stuart, James, son of Mary, Queen of Scots *see* James VI & I of Scotland and England
Stuart, James, son of Charles II of England, Scotland and Ireland *see*

James VII & II of England, Scotland, and Ireland
Stuart, James, Duke of Cambridge and Baron of Dauntsey, son of James VII & II of England, Scotland and Ireland, 158
Stuart, James Francis Edward, 171, 172, 174, 178, 202
Stuart, Jane, illegitimate half-sister of Mary, Queen of Scots, 98
Stuart, Louisa Maria Theresa, 173, 174, 183
Stuart, Margaret, daughter of James VI & I of England, Scotland and Ireland, 126
Stuart, Mary *see* Mary, Queen of Scots
Stuart, Mary, daughter of James VI & I of England, Scotland and Ireland, 128, 129
Stuart, Mary, daughter Queen Anne, 186
Stuart, Mary, another daughter of Queen Anne, 189
Stuart, Mary Henrietta, daughter of Charles I of England, Scotland and Ireland, 137–139, 140, 148, 149, 156, 157, 167, 175, 176
Stewart, Philip, 92
Stuart, Robert, illegitimate half-brother of Mary, Queen of Scots, 98, 103
Stuart, Robert, son of James VI & I of England, Scotland and Ireland, 126
Stuart, Sophia, daughter of James VI & I of England, Scotland and Ireland, 128, 129
Stuart, William, son of Queen Anne, 188, 189
Swynford, Katherine, 4

Tangier, 150
Tarascon Castle, 22
Teerlinc, Levina, 32
Temple Newsam House, 92
Ter Heijde, 177
The Hague, 139, 140, 148, 167, 171, 175, 177, 178
Throndsen, Anna, 105, 107, 109, 118
Tillycoultry, 18
Touraine, 9
Tours, 9
Treaty of Perpetual Peace, 42, 43
Treaty of Union *see* Acts of Union

Trent, 1545 Council of, 83
Trinity College Church, 23–25
Troyes, 1420 Treaty of, 7
Tudor, Arthur, 38, 41–43
Tudor, Edward *see* Edward VI of England
Tudor, Elizabeth, Queen Regnant of England *see* Elizabeth I of England
Tudor, Henry (1457–1509) *see* Henry VII of England
Tudor, Henry (1491–1547) *see* Henry VIII of England
Tudor, Margaret, x, xvi, xvii, 15, 38–52, 57, 65, 66, 68, 69, 75, 92, 94, 193
  wedding, x, 42, 43
  coronation, 46, 47
  death, x, 52, 53
Tudor, Mary, Queen Consort of France, xvi, xvii, 38, 42, 64
Tudor, Mary, Queen Regnant of England *see* Mary I of England
Tyburn, 137

Ulrich III of Mecklenburg-Guestrow, 120
Union with England Act *see* Acts of Union
Union with Scotland Act *see* Acts of Union
Unst, 118

Valois, Charles de 54
Valois, Charlotte de, 54
Valois, Francis de, son of Francis I of France, 54
Valois, Francis de, later Francis II *see* Francis II of France
Valois, Henri de *see* Henri II of France
Valois, Madeleine de, 54–59
  wedding, x, 60, 61
  death, x, 61, 62
Valois, Margaret de, 54, 56, 57
Vannes, 133
Versailles, 163, 173
Vikings, 18
Vila Viçosa, 148
Villiers, Elizabeth, 182
Vinci, Leonardo da, 54

Wales, Princess Charlotte of, 192
Wales, Prince George of, 192
Wales, Prince Louis of, 192

Wales, Prince William of, 192
War of the Grand Alliance *see* Nine Years' War
War of the League of Augsburg *see* Nine Years' War
War of the Spanish Succession, 190
Warbeck, Perkin, 39–41
Warkworth Castle, 23
Wars of the Roses, 20–22, 33
Wars of the Three Kingdoms, 137–140
Wassenhove, Joos van, 31
Wemyss Castle, 93
Werle, 130
Westminster
    Abbey, 22, 129, 136, 137, 146, 158, 165, 170, 179, 181, 183, 190, 191
    Hall, 141
    Palace, 38, 42
Whitehall Palace, 76, 87, 88, 144–147, 164, 166, 169–171, 181, 185
    Banqueting House, 87, 181
    Chapel Royal, 138
Whithorn Priory, 36, 75
Willem Hendrik of Orange *see* William III of England, Scotland and Ireland
William I of Scotland, xviii
William II of Orange, 137, 138, 156, 166
William III of England, Scotland and Ireland, 153, 168, 169, 171–178, 181, 182
    wedding, 177
    coronation, 179, 180
    death, 183
Williams, Oliver *see* Cromwell, Oliver, Lord Protector of England
Williams, Richard, 142
Willoughby, Maria, 67
Winchester
    Bishop, 5
    Palace, 4
Windsor Castle, 1, 3, 127
Windsor, 156, 169, 189
Wittenberg, 80
Worcester House, 157
Wycliffe, John, 80

Yolande, Queen Consort of Scotland, xv
Yonge, Peter, 122
York, Cecily, 35, 36, 39
York, Elizabeth of, 38, 43
York, Margaret of, 31–33, 35, 40, 42
Yorkshire, xxvi, 92, 139

Zeeland, 33
Zutphen, 33

Dear Reader,

We hope you have enjoyed this book, but why not share your views on social media? You can also follow our pages to see more about our other products: facebook.com/penandswordbooks or follow us on X @penswordbooks

You can also view our products at www.pen-and-sword.co.uk (UK and ROW) or www.penandswordbooks.com (North America).

To keep up to date with our latest releases and online catalogues, please sign up to our newsletter at: www.pen-and-sword.co.uk/newsletter

If you would like a printed catalogue with our latest books, then please email: enquiries@pen-and-sword.co.uk or telephone: 01226 734555 (UK and ROW) or email: uspen-and-sword@casematepublishers.com or telephone: (610) 853-9131 (North America).

We respect your privacy and we will only use personal information to send you information about our products.

Thank you!